D1175096

Alcoholics Anonymous Comes of Age

Alcoholics Anonymous

Comes of Age

A BRIEF HISTORY OF A.A.

ALCOHOLICS ANONYMOUS WORLD SERVICES, INC.

NEW YORK

ALCOHOLICS ANONYMOUS COMES OF AGE

Copyright © 1957 by Alcoholics Anonymous Publishing, Inc.
(now known as A.A. World Services, Inc.)
Printed in the United States of America

FIRST PRINTING 1957

SECOND PRINTING 1967
THIRD PRINTING 1970
FOURTH PRINTING 1971
FIFTH PRINTING 1973
SIXTH PRINTING 1975
SEVENTH PRINTING 1977
EIGHTH PRINTING 1979

Library of Congress catalog card number: 57-10949
ISBN 0-916856-02-X
AMERICAN BOOK—STRATFORD PRESS, INC., NEW YORK

Contents

Illustrations will be found following page 114

Landmarks in A.A. History

DATE	
1962	The publication of "Twelve Concepts for World Service" written by Bill W.
1963	First Regional Trustees elected to the General Service Board. This proceedure replaces the Area Trustee, heretofore elected from a single state. Under the new procedure, the U.S. is divided into six regions
1963-1967	This period is characterized by rapid growth overseas. It is accelerated by our increased world service activity, such as more advisory correspondence, establishment of new literature centers, large numbers of new and effective translations, better inculcation of A.A. traditions, etc.
1965	30th Anniversary Convention in Toronto, Canada, in July. Attendance 10,000 plus. The Declaration, later so widely used—"I Am Responsible. When anyone, anywhere, reaches out for help, I want the hand of A.A. always to be there. And for that: I am responsible"— is the keynote of this gathering Gift pocket-size edition of *Twelve Steps and Twelve Traditions* released at Toronto Color film documentary produced for group use only, in which Bill and Lois tell the early A.A. story
1966	Change in ratio of Trustees of the General Service Board to provide for a two-thirds majority of alcoholic members, the historic occasion on which the A.A. Fellowship accepts top responsibility for the future conduct of all its affairs. With this change, the number of Regional Trustees rises to eight— six from the U.S., two from Canada
1967	Publication of book *The A.A. Way of Life* (now titled *As Bill Sees It*), featuring extracts from Bill W.'s writings. In this period, the number of A.A. groups increases from 5,927 to 13,279; groups overseas come to represent about 20% of the A.A. population
1955-1967	

1969	First World Service Meeting held in New York, October 9-11, with delegates from 14 countries
1970	35th Anniversary International Convention held at Miami Beach, Florida. Approximately 11,000 in attendance. Bill's last public appearance. The keynote is the Declaration of Unity—"This we owe to A.A.'s future: to place our common welfare first; to keep our Fellowship united. For on A.A. unity depend our lives, and the lives of those to come"
1971	Bill dies January 24 at Miami Beach, Florida. His name, picture, and story carried worldwide in public media for the first time A.A. groups worldwide hold memorial services February 14
1972	Second World Service Meeting, held in New York, October 5-7, with delegates from 15 countries. (Meetings biennially thereafter)
1973	Publication of booklet *Came to Believe . . .* , expressing a wide range of individual members' spiritual views
1973, April	Distribution of the book *Alcoholics Anonymous* reaches the 1,000,000 mark
1975	40th Anniversary International Convention held at Denver, Colorado. Over 19,000 join Lois in repeating the theme, "Let It Begin With Me"
1975	Publication of booklet *Living Sober*, detailing some practical methods A.A. members have used for not drinking
1976	Worldwide estimates: more than 1,000,000 members; almost 28,000 groups Third edition of *Alcoholics Anonymous* published
1978	Grapevine circulation exceeds 100,000 Distribution of *Alcoholics Anonymous* passes the 2,000,000 mark

Foreword

This book is for A.A. members and their friends. It is for all who are interested to know the history of how A.A. started, how its principles of Recovery, Unity, and Service were evolved, and by what means this fellowship has grown and spread its message around the world. Here is an inside and wide-angled view of Alcoholics Anonymous.

The first part of the book presents a panoramic sketch of the historic St. Louis Convention at which the fellowship of Alcoholics Anonymous came of age and assumed full responsibility for all its affairs.

The second part includes three talks, edited and enlarged, on the history of A.A. Recovery, Unity, and Service, which were given by co-founder Bill W. at the St. Louis gathering.

The third part is devoted to addresses of a number of A.A.'s friends, all of them notable in their several fields: Dr. Harry M. Tiebout, psychiatrist, Dr. W. W. Bauer of the American Medical Association, Father Edward Dowling of the Jesuit order, Dr. Samuel M. Shoemaker, Episcopal clergyman, and Mr. Bernard B. Smith, New York attorney and former Chairman of the General Service Board of Alcoholics Anonymous. These friends tell of their association with Alcoholics Anonymous, the part they played in its development, and their view of what the future holds for this society.

Dear Friends,

As you read coming pages, it will be seen that their historical content is not arranged in a conventional, straight-line time-sequence.

For the limited purposes of this book, it was deemed better to throw special emphasis on our A.A. Legacies of Recovery, Unity and Service by separately telling the stories of those crucial developments. This has the merit of focusing attention upon them, one concept at a time. Nevertheless some members may prefer to start reading at page 51, which leads quickly into the early A.A. story as it relates to our present-day program of recovery.

The title of this volume, *A.A. Comes of Age,* is now and then questioned because it conveys to some people the idea that we A.A.'s really think we have "grown up"; that we have already achieved great emotional maturity.

In reality, the expression "comes of age" is used by us in a very different sense. We simply say that we have arrived at the time of life when adult responsibilities have to be faced and dealt with, as best we are able. To this end we do try to rely upon ourselves—and upon God.

Faithfully yours,

Bill W.

March, 1967

I

When A.A. Came of Age

BY BILL W.,

co-founder, Alcoholics Anonymous

DURING the first three days of July, 1955, Alcoholics Anonymous held a Convention in St. Louis, commemorating the twentieth anniversary of its founding. There our fellowship declared itself come to the age of full responsibility, and there it received from its founders and old-timers permanent keeping of its three great legacies of Recovry, Unity, and Service.

I will always remember those three days as among the greatest experiences of my life.

At four o'clock in the afternoon of the final day about 5,000 A.A. members and their families and friends were seated in the Kiel Auditorium at St. Louis. All of the United States and Canadian Provinces were represented. Some had traveled from far lands to be there. On the auditorium stage were the General Service Conference of Alcoholics Anonymous, including some seventy-five delegates from the United States and Canada, Trustees of A.A.'s General Service Board, directors and secretarial staffs of our world services at New York, my wife Lois, my mother, and I.

The General Service Conference of Alcoholics Anonymous was about to take over the custody of A.A.'s Twelve Traditions and the guardianship of its world services. It was to be named as the permanent successor to the founders of A.A. Speaking for co-founder Dr.

Bob and for A.A.'s old-timers everywhere, I made the delivery of the Three Legacies of Alcoholics Anonymous to our whole society and its representative Conference. From that time A.A. went on its own, to serve God's purpose for so long as it was destined, under His providence, to endure.

Many events in the days preceding had led up to this moment. The total effect was that 5,000 people got a vision of A.A. such as they had never known before. They were exposed to the main outlines of A.A. history. With some of us oldsters they relived the exciting experiences that led to the creation of the Twelve Steps of recovery and the book *Alcoholics Anonymous*. They heard how the A.A. Traditions were beaten out on the anvils of group experience. They got the story of how A.A. had established beachheads in seventy foreign lands. And when they saw A.A.'s affairs delivered entirely into their own hands, they experienced a new realization of each individual's responsibility for the whole.

At the Convention it was widely appreciated for the first time that nobody had *invented* Alcoholics Anonymous, that many streams of influence and many people, some of them nonalcoholics, had helped, by the grace of God, to achieve A.A.'s purpose.

Several of our nonalcoholic friends of medicine, of religion, and of A.A.'s Board of Trustees had come all the hot and dusty way to St. Louis to share that happy occasion and to tell us about their own experience of participation in the growth of A.A. There were men like clergyman Sam Shoemaker, whose early teachings did so much to inspire Dr. Bob and me. There was the beloved Father Dowling [1] whose personal inspiration and whose recommendation of A.A. to the world did so much to make our society what it is. And there was Dr. Harry Tiebout,[2] our first friend of psychiatry, who very early began to use A.A. concepts in his own practice, and whose good humor, humility, penetrating insight, and courage have meant so much to all of us.

It was Dr. Tiebout, helped by Dr. Kirby Collier of Rochester and Dwight Anderson of New York, who persuaded the Medical Society of the State of New York in 1944 and later the American

[1] Father Dowling died in 1960.
[2] Dr. Tiebout died in 1966.

Psychiatric Association in 1949 to let me, a layman, read papers about A.A. at their annual gatherings, thus hastening the acceptance of the then little-known A.A. by physicians all over the globe.

The value of Dr. Tiebout's contribution, then and since, is beyond calculation. When we first met Harry, he was serving as Chief Psychiatrist at one of America's finest sanitariums. His professional skill was widely recognized by patients and colleagues alike. At that time the modern art of psychiatry was just passing out of its youth and had begun to claim world-wide attention as one of the great advances of our times. The process of exploring the mysteries and motives of the unconscious mind of man was already in full swing.

Naturally, the explorers, representing the several schools of psychiatry, were in considerable disagreement respecting the real meaning of the new discoveries. While the followers of Carl Jung saw value, meaning, and reality in religious faith, the great majority of psychiatrists in that day did not. They mostly held to Sigmund Freud's view that religion was a comforting fantasy of man's immaturity; that when he grew up in the light of modern knowledge, he would no longer need such support.

This was the background against which, in 1939, Dr. Harry had seen two spectacular A.A. recoveries among his own patients. These patients, Marty and Grennie, had been the toughest kind of customers, both as alcoholics and as neurotics. When after a brief exposure to A.A. they abruptly stopped drinking (for good, by the way) and at once began to show an astonishing change in outlook and attitude, Harry was electrified. He was also agreeably astonished when he discovered that as a psychiatrist he could now really reach them, despite the fact that only a few weeks previously they had presented stone walls of obstinate resistance to his every approach. To Harry, these were facts, brand-new facts. Scientist and man of courage that he is, Harry faced them squarely. And not always in the privacy of his office, either. As soon as he became fully convinced, he held up A.A. for his profession and for the public to see. (Note the index of his medical papers.) [3] At very considerable risk to his professional standing Harry Tiebout ever since has continued to endorse A.A. and its work to the psychiatric profession.

Dr. Tiebout was paired on the Convention's medical panel with Dr. W. W. Bauer of the American Medical Association, who held out the hand of friendship to A.A. and recommended us warmly.

These good medical friends were not in the least surprised at the testimony of Dr. Earle M., the A.A. member of the panel. A notable in medical circles from coast to coast, Dr. Earle flatly stated that despite his medical knowledge, which included psychiatry, he had nevertheless been obliged humbly to learn his A.A. from a butcher. Thus he confirmed all that Dr. Harry had told us about the necessity of reducing the alcoholic's ballooning ego, before entering A.A. and afterward.

The inspiring talks of these doctors reminded us of all the help that A.A.'s friends in medicine had given us over the years. Many A.A.'s at the Convention had been at the San Francisco Opera House on the evening in 1951 when Alcoholics Anonymous received the Lasker Award—the gift of Albert and Mary Lasker—from the 12,000 physicians of the American Public Health Association.[4]

The addresses which the Rev. Samuel Shoemaker,[5] Father Edward Dowling, Dr. Harry Tiebout, and Dr. W. W. Bauer made before the Convention can be read beginning on page 235 of this book. Along with them we publish the talk of another friend, Bernard B. Smith, the New York lawyer who has served us so faithfully and brilliantly in recent years as Chairman of A.A.'s Board of Trustees. He will be remembered forever as the nonalcoholic whose singular skill and ability to reconcile different viewpoints were deciding factors in the formation of the General Service Conference upon which A.A.'s future so heavily depends. Like the other speakers, Bernard Smith tells not only what A.A. means to alcoholics and to the world at large but

[3] See Appendix E:b for Dr. Tiebout's papers.
[4] See Appendix D, Lasker Award citation.
[5] Rev. Sam Shoemaker died in 1963.

also what A.A. principles as practiced in his own life have meant to him.

Several other of our old-time friends made inspiring contributions to the gathering. Their talks, indeed all of the St. Louis meetings, were recorded on tapes in full and thus are available. [These tapes are no longer available.] We regret that the limited compass of this volume does not permit the inclusion of all of them here.

On the very first day of the Convention, for example, one of A.A.'s oldest and most valued friends, Mr. Leonard V. Harrison, chaired a session called "A.A. and Industry." Leonard, who is still a Trustee, has endeared himself to us over a period of more than ten years' service on our Board. He preceded Bernard Smith as our Board Chairman, and he saw A.A. through its frightfully wobbly time of adolescence, a time when nobody could say whether our society would hang together or blow up entirely. What his wise counsel and steady hand meant to us of A.A. in that stormy period is quite beyond telling.

Mr. Harrison then introduced a newer friend, Henry A. Mielcarek, who is engaged by Allis-Chalmers to look after the alcoholic problem in that great company. Ably seconded by Dave, an A.A. member holding a similar position at Du Pont, Mr. Mielcarek opened the eyes of the audience to the possibilities of the application of A.A. and its principles in industry. Our vision of A.A. in industry was taken a step farther by the final speaker, Dr. John L. Norris of the Eastman Kodak Company. He had come to the Convention in a double role. One of the pioneers in the introduction of A.A. into industry, he was also a long-time Trustee on A.A.'s General Service Board, a most selfless and devoted worker. Again those of us who sat in the audience asked ourselves: What would we have ever done without friends like these?

During the second day of the Convention there was a meeting on "A.A. in Institutions." The speakers took us on a journey into what were once the two darkest pits in which the alcoholic could suffer, the prison and the mental hospital. We were told how a new hope and a new light had entered these places of one-time darkness. Most of us were astounded when we learned the extent of the A.A. penetration, with groups today in 265 hospitals and 335 prisons[6] throughout the world. Formerly only about 20 per cent of the alcoholic parolees from institutions and prisons ever made the grade. But since the advent of A.A., 80 per cent of these parolees have found permanent freedom.

Two A.A.'s sparked this panel, and here again our faithful non-alcoholic friends were represented. There was Dr. O. Arnold Kilpatrick, psychiatrist in charge of a New York State mental institution, who told us of the wonderful progress of A.A. in his hospital. He was followed by Mr. Austin MacCormick, one-time Commissioner of Correction in New York City and now Professor of Criminology at the University of California. Here was an old-time friend indeed, a kind and devoted fellow worker who had served a considerable hitch as a Trustee in the days of A.A.'s Alcoholic Foundation. When he moved west, it was California's gain and a corresponding loss to A.A.'s Headquarters. And now here he was again, telling how he had kept in touch with prison authorities throughout America. As Dr. Kilpatrick had confirmed A.A.'s progress in mental institutions, so Austin MacCormick, with an authority born of experience, reported the steadily increasing influence of A.A. groups in prisons. Again our vision was extended and our spirits were kindled.

During the Convention many just plain A.A. meetings were held. At those meetings, and in the corridors, coffee shops, and hotel rooms, we were continually and gratefully thoughtful of our friends and of all that Providence had appointed them to do for us. Our thoughts often went out to those who were not there: those who had passed on, those who were ill, and those who just couldn't make it. Among the latter we sorely missed Trustees Jack Alexander, Frank Amos, Dr. Leonard Strong, Jr., and Frank Gulden.

Most of all, of course, we talked about co-founder Dr. Bob and his wife, Anne. A handful of us could recall those first days in 1935 at Akron where the spark that was to become the first A.A. group was struck. Some of us could retell tales that had been told in Dr. Bob's

[6] These figures as of 1957. In 1978, there were over 1,200 groups in correctional facilities and over 1,400 in treatment facilities worldwide.

living room in their house on Ardmore Avenue. And we could re-member Anne as she sat in the corner by the fireplace, reading from the Bible the warning of James, that "faith without works is dead." Indeed, we had with us at the Convention young Bob and sister Sue, who had seen the beginnings of A.A.'s first group. Sue's husband, Ernie, A.A. number four, was there, too. And old Bill D., A.A. num-ber three, was represented by his widow, Henrietta.

We were all overjoyed to see Ethel, the longest-sober lady of the Akron-Cleveland region, whose moving story can now be read in the second edition of the A.A. book. She reminded us of all the early Akron veterans—a dozen and a half of them—whose stories were the backbone of the first edition of the book *Alcoholics Anonymous* and who, together with Dr. Bob, had created the first A.A. group in the world.

As the stories unfolded we saw Dr. Bob entering the doors of St. Thomas Hospital, the first religious hospital to receive prospective members of A.A. for treatment on a regular basis. Here there de-veloped that great partnership between Dr. Bob and the incomparable Sister Ignatia [7] of the Sisters of Charity of St. Augustine. Her name brings to mind the classic story about the first drunk she and Dr. Bob treated. Sister Ignatia's night supervisor wasn't very keen about alco-holics, especially the d.t. variety, and Dr. Bob had arrived with a request for a private room for his first customer. Sister Ignatia said to him, "Doctor, we do not have any beds, much less private rooms, but I will do what I can." And then into the hospital's flower room she slyly bootlegged A.A.'s first jittering candidate for admission. From this uncertain start of hospitalization in our pioneering time, we watched the growing procession of alcoholic sufferers as they passed through the doors of St. Thomas and out into the world again, most of them never to return to the hospital except as visitors. From 1939 to the time Dr. Bob took his leave of us in 1950, over 5,000 had thus been treated. And so the ministry of Dr. Bob, his wife Anne, Sister Ignatia, and Akron's early timers set an example for the prac-tice of A.A.'s Twelve Steps that will remain for all time.

[7] Sister Ignatia died in 1966.

This great tradition lives on in the person of Sister Ignatia. She continues her labor of love today at Cleveland's St. Vincent Charity Hospital, where grateful A.A.'s of that area have contributed labor and money to reconstruct an old wing of the place which has been christened "Rosary Hall" and set aside for the special use of the Sister and her co-workers. Already 5,000 cases have been treated.[8]

Many an A.A. member today believes that among the best gateways to sobriety are the alcoholic wards of the religious hospitals that cooperate with us. Surely those who have passed through St. Thomas at Akron and St. Vincent's Charity at Cleveland will heartily agree with this. It is our hope that in due time religious hospitals of all denominations will follow the example of these great originals. What Sister Ignatia and her associates at St. Thomas have already done is a very brave beginning. But the future may honor them even more for the great works that their example set in motion.

In 1949, ten years after the start of Dr. Bob's and Sister Ignatia's pioneering, the importance of this work was deeply realized by A.A.'s throughout Ohio. A committee was formed to place a plaque in the alcoholic ward at St. Thomas Hospital, a memorial which would clearly show what so many of us really thought and felt. I was asked to write the inscription and preside at the dedication. Though Anne had recently passed away, Dr. Bob could still be with us. Characteristically, Sister Ignatia would not let her name appear on the inscription. It was on Saturday afternon, April 8, 1949, that we unveiled and presented the memorial plaque to the hospital. Its inscription read as follows:

IN GRATITUDE

THE FRIENDS OF DR. BOB AND ANNE S.
AFFECTIONATELY DEDICATE THIS MEMORIAL
TO THE SISTERS AND STAFF OF
ST. THOMAS HOSPITAL.

[8] As of 1957.

AT AKRON, BIRTHPLACE OF ALCOHOLICS
ANONYMOUS, ST. THOMAS HOSPITAL BECAME
THE FIRST RELIGIOUS INSTITUTION EVER
TO OPEN ITS DOOR TO OUR SOCIETY.

MAY THE LOVING DEVOTION OF THOSE WHO
LABORED HERE IN OUR PIONEERING TIME
BE A BRIGHT AND WONDROUS EXAMPLE
OF GOD'S GRACE EVERLASTINGLY SET
BEFORE US ALL.

Everyone remembers Dr. Bob's famous final admonition to Alcoholics Anonymous: "Let's not louse this thing up; let's keep it simple." And I recall my own tribute in the *A.A. Grapevine* to his great simplicity and strength . . .

Serenely remarking to his attendant, "I think this is it," Dr. Bob passed out of our sight and hearing November sixteenth, 1950 at noonday. So ended the consuming malady in the course of which he had shown us how high faith can rise over grievous distress. As he had lived, so he died, supremely aware that in his Father's house are many mansions.

Among all those he knew, memory was at floodtide. But who could really say what was thought and felt by the five thousand sick ones to whom he personally ministered and freely gave a physician's care? Who could possibly record the reflections of his townsmen who had seen him sink almost into oblivion, then rise to anonymous world renown? Who could express the gratitude of those tens of thousands of A.A. families who had so often heard of him but had never seen him face to face? And what were the emotions of those nearest him as they thankfully pondered the mystery of his regeneration fifteen years before and all its vast consequence since? Only the smallest fraction of this great blessing could be comprehended. We could only say, "What indeed hath God wrought?"

Never would Dr. Bob have us think him a saint or a superman. Nor would he have us praise him or grieve his passing. We can almost hear him saying to us, "Seems to me you folks are making heavy going. I'm not to be taken so seriously as all that. I was only a first link in that chain of Providential circumstances which is called A.A. By grace and good fortune my link did not break, though my faults and failures often might have brought on that unhappy result. I was just another alcoholic trying to get along, under the grace of God. Forget me, but go you and do likewise. Add your own link to our chain. With God's help, forge that chain well and truly." It was in this manner, if not in these exact words, that Dr. Bob actually did estimate himself and counsel us.

Meeting a few months after Dr. Bob's death, the first General Service Conference of Alcoholics Anonymous voted in 1951 to present each of Dr. Bob's heirs, young Bob and Sue, with a scroll which struck a final note. It read as follows:

DR. BOB

IN MEMORIAM

Alcoholics Anonymous herein records its timeless gratitude for the life and works of Dr. Robert Holbrook S., a Co-Founder.

Known in affection as "Dr. Bob" he recovered from alcoholism on June 10, 1935; in that year he helped form the first Alcoholics Anonymous Group; this beacon he and his good wife Anne so well tended that its light at length traversed the world. By the day of his departure from us, November 16, 1950, he had spiritually and medically helped countless fellow sufferers.

Dr. Bob's was the humility that declines all honors, the integrity that brooks no compromise; his was a devotion to man and God which in bright example will shine always.

The World Fellowship of Alcoholics Anonymous presents this testament of gratitude to the heirs of Dr. Bob and Anne S.

Thinking of the early years in Akron reminded us also of the pioneering days in the East; of the struggle to start A.A.'s Group Number Two at New York in the fall of 1935. Earlier in the year, before meeting Dr. Bob, I had worked with many alcoholics, but there had been no success in New York until my return home in September. I told the Convention how the idea began to catch on: of the first meetings in the parlor at 182 Clinton Street, Brooklyn; of the forays to New York's Calvary Mission and Towns Hospital in the feverish search for more prospects; of the sprinkling of those who sobered up and of the many who dismally flopped. My wife Lois recalled how for three years our Clinton Street home had been filled from cellar to garret with alcoholics of every description and how to our dismay they skidded back into drink, seeming failures all. (Some of them did sober up later on, perhaps in spite of us!)

Out in Akron, in the houses of Dr. Bob and Wally, the home-sobering treatment fared better. In fact, Wally and his wife probably made an all-time high record for home treatment and rehabilitation of A.A.'s newcomers. Their percentage of success was great and their example was widely followed for a time in the homes of other Akron-ites. As Lois once said, it was a wonderful laboratory in which we experimented and learned—the hard way.

I reminded Jerseyites at the Convention of early meetings in Upper Montclair and South Orange and in Monsey, New York, when Lois and I moved over there about the time the A.A. book came off the press in the spring of 1939, after the foreclosure of the Brooklyn home of her parents where we had been living. The weather was warm, and we lived in a summer camp on a quiet lake in western New Jersey, the gracious loan of a good A.A. friend and his mother. Another friend let us use his car. I recalled how the summer had been spent trying to repair the bankrupt affairs of the A.A. book, which money-wise had failed so dismally after its publication. We had a hard time keeping the sheriff out of our little cubicle of an office at 17 William Street, Newark, where most of the volume had been written.

We attended New Jersey's first A.A. meeting, held in the summer of 1939, at the Upper Montclair house of Henry P., my partner in the now shaky book enterprise. There we met Bob and Mag V., our great friends-to-be. When at Thanksgiving snow fell on our summer camp, they invited us to spend the winter with them at their house in Monsey, New York.

That winter with Mag and Bob was both rough and exciting. Nobody had any money. Their house was a one-time mansion gone ramshackle. The furnace and the water pump quit by turns. An earlier member of Mag's family had built an addition of two huge rooms, one downstairs and one upstairs, which boasted no heat at all. The upper room was so cold they called it "Siberia." We fixed this with a second-hand coal stove which cost $3.75. It continually threatened to fall apart, and why we never burned the house down I'll never understand. But it was a very happy time; besides sharing all they had with us, Bob and Mag were expansively cheerful.

The big excitement came with the start of the first mental hospital group. Bob had been talking to Dr. Russell E. Blaisdell, head of New York's Rockland State Hospital, a mental institution, which stood nearby. Dr. Blaisdell had accepted the A.A. idea on sight for his alcoholic inmates. He gave us the run of their ward and soon let us start a meeting within the walls. The results were so good that a few months later he actually let busloads of committed alcoholics go to the A.A. meetings which by then had been established in South Orange, New Jersey, and in New York City. For an asylum superintendent this was certainly going way out on the limb. But the alcoholics did not let him down. At the same time the A.A. meeting was established on a regular basis in Rockland itself. The grimmest imaginable cases began to get well and stay that way when released. Thus began A.A.'s first working relation with a mental hospital, since duplicated more than 200 times. Dr. Blaisdell had written a bright page in the annals of alcoholism.

In this connection it should be noted that three or four alcoholics previously had been released into A.A. from Jersey's Greystone and Overbrook asylums, where friendly physicians had recommended us. But Dr. Blaisdell's Rockland State Hospital was the first to enter into full scale co-operation with A.A.

Lois and I finally recrossed the Hudson River to stay in New York City. Small A.A. gatherings were being held at that time in newcomer Bert's tailor shop. Later this meeting moved to a small room in Steinway Hall and thence into permanent quarters when A.A.'s first clubhouse, "The Old Twenty-Fourth," was opened. Lois and I went there to live.

As we looked back over those early scenes in New York, we saw often in the midst of them the benign little doctor who loved drunks, William Duncan Silkworth, then Physician-in-Chief of the Charles B. Towns Hospital in New York, a man who was very much a founder of A.A. From him we learned the nature of our illness. He supplied us with the tools with which to puncture the toughest alcoholic ego, those shattering phrases by which he described our illness: *the obsession of the mind* that compels us to drink *and the allergy of the body* that condemns us to go mad or die. These were indispensable passwords. Dr. Silkworth taught us how to till the black soil of hopelessness out of which every single spiritual awakening in our fellowship has since flowered. In December, 1934, this man of science had humbly sat by my bed following my own sudden and overwhelming spiritual experience, reassuring me. "No, Bill," he had said, "you are not hallucinating. Whatever you have got, you had better hang on to; it is so much better than what you had only an hour ago." These were great words for the A.A. to come. Who else could have said them?

When I wanted to go to work with alcoholics, Dr. Silkworth led me to them right there in his hospital, and at great risk to his professional reputation.

After six months of failure on my part to dry up any drunks, he again reminded me of Professor William James' observation that truly transforming spiritual experiences are nearly always founded on calamity and collapse. "Stop preaching at them," Dr. Silkworth had said, "and give them the hard medical facts first. This may soften them up at depth so that they will be willing *to do anything* to get well. Then they may accept those spiritual ideas of yours, and even a higher Power."

Four years later, Dr. Silkworth had helped to convert Mr. Charles B. Towns, the hospital's owner, into a great A.A. enthusiast and had encouraged him to loan $2,500 to start preparation of the book *Alcoholics Anonymous,* a sum, by the way, which was later increased to over $4,000. Then, as our only medical friend at the time, the good doctor boldly wrote the introduction to our book, where it remains to this day and where we intend to keep it always.

Perhaps no physician will ever give so much devoted attention to so many alcoholics as did Dr. Silkworth. It is estimated that in his lifetime he saw an amazing 40,000 of them. In the years before his death in 1951, in close co-operation with A.A. and our red-headed powerhouse nurse, Teddy, he had ministered to nearly 10,000 alcoholics at New York's Knickerbocker Hospital alone. None of those he treated will ever forget the experience, and the majority of them are sober today. Silky and Teddy were much inspired by Dr. Bob and Sister Ignatia at Akron and will always be regarded as their Eastern counterparts in our pioneering time. These four set the shining example and laid the basis for the wonderful partnership with medicine which we enjoy today.

We could not take leave of New York without paying grateful tribute to those who made today's world services possible: the very early pioneers of the Alcoholic Foundation, forerunner of A.A.'s present General Service Board.

First in order of appearance was Dr. Leonard V. Strong, Jr., my brother-in-law. When Lois and I were alone and deserted, he, together with my mother, saw us through the worst of my drinking. It was Dr. Strong who introduced me to Mr. Willard Richardson, one of the finest servants of God and man that I shall ever know. This introduction led directly to the formation of the Alcoholic Foundation. Dick Richardson's steady faith, wisdom, and spiritual quality were our main anchors to windward during the squalls that fell on A.A. and its embryo service center in the first years, and he carried his conviction and enthusiasm to still others who labored for us so well. With selfless care and devotion, Dr. Strong served as secretary to our Board of Trustees from its beginning in 1938 until his own retirement in 1955.

Dick Richardson was an old friend and confidant of the John D. Rockefellers, Senior and Junior. The result was that Mr. Rockefeller,

Jr., became deeply interested in A.A. He saw that we had the small sum necessary to launch our service project, yet not enough to professionalize it, and he gave a dinner in 1940 to many of his friends so they might meet some of us and see A.A. for themselves. This dinner, at which Dr. Harry Emerson Fosdick and the neurologist Dr. Foster Kennedy talked, was a significant public recommendation of our fellowship at a time when we were few and unknown. Sponsoring such a dinner could have brought Mr. Rockefeller under much ridicule. He did it nevertheless, giving a very little of his fortune and much of himself.

Mr. Richardson brought still other friends to our aid. There was Mr. Albert Scott, head of an engineering firm and Chairman of the Board of Trustees of the Riverside Church in New York, who presided over the famous meeting in late 1937 in Mr. Rockefeller's office which was the first gathering of some of us alcoholics with our new friends. Here Mr. Scott asked the searching and historic question: "Won't money spoil this thing?" Dr. Bob, Dr. Silkworth, and I attended that meeting, and there were present also two more friends of Mr. Richardson's who were destined to exert great influence on our affairs.

Early in the spring of 1938 our new friends helped us to organize the Alcoholic Foundation, and Mr. A. LeRoy Chipman tirelessly served for many years as its treasurer. In 1940 it seemed desirable for the Foundation to take over Works Publishing, Inc., the little company we had formed to handle the book, and two years later Mr. Chipman did most of the work in raising the $8,000 which was needed to pay off the shareholders and Mr. Charles B. Towns in full, thus making the Foundation the sole owner of the A.A. book and putting it in trust for our society for all time. Recently Mr. Chipman had to retire from the Board of Trustees because of illness and to his deep disappointment was unable to come to St. Louis. Nor could Dick Richardson be with us, for he had died some years before.

Present at that early 1940 meeting was yet another of Mr. Richardson's friends, Frank Amos, a newspaper and advertising executive and a Trustee of A.A., only lately retired. In 1938 Frank went out to Akron to meet Dr. Bob and to make a careful survey of what had transpired there. It was his glowing report of Dr. Bob and Akron's Group Number One that had caught Mr. Rockefeller's interest and had further encouraged the formation of the Foundation. This Foundation was to become the focal point of A.A.'s world services, which have been responsible for much of the unity and growth of our whole fellowship. Frank Amos was accessible at his office or home in New York at almost any time of day or night, and his counsel and faith were of immense help to us.

As we New Yorkers continued to reminisce the small hours away at St. Louis, we thought of Ruth Hock, the devoted nonalcoholic girl who had taken reams of dictation and had done months of typing and retyping when the book *Alcoholics Anonymous* was in preparation. She often went without pay, taking the then seemingly worthless stock of Works Publishing instead. I recall with deep gratitude how often her wise advice and her good humor and patience helped to settle the endless squabbles about the book's content. Many an oldtimer at St. Louis also remembered with gratitude those warm letters Ruth had written to him when he was a loner struggling to stay sober out there in the grass roots.

Ruth was our first National Secretary, and when she left in early 1942 Bobbie B. took her place. Bobbie for several years faced almost single-handed the huge aftermath of group problems that followed in the wake of Jack Alexander's feature article on A.A. in the *Saturday Evening Post*. Writing thousands of letters to struggling individuals and wobbly new groups, she made all the difference during that time when it seemed very uncertain that A.A. could hang together at all.

While I was still reminiscing about old times in New York, the names of more of my alcoholic friends loomed up. I remembered Henry P., my partner in Works Publishing and the book enterprise. Among all the prospects Dr. Silkworth had pointed out to me at Towns Hospital, Henry in 1935 was the first one to sober up. He had been a big-time executive and salesman, and he turned his really prodigious enthusiasm into the formation of the New York group. Many a Jerseyite can remember his impact over there, too. When in 1938 the Foundation found it could not raise money to publish the A.A. book, it was largely Henry's insistence that caused us to set up Works Publishing, Inc., and while we were working on the book his endless hounding of the subscribers to Works Publishing kept enough money trickling in (barely enough!) to finish the job.

About that time there appeared on the New York scene another character, Fitz M., one of the most lovable people that A.A. will ever know. Fitz was a minister's son and deeply religious, an aspect of his nature which is revealed in his story entitled "Our Southern Friend" in the Big Book. Fitz fell at once into hot argument with Henry about the religious content of the coming volume. A newcomer named Jimmy B., who like Henry was an ex-salesman and former atheist, also got into the hassles. Fitz wanted a powerfully religious document; Henry and Jimmy would have none of it. They wanted a psychological book which would lure the reader in; when he finally arrived among us, there would then be enough time to tip him off about the spiritual character of our society. As we worked feverishly on this project Fitz made trip after trip to New York from his Maryland home to insist on raising the spiritual pitch of the A.A. book. Out of this debate came the spiritual form and substance of the document, notably the expression, *"God as we understood Him,"* which proved to be a ten-strike. As umpire of these disputes, I was obliged to go pretty much down the middle, writing in spiritual rather than religious or entirely psychological terms.

Fitz and Jimmy were equally ardent to carry the A.A. message. Jimmy started the Philadelphia group in 1940, while Fitz took the good news to Washington. The first meeting in Philadelphia was held in the home of George S. George was one of A.A.'s first loners. He had sobered up after reading the article "Alcoholics and God" written in 1939 by Morris Markey and published in the September issue of *Liberty* magazine by its then editor Fulton Oursler, who was to do much more for us later on. George's case was a very severe one, even for those days of "last gaspers." When the issue of *Liberty* first arrived, George was in bed drinking whiskey for his depression and taking laudanum for his colitis. The Markey piece hit George so hard that he went ex-grog and ex-laudanum instantly. He wrote to New York, and we gave his name to salesman Jimmy, who traveled that territory, and that's how A.A. started in the City of Brotherly Love.

Philadelphia A.A. soon attracted the attention of three noted Philadelphia physicians, Drs. A. Wiese Hammer, C. Dudley Saul, and John F. Stouffer, the latter of the Philadelphia General Hospital. The outcome of this interest was the best of hospital care for alcoholics and the opening of a clinic. And it was Dr. Hammer's friendship with Mr. Curtis Bok, owner of the *Saturday Evening Post,* that led to the publication in 1941 of Jack Alexander's article. These friends could hardly have done more for us.

Fitz, living near Washington, D.C., had no such breaks. Near-failure dogged his efforts for years. But he finally planted seed there that bore fruit and before his death in 1943 he saw that seed flower. His sister Agnes rejoiced with him. She had loaned him and me $1,000 from her modest resources when, after the A.A. book fiasco in 1939, the future had looked the darkest. To her I send our everlasting thanks.

The year 1939 saw the arrival among us of still another unforgettable character, a woman alcoholic known to so many of us as Marty. At Blythewood Sanitarium in Greenwich, Connecticut, she had been a patient of Dr. Harry Tiebout's, and he had handed her a prepublication manuscript copy of the A.A. book. The first reading made her rebellious, but the second convinced her. Presently she came to a meeting held in our living room at 182 Clinton Street, and from there she returned to Blythewood carrying this classic message to a fellow patient in the sanitarium: "Grennie, we aren't alone any more."

Marty pioneered a group in Greenwich so early in 1939 that some folks now think this one should carry the rating of A.A.'s Group Number Three. Backed by Dr. Harry and Mrs. Wylie, owner of

Blythewood, the first meetings were held on the sanitarium's grounds. Marty was one of the first women to try A.A., and she became in later years among the most active workers we have, as well as a pioneer in the field of education and rehabilitation for alcoholics. Today she holds the longest sobriety record in A.A. for her sex. There had been another earlier woman pioneer, Florence R., who had come among us in 1937. Her story was printed in the first edition of *Alcoholics Anonymous*. With great valor she had tried to help Fitz at Washington, but she became involved in the early wave of failure there and died of alcoholism.

Old-time midwesterners at the Convention could remember that while all this was going on in Akron and New York, certain candles were being lighted in Cleveland which presently sent up a flame that could be seen country-wide. A few older Clevelanders remembered how some of them had gone to the Akron meetings, then held in the home of Oxford Groupers T. Henry and Clarace Williams. There they had met Dr. Bob and Anne and had looked with wonder upon alcoholics who had stayed sober one and two and three years. They had met and listened to Henrietta Seiberling, the nonalcoholic who had brought Dr. Bob and me together in her house three years previously—one who had understood deeply and cared enough and who was already seen as one of the strongest links in the chain of events that Providence was unfolding. On other evenings, Clevelanders had gone to Dr. Bob's Akron home, sitting with him and Anne over cups of coffee at their kitchen table. Eagerly they had absorbed knowledge of their problem and its solution and had breathed deeply of the remarkable spiritual atmosphere of the place. They became friends with old Bill D., A.A. number three. At other times Dr. Bob had taken them to St. Thomas Hospital, where they met Sister Ignatia, saw her at work, and in their turn talked to the newcomers on the beds. Returning to Cleveland, they began to dig up their own prospects and got to know for the first time the pains, the joys, and the benefits of A.A.'s Twelve Steps.

Clarence S. and his wife Dorothy were among the earliest contingent to come from Cleveland to the Akron meeting. By the early summer of 1939 a group had commenced to form around them in Cleveland where, by fall, they could count a score or more of promising recoveries.

At this point the *Cleveland Plain Dealer* ran a series of pieces that ushered in a new period for Alcoholics Anonymous, the era of mass production of sobriety.

Elrick B. Davis, a feature writer of deep understanding, was the author of a series of articles that were printed in the middle of the *Plain Dealer's* editorial page, and these were accompanied every two or three days by red-hot blasts from the editors themselves. In effect the *Plain Dealer* was saying, "Alcoholics Anonymous is good, and it works. Come and get it."

The newspaper's switchboard was deluged. Day and night, the calls were relayed to Clarence and Dorothy and from them to members of their little group. Earlier in the year, through the good offices of Nurse Edna McD. and the Rev. Kitterer, Administrator of Deaconess Hospital, an A.A. entry was made into this institution. But this one hospital could not begin to cope with the situation that now confronted Cleveland. For weeks and weeks A.A.'s ran about in desperate haste to make Twelfth Step calls on the swelling list of prospects. Great numbers of these had to be tossed into other Cleveland hospitals such as Post Shaker, East Cleveland Clinic, and several more. How the bills were paid nobody ever quite knew.

Sparked by Clarence and Dorothy, clergymen and doctors began to give great help. Father Nagle and Sister Victorine at St. Vincent's Charity Hospital were meeting the new tide with love and understanding, as was Sister Merced at St. John's. Dr. Dilworth Lupton, the noted Protestant clergyman, preached and wrote warmly about us. This fine gentleman had once tried to sober up Clarence, and when he saw A.A. do the job he was astonished. He published a pamphlet, widely used in Cleveland, entitled "Mr. X and Alcoholics Anonymous." "Mr. X" of course was Clarence.

It was soon evident that a scheme of personal sponsorship would have to be devised for the new people. Each prospect was assigned an older A.A., who visited him at his home or in the hospital, instructed him on A.A. principles, and conducted him to his first meeting. But in the face of many hundreds of pleas for help, the supply of elders could not possibly match the demand. Brand-new A.A.'s, sober only a month or even a week, had to sponsor alcoholics still drying up in the hospitals.

Homes were thrown open for meetings. The first Cleveland meeting started in June, 1939, at the home of Abby G. and his wife Grace. It was composed of Abby and about a dozen others who had been making the journey to Akron to meet at the Williams home. But Abby's group presently ran out of space. So one segment began to meet in the home of Cleveland's financier, Mr. T. E. Borton, at his generous invitation. Another part of the group found quarters in a hall in the Lakewood section of Cleveland and became known as the Orchard Grove Group. And still a third offshoot of Abby's meeting went under the name of the Lee Road Group.

These multiplying and bulging meetings continued to run short of home space, and they fanned out into small halls and church basements. Luckily the A.A. book had come off the press six months before, and some pamphlets were also available. These were the guides and time-savers that probably kept the hectic situation from confusion and anarchy.

We old-timers in New York and Akron had regarded this fantastic phenomenon with deep misgivings. Had it not taken us four whole years, littered with countless failures, to produce even a hundred good recoveries? Yet there in Cleveland we saw about twenty members, not very experienced themselves, suddenly confronted by hundreds of newcomers as a result of the *Plain Dealer* articles. How could they possibly manage? We did not know.

But a year later we *did* know; for by then Cleveland had about thirty groups and several hundred members. Growing pains and group problems had been terrifying, but no amount of squabbling could dampen the mass demand for sobriety. Yes, Cleveland's results were of the best. Their results were in fact so good, and A.A.'s membership elsewhere was so small, that many a Clevelander really thought A.A. had started there in the first place.

The Cleveland pioneers had proved three essential things: the value of personal sponsorship; the worth of the A.A. book in indoctrinating newcomers, and finally the tremendous fact that A.A., when the word really got around, could now soundly grow to great size.

Many of the essentials of A.A. as we now understand them were to be found already in the pioneering groups in Akron, New York, and Cleveland as early as 1939. But there remained much more to be done and lots of questions to be answered. Would many A.A.'s, for example, moving out of the old original groups, be successful in new towns and cities? In those days the first few of our early A.A. travelers, the forerunners of thousands, were on the move.

We had watched one named Earl T. as, soundly indoctrinated by Dr. Bob and the Akronites, he returned home to Chicago in 1937. With much concern we had followed his constant but fruitless efforts to start a group there, a struggle that lasted two whole years, despite the help of Dick R., his first "convert," and Ken A., who had migrated from the Akron group in 1938. Then in mid-1939 two Chicago doctors came upon the scene. Earl's friend, Dr. Dan Craske, handed him two floundering patients. One of them, Sadie, began to stay dry.

A little while later a Dr. Brown of Evanston exposed several patients to Earl. Among them were Sylvia, Luke, and Sam and his wife Tee, all of whom have remained sober to this day. Sylvia, however, got off to a slow start. In desperation she visited Akron and Cleveland, the founding centers in Ohio. Here she was exposed to Henrietta and Dr. Bob, and was worked over by Clarence and Dorothy, the Cleveland elders. Still she drank on. She returned to her home in Chicago, where for reasons best known to herself and God, she suddenly got sober and stayed that way.

Chicago now had the solid nucleus from which its coming great growth could issue. Continually encouraged by Dr. Brown, vastly helped by Sylvia's nonalcoholic personal secretary, Grace Cultice, and cheered on by Earl's wife Katie, the Chicagoans started to search for still more prospects. Meetings soon began, both in Earl's home and in Sylvia's.

As A.A. in Chicago slowly grew and prospered, Grace was continually at the business end of Sylvia's phone, and she became the group's first secretary. When the *Saturday Evening Post* article appeared in 1941, the traffic became very heavy. Sylvia's place became a sort of Chicago Grand Central, and things were just about as rugged with Earl and Katie. Something had to be done. So they rented a one-room office in the Loop, and secretary Grace was installed there to direct the stream of applicants for Twelfth Step attention, hospitalization, or other help. This was A.A.'s first organized local service center, the forerunner of the many Intergroup Associations we maintain in large cities nowadays. Many an A.A. group within a several-hundred-mile radius of Chicago can trace its origin to the work of that center—notable early ones being Green Bay, Wisconsin, and Minneapolis, Minnesota.

Meanwhile, Katie realized that many A.A. families needed the program as much as their alcoholics did, and she vigorously carried on the precedent already set by Anne and Lois who—in their homes, in their A.A. travels with Dr. Bob and myself, and even upstairs in New York's Old Twenty-Fourth Street Club—had urged A.A.'s Twelve Steps upon nonalcoholic wives and husbands as a way of restoring family life to normal.

No one knows exactly when the first Family Group as such started. One of the largest, most vigorous, and best accepted of the early family centers developed in Toronto, Canada. There they wrought so well that many A.A. groups in the area customarily invite Family Group speakers to their meetings. By 1950, the Toronto Family Group had created such a wide and deep impression that their speakers were featured at the Cleveland International A.A. Convention of that year. And what was true of Toronto was equally true of Long Beach, California, and Richmond, Virginia. Indeed, some of these latter Family Groups may quite possibly have antedated Toronto somewhat. In any case it is sure that Anne, Lois, and Katie long ago planted the ideas which have since flowered into hundreds of Al-Anon Family Groups, one of the most encouraging developments in the whole A.A. picture in recent years.

Another early A.A. traveler was Archie T. He had been tenderly nursed back to sobriety in the home of Dr. Bob and Anne at Akron. Still sick, frail, and frightened, he returned to his native city, Detroit, the scene of his downfall, where his personal reputation and financial credit still stood at zero. We saw Archie make amends everywhere he could. We saw him delivering dry cleaning out of a broken-down jalopy to the back doors of his one-time fashionable friends in Grosse Pointe. We saw him, helped by a dedicated nonalcoholic, Sarah Klein, start a group that met in her basement. Archie and Sarah next straightened out a man named Mike, a manufacturer, and a socialite lady named Anne K. These were the ones from whom stemmed Detroit's huge membership of later years.

Then there was Larry J., a newspaperman who had barely escaped death by d.t.'s and exhaustion. Despite a lung ailment that required him to spend much time in an oxygen tent, he courageously set out from Cleveland to Houston, Texas, and on the train he experienced a spiritual awakening that made him feel, as he said, "all in one piece again." On his arrival in Houston, Larry wrote a series of pieces for the *Houston Press* that attracted the attention of the townsmen and their Bishop Quinn, and thus finally, after heartbreaking setbacks, the first group in Texas emerged. Larry's first good prospects were salesman Ed, who was to carry the message to Austin; Army Sergeant Roy, who made the start at Tampa, Florida, and who later helped greatly in Los Angeles; and one Esther, who presently moved to Dallas, where, with characteristic enthusiasm and energy, she founded A.A. in that town and became dean of all the alky ladies in the astonishing state of Texas.

Meanwhile Cleveland A.A. had sobered up Rollie H., a famous athlete. Newspaper stories about this event were sensational and they brought in many new prospects. Nevertheless this development was one of the first to arouse deep concern about our personal anonymity at the top public level.

Still another famous early itinerant was Irwin M., a Cleveland A.A. who had become a champion salesman of Venetian blinds to department stores in the deep South. He used to range a territory bounded by Atlanta and Jacksonville on one side and Indianapolis, Birmingham, and New Orleans on the other. Irwin weighed 250 pounds and was full of energy and gusto. The prospect of Irwin, as a missionary, scared us rather badly. At the New York Headquarters we had on file a long list of topers in many a Southern city and town, people who had not been personally visited. Irwin had long since broken all the rules of caution and discreet approach to newcomers, so it was with reluctance that we gave him the list. Then we waited—but not for long. Irwin ran them down, every single one, with his home-crashing tornado technique. Day and night, besides, he wrote letters to his prospects and got them to writing each other.

Stunned but happy Southerners began to send their thanks to Headquarters. As Irwin himself reported, many a first family of the South had been an easy pushover. He had cracked the territory wide open and had started or stimulated many an original group.

Still thinking of the South, we remembered the Richmond A.A.'s who believed in getting away from wives and drinking only beer, but who became more orthodox through the ministrations of the Virginia squire, Jack W., and certain A.A. travelers. We thought, too, of the Jersey boiler inspector, the tireless Dave R., who had descended upon Charlotte, North Carolina; and of Fred K., another Jersey man, who set the A.A. ferment going in Miami; and of super-promoter Bruce H., who, working in Jacksonville and its environs, was the first to use radio to carry the message.

Shortly after the beginning of A.A. in Atlanta, that shaky group was sparked by the appearance of Sam, a high-powered Yankee preacher, temporarily minus frock and salary. Sam spoke with great effect from both pulpit and A.A. platform. He created a sort of "Chautauqua" brand of A.A. which was mildly deprecated by some members but cheered on by others. Sam has since passed away, but his work is remembered gratefully.

Many more of these early people and early stories came flooding back to mind as we in St. Louis continued to review the history of A.A.'s growth. We remembered the excitement of the formation of the first A.A. group solely by mail in Little Rock, Arkansas; the first Canadian group in Toronto and soon after those in Windsor and Vancouver, B.C.; the first beginning in Australia and Hawaii, creating a pattern later followed in some seventy foreign lands and U.S. possessions; the affecting tale of the little Norwegian from Greenwich, Connecticut, who had sold all he had to go to Oslo to help his brother and thus started the group there; the Alaskan group that had taken shape because a prospector out in the wilds found an A.A. book in an old oil drum; the Utah alkies who dried up in A.A. and struck uranium in the process; the spread of A.A. to South Africa, Mexico, Puerto Rico, South America, England, Scotland, Ireland, France, and Holland, and then to Japan and even Greenland and Iceland; the story of Captain Jack in a Standard Oil tanker, spreading A.A. as he sailed. In such happy reminiscences we at St. Louis reviewed A.A.'s crossing of the barriers of distance, race, creed, and tongue and saw our fellowship reaching to the four corners of the earth.

These tales brought Lois and me wonderful recollections of our six weeks' journey abroad in 1950.

We could remember the heated arguments between the Swedes of Stockholm and the Swedes of Göteborg over whether A.A. should be based on Stockholm's "Seven Steps" or America's "Twelve." We recalled meeting the founder of the wonderful group in Helsinki, Finland. We could still see the Danes at Copenhagen as their "Ring i Ring" wondered whether A.A. or antabuse was their answer. We remembered Henk Krauweel, in whose home we were guests while in Holland. Henk, a social worker and nonalcoholic, was engaged by the city of Amsterdam to see what he could do for the drunks there. He had been able to do very little until one day he ran across A.A.'s

Twelve Steps. Translating them into Dutch, he handed them to some of his charges. To his astonishment, several tough cases went dry. And by the time we arrived he could show us plenty more. A.A. was solid in the Netherlands and well on its way. Our great friend Henk Krauweel has since become one of Europe's leading authorities on the total alcohol problem.

In Paris we found several scattered American A.A.'s who acted mostly as a reception committee for A.A. travelers, some dry and some in deep trouble. The Frenchmen at Paris were still pretty shy about A.A. and they were possessed of the wonderful rationalization that wine was not liquor at all and was therefore quite harmless!

In London and Liverpool we met many very anonymous Englishmen. In those days their meetings had a definite parliamentary atmosphere, including a gavel which was struck at appropriate moments. Of course the Irish A.A. was everything we expected and more. The South-of-Ireland A.A.'s at Dublin were on a most genial basis with the North Irelanders at Belfast, despite an occasional burst of rock throwing among their compatriots in the streets. We watched as the seeds of A.A. pushed up their sprouts in Scotland, and when we encountered Scottish hospitality we knew for sure that the Scotsman A.A. is neither penurious nor dour.

To Lois and me this overseas experience was like turning the clock back to early times at home. Depending on their stage of progress, the foreign groups of that day were either flying blind, were hopefully pioneering, or had reached the fearsome and sometimes quarrelsome state of adolescence. They were re-enacting all of our American experiences of fifteen, ten, and five years before. We returned home with the sure conviction that nothing could stop their progress, that they could surmount all barriers of social caste or language. In the seven years since our 1950 visit, the A.A. achievement overseas has far exceeded our highest hopes.

I have saved our Norwegian impression for the final part of this foreign account, because the story of the beginning there is a classic. It all started in Greenwich, Connecticut, in a coffee shop owned by a quiet little Norwegian and his devoted wife. The Greenwich group had lifted him to sobriety and his shop had become a popular rendezvous for them.

The little Norwegian had not written and had not heard from home in the twenty years he had been a virtual derelict. But now, feeling sure of himself, he sent a letter bringing the folks back there up to date and telling them all about himself and his escape from alcoholic oblivion via A.A.

He soon received an excited and pleading letter, telling him of the awful plight of his brother, a typesetter on an Oslo newspaper. The brother, his relatives said, was not long for his job and maybe not long for this world. What could be done?

The little Norwegian in Greenwich took counsel with his wife. They sold their coffee shop, all they had in the world, and bought a round-trip to Oslo, with only a little to spare. A few days later they saw their homeland. From the airfield they hurried down the east bank of Oslo fjord to the stricken brother's house. It was just as they had been told; the brother was close to the jumping-off place.

But Brother was obstinate. The man from Greenwich told his A.A. story and retold it. He translated the Twelve Steps of A.A. and a small pamphlet he had brought along. But it was no use; Brother would have none of it. Said the travelers, "Have we come all the way to Oslo just for this? Our money will soon run out and we shall have to go back." Brother said nothing.

So the Norwegian from Greenwich began to canvass the clergymen and some of the doctors in Oslo. They were polite but not interested. Much cast-down, the A.A. and his wife made their plans to return to America.

Then the impossible happened. Brother suddenly called out and said, "Tell me more about those anonymous alcoholics in America. Explain again their Twelve Steps to me." He sobered up almost at once and was able to watch his brother's plane take to the air for New York. He had got the message all right, but he was alone now. What could he do?

The instant he got back to work he started modest ads in his own newspaper, one every day for a month. Nothing happened until the very last day. Then the wife of one of Oslo's sidewalk florists wrote him a letter asking help for her husband. When the florist heard the story and studied the Twelve Steps he too dried up. The two-man group continued the newspaper notices that A.A. had come to town. Soon they had a third sober member. Among others who followed was a patient of Dr. Gordon Johnson's, Oslo's leading psychiatrist. Dr. Johnson, a deeply religious man, at once saw the implications of A.A.'s Twelve Steps and immediately threw the whole weight of his reputation behind the uncertain little group.

Three years later Lois and I looked through the customs gate at Oslo Airport upon a large welcoming delegation. Very few words of English could they speak, but they didn't have to. We could see and feel what they had. On the way to the hotel we learned that Norway already had hundreds of A.A.'s now spread into many groups. It was unbelievable, yet there they were.

What happened to the little Norwegian from Greenwich? He came home and somehow started another coffee shop. Four years later he suffered a heart attack and died. But not before he had seen A.A. grow great in Norway.

One more word about Norway. Quite unknown to the rest of that country, a group had sprung up in Bergen at about the same time that Oslo got underway. Hans H., a Scandinavian-American, had returned to his home town with an A.A. book. Having perfect command of English, he could translate it into Norwegian as he read aloud to a tiny band of alcoholics that he had somehow gathered about him. With the benefit of this auspicious beginning several laid hold of sobriety and thereafter spread the message in this city to such good effect that Bergen today can point to sixteen A.A. groups as the remarkable result.

At many another Convention meeting the panorama of A.A. in action today was unfolded. A.A. clubs, now numbered by the hundreds, had their problems aired and their assets and liabilities weighed.

There was a lively swapping of experience on how best we could give brother and sister sufferers in mental hospitals and prisons a still better break while they were in these places and when they left them. Great numbers of these folks were already making good and had become our fast friends and co-workers on the outside, and we realized how foolish had been our early fears of the alcoholic bearing a double stigma. In still another seminar secretaries and committeemen of scores of local central services, the so-called Intergroup Associations, exposed their many problems for each other's inspection and advice, always seeking to remedy the functional weaknesses of the many newer service bodies just trying to get under way.

In another meeting the whole subject of money in A.A. got a most healthy kicking around. A.A.'s principle of "no compulsory fees or dues" *can* be construed and rationalized into "no voluntary group or individual responsibility at all," and this fallacy was exploded with a bang. There was complete unanimity that through voluntary contributions the legitimate bills of groups, areas, and A.A. as a whole *must* be paid or we could not properly carry our message. It was agreed that no A.A. treasury ought to get overstuffed or rich. Nevertheless, it was emphasized that the notion of keeping A.A. "simple" and "spiritual" by eliminating vital services that happened to cost a little time, trouble, and money was risky and absurd. It was the opinion of the meeting that oversimplification, which might lead us to muff our Twelfth Step work, area-wide and world-wide, could not be called either really simple or really spiritual.

Then there was a very moving get-together of lone A.A. members who had come in from the far reaches and isolated outposts to share the unusual view of our fellowship that St. Louis afforded. To no others could the Convention mean so much. They got a fresh sense of belonging, and they realized that their isolation was never so complete as they had sometimes felt it to be. They knew, as few did, how greatly A.A.'s literature and world services could help, for their sobriety had depended heavily upon the Big Book and upon those constant letters that came to them from Headquarters and fellow loners.

They had developed all sorts of gimmicks and disciplines to bulwark themselves and to perfect their conscious contact with God, who, they had joyfully discovered, could just as well be felt and heard whether one dwelt in a ship crossing the equator or next door to the polar icecap.

Typical of the loner stories was that of the Australian sheepman who lived 2,000 miles from the nearest town where yearly he sold his wool. In order to be paid the best prices he had to go to town during a certain month. But when he heard that a big regional A.A. meeting was to be held at a later date when wool prices would have fallen, he had gladly taken a heavy money loss in order to make his journey then. That's how much an A.A. meeting could mean to him. This was something that every loner at St. Louis could well understand.

At another interesting gathering the founders of many groups assembled to swap information on how best to get going in a new locality. Since more than 7,000[9] A.A. groups with a total membership of over 200,000 had already been spawned over the years and new ones were taking shape somewhere in the world almost every day, there were plenty of experiences to share.

In still another section of the Convention there was much to be learned about A.A.'s *Grapevine,* our magazine of more than 40,000[10] monthly circulation and our biggest and best means of communicating current A.A. thought and experience in staying sober, in hanging together, and in serving. Among members of the *Grapevine's* staff on hand were editor Don, three editorial assistants, a photographer, and a number of artists and magazine experts. By talks and exhibits they showed how the *Grapevine's* well-illustrated pages could be a lively and convincing means of introducing A.A. to the new or potential member, and how its articles could provide solid material for closed meetings and discussion. The *Grapevine* was seen as the monthly mirror of A.A. in action, always the same principle yet ever grow-

[9] As of 1978, there were over 30,000 groups worldwide and an estimated total of over 1,000,000 members.
[10] Circulation in 1979 is over 115,000.

ing and ever finding better ways of doing and thinking on new fronts of our exciting adventure in living and working together.

Then there was a session called "Presenting the Headquarters Staff." The staff was headed by manager Hank G., and it included fellow workers with talents in finance, public relations, and the like, and five capable A.A. women staff members. There was an extensive set of exhibits showing the wide range of activities of our top services. To the onlookers the World Headquarters of Alcoholics Anonymous was no longer the source of dry statistics about tons of literature, thousands of calls for help and letters in reply, and hundreds of problems of groups and of public information, or just the source of pleas for voluntary contributions. Here were the flesh-and-blood folks who were actually *doing* these things, and a well-trained, eager, and dedicated group they were, just like the *Grapevine* gang.

Countless A.A.'s at the Convention got to know our Trustees, those faithful alcoholic and nonalcoholic friends who had served us so long. Many a grass-rooter talked with Archie Roosevelt and learned that this exuberant and genial man had recently joined the Board and had taken on the sometimes thankless and always time-consuming job of being its treasurer. Grass-rooters and city people alike began to say, "Well, if our new nonalcoholic friend Archie can spend years looking after A.A.'s general finances, then we guess that we can certainly spare the minute it takes twice yearly to reach into our pockets for those two dollars that Archie needs to balance A.A.'s budget."

Right up front among the biggest eye-openers of the Convention were Al-Anon Family Group meetings, which bore the titles: "Meet the Staff," "The Children of Alcoholics," "Adjustment Between Husbands and Wives," and "The Twelve Steps." In St. Louis many a skeptical A.A. had his first look at this movement within a movement and learned with astonishment that the Family Groups had jumped from 70 to 700 in only three years and that right now a brand-new one was popping up in the world about every day. Lois and speakers from many areas told us that the Family Groups had a world clearinghouse much like A.A.'s Headquarters and that already there was literature, the beginning of a magazine, and even a new book.

Many A.A.'s had wondered what these Family Groups were all about. Were they gossip clubs, commiseration societies? Were they coffee and cake auxiliaries? Did they divert A.A. from its single purpose of sobriety? The Family Group meetings provided the answers: These new groups were *not* also-rans to A.A., nor were they gossip factories. The families of alcoholics—wives, husbands, mothers, fathers, and children—were pointing A.A.'s principles right straight at themselves and at nobody else.

The Family Group speakers asked and answered plenty of questions like these: "Weren't we just as powerless over alcohol as the alcoholics themselves? Sure we were." "And when we found that out, weren't we often filled with just as much bitterness and self-pity as the alcoholic ever had been? Yes, that was sometimes a fact." "After the first tremendous relief and happiness which resulted when A.A. came along, hadn't we often slipped back into secret and deep hurt that A.A. had done the job and we hadn't? For many of us, that was certainly so." "Not realizing that alcoholism is an illness, hadn't we taken sides with the kids against the drinking member? Yes, we had often done that, to their damage. No wonder, then, that when sobriety came, the emotional benders in our homes often went right on and sometimes got worse."

As the A.A.'s listened, the Family Group speakers continued: "Could we find an answer for all of this? At first, no. The A.A. meetings sometimes helped us, but not enough. We got a better understanding of the alcoholic problem but not enough of our own condition. We thought A.A.'s Twelve Steps were wonderful for alcoholics, but didn't think *we* had to take them too seriously. After all, *we* had been doing our best. There was nothing much wrong with *us*. So we reasoned, and so we complained when things continued to go badly at home. Or often, if things went well, we turned complacent or maybe rather jealous of all the time our partners thought they had to spend on A.A.

"But when the Family Groups were formed, these notions and attitudes began to change, and the change was mainly in us. The transformation really set in when we began to practice A.A.'s Twelve Steps in daily living, in all our affairs, and in the company of those who were able to understand our problems as no alcoholic partner could.

"In the Family Groups we see men and women, even those with active alcoholics on their hands, shake off their miseries and begin to live serenely, without blame or recrimination. We have seen many a partner, whose mate was sober in A.A. but still hard to live with, completely alter his or her thinking. Finally we have seen badly bent children straighten around and begin to respect and love their parents once more. We have seen many kinds of pride and fear and domination and nagging and maddening possessiveness just melted away by the Twelve Steps as we practice them in the home. Like our A.A. partners, we Family Groupers are now getting the tremendous dividend which comes from the practice of Step Twelve, 'carrying the message.' And the message of our Family Group is this: 'You can have more than alcoholic sobriety in your own family; you can have emotional sobriety, too. Even if the rest of the family about you hasn't yet found stability, you can still have *yours*. And your own emotional sobriety often can hasten the happy day of change for them.'"

Many an A.A. member who saw the Family Groups in action in St. Louis said afterwards, "This is one of the best things that has happened since A.A. began."

When they saw the Convention's pressroom, many visitors realized for the first time that good communications, within and without, were the actual arteries in which A.A.'s life-giving blood circulates among us and thence out to brother and sister sufferers everywhere. Something more than slow word-of-mouth message-carrying obviously has been required. Certainly not much Twelfth Step work ever could have been done until the sick ones and their families had been reached and persuaded that A.A. might offer hope for them. This kind of communication often required the good will of clergymen, doctors, employers, and friends—indeed, the good will of the public at large. For years A.A.'s Headquarters had used every possible means of enlisting such good will, and in addition to our own efforts our friends of the press—newspapers, magazines, and later radio and television—had told our story faithfully and often and had reported eventful A.A. occasions whenever they occurred. Thus they had drawn thousands of alcoholics into our membership and were still doing so.

They had not done this, of course, without help from us. Years ago we found that accurate and effective publicity about A.A. simply does not manufacture itself. Our over-all public relations couldn't be left entirely to chance encounters between reporters and A.A. members, who might or might not be well informed about our fellowship as a whole. This kind of unorganized "simplicity" often garbled the true story of A.A. and kept people away from us. A badly slanted press could prolong preventable suffering and even result in unnecessary deaths.

When in 1941 the *Saturday Evening Post* assigned Jack Alexander to scout A.A. for a feature story, we had already learned our lesson. Therefore nothing was left to chance. Had Jack been able to get to St. Louis for the Convention he himself could have told how skeptical he had been of this assignment. He had just finished doing a piece on the Jersey rackets, and he didn't believe anybody on a stack of Bibles a mile high.

After Jack checked in with us at Headquarters, we took him in tow for nearly a whole month. In order to write his powerful article, he had to have our fullest attention and carefully organized help. We gave him our records, opened the books, introduced him to nonalcoholic Trustees, fixed up interviews with A.A.'s of every description, and finally showed him the A.A. sights from New York and Philadelphia all the way to Chicago, via Akron and Cleveland. Although he was not an alcoholic, Jack soon became a true A.A. convert in spirit. When at last he sat down at his typewriter, his heart was in it. He was no longer on the outside of A.A. looking in; he was really inside looking out. As soon as the article appeared, 6,000 frantic inquiries hit our New York post office. Jack's piece made Alcoholics Anonymous a national institution, and it also made him one of our greatest friends and, finally, one of our Trustees.

The kind of help we gave Jack Alexander—our organized service of public information—is the vital ingredient in our public relations that most A.A.'s have never seen. But in the St. Louis pressroom the visitors did see one aspect of it, working this time for the Convention itself. There sat A.A.'s Ralph, handling our contacts with the press. He was surrounded by phones, typewriters, piles of releases, clip-sheets, telegrams in and out—all the gadgets of his trade. Now what was he doing and why? Could this be a ballyhooed promotion stunt, something quite contrary to A.A. Traditions?

Not a bit of it. Ralph was handling this job simply to help our friends of press, radio, and television. The whole world wanted to know about our twentieth anniversary. Newspapers and magazines wanted interviews and press releases. Radio and television broadcasters wanted to arrange for interviews. People wanted us to explain what we meant when we said that A.A. had "come of age."

Our friends in A.A. and millions outside wanted to read and hear and see, and it was certainly up to us to help. It was not always a question of our communicating with *them:* lots of them wanted to communicate with *us,* especially alcoholics and families who were still suffering. The city fathers of St. Louis sent their warmest congratulations, and this reminded us of their generosity in giving the use of the Kiel Auditorium free of charge. We were further reminded of the wonderful cordiality of the local groups in town, the hospitable clubs and the many parties.

Telegrams came to us in the Kiel Auditorium from A.A. people and groups everywhere. One of the brightest highlights of the Convention appeared in this message:

Dateline: The White House; Sender: The President of the United
States
Please convey to all who participate in your Twentieth Anniversary gathering my good wishes for a successful meeting. Your society's

record of growth and service is an inspiration to those who, through research, perseverance and faith, move forward to the solution of many serious personal and public health problems.

Dwight D. Eisenhower.

When this telegram was read to the Convention, we experienced great elation mixed with deep humility. A.A. had indeed come of age. In the eyes of the world we had now become full and responsible citizens once more.

The last day of the Convention moved from morning crescendo to afternoon climax. At 11:30 A.M. we began the meeting "God as We Understand Him." Deep silence fell as Dr. Jim S., the A.A. speaker, told of his life experience and the serious drinking that led to the crisis which had brought about his spiritual awakening. He re-enacted for us his struggle to start the very first group among Negroes, his own people. Aided by a tireless and eager wife, he had turned his home into a combined hospital and A.A. meeting place, free to all. As he told how early failure had finally been transformed under God's grace into amazing success, we who listened realized that A.A. not only could cross seas and mountains and boundaries of language and nation but could surmount obstacles of race and creed as well.

A great cheer of welcome greeted Father Ed Dowling as, indifferent to his grievous lameness, he made his way to the lectern. Father Dowling of the Jesuit order in St. Louis is intimately known to A.A.'s for a thousand miles and more around. Many in the Convention audience remembered with gratitude his ministry to their spiritual needs. St. Louis old-timers recalled how he helped start their group; it had turned out to be largely Protestant, but this fazed him not a bit. Some of us could remember his first piece about us in *The Queen's Work,* the sodality's magazine. He had been the first to note how closely in principle A.A.'s Twelve Steps paralleled a part of the Exercises of St. Ignatius, a basic spiritual discipline of the Jesuit order. He had boldly written in effect to all alcoholics and especially to those of his own faith: "Folks, A.A. is good. Come and get it." And this they certainly had done. His first written words were the beginning of a wonderfully benign influence in favor of our fellowship, the total of which no one will ever be able to compute.

Father Ed's talk to us at the Convention that Sunday morning flashed with humor and deep insight. As he spoke, the memory of his first appearance in my own life came back to me as fresh as though it were yesterday: One wintry night in 1940 in A.A.'s Old Twenty-Fourth Street Club in New York I had gone to bed at about ten o'clock with a severe dose of self-pity and my imaginary ulcer. Lois was out somewhere. Hail and sleet beat on the tin roof over my head; it was a wild night. The Club was deserted except for old Tom, the retired fireman, that diamond in the rough lately salvaged from Rockland asylum. The front doorbell clanged, and a moment later Tom pushed open my bedroom door. "Some bum," said he, "from St. Louis is down there and wants to see you." "Oh, Lord!" I said. "Not another one! And at this time of night. Oh, well, bring him up."

I heard labored steps on the stairs. Then, balanced precariously on his cane, he came into the room, carrying a battered black hat that was shapeless as a cabbage leaf and plastered with sleet. He lowered himself into my solitary chair, and when he opened his overcoat I saw his clerical collar. He brushed back a shock of white hair and looked at me through the most remarkable pair of eyes I have ever seen. We talked about a lot of things, and my spirits kept on rising, and presently I began to realize that this man radiated a grace that filled the room with a sense of presence. I felt this with great intensity; it was a moving and mysterious experience. In years since I have seen much of this great friend, and whether I was in joy or in pain he always brought to me the same sense of grace and the presence of God. My case is no exception. Many who meet Father Ed experience this touch of the eternal. It is no wonder that he was able to fill all of us there in the Kiel Auditorium with his inimitable spirit on that wonderful Sunday morning.

There came next to the lectern a figure that not many A.A.'s had seen before, the Episcopal clergyman Sam Shoemaker. It was from him that Dr. Bob and I in the beginning had absorbed most of the principles that were afterward embodied in the Twelve Steps of Alcoholics Anonymous, steps that express the heart of A.A.'s way of life Dr. Silkworth gave us the needed knowledge of our illness, but Sam Shoemaker had given us the concrete knowledge of what we could do about it. One showed us the mysteries of the lock that held us in prison; the other passed on the spiritual keys by which we were liberated.

Dr. Sam looked scarcely a day older than he had almost twenty-one years earlier when I first met him and his dynamic group at Calvary's parish house in New York. As he began to speak, his impact fell upon us there in the Kiel Auditorium just as it had upon Lois and me years before. As always, he called a spade a spade, and his blazing eagerness, earnestness, and crystal clarity drove home his message point by point. With all his vigor and power of speech, Sam nevertheless kept himself right down to our size. Here was a man quite as willing to talk about *his* sins as about anybody else's. He made himself a witness of God's power and love just as any A.A. might have done.

Sam's appearance before us was further evidence that many a channel had been used by Providence to create Alcoholics Anonymous. And none had been more vitally needed than the one opened through Sam Shoemaker and his Oxford Group associates of a generation before. The basic principles which the Oxford Groupers had taught were ancient and universal ones, the common property of mankind. Certain of the former O.G. attitudes and applications had proved unsuited to A.A.'s purpose, and Sam's own conviction about these lesser aspects of the Oxford Groups had later changed and become more like our A.A. views of today. But the important thing is this: the early A.A. got its ideas of self-examination, acknowledgment of character defects, restitution for harm done, and working with others straight from the Oxford Groups and directly from Sam Shoemaker, their former leader in America, and from nowhere else. He will always be found in our annals as the one whose inspired example and teaching did most to show us how to create the spiritual climate in which we alcoholics may survive and then proceed to grow. A.A. owes a debt of timeless gratitude for all that God sent us through Sam and his friends in the days of A.A.'s infancy.

As we approached our last session, a number of great questions still remained in the collective mind of the Convention. What would happen when A.A.'s originators and old-timers had gone? Would A.A. continue to grow and prosper? Could we go on functioning as a whole, no matter what perils the future brought? Had A.A. *really* come to the age of full responsibility? Could members and groups world-wide now safely assume complete control and guidance of A.A.'s principal affairs? Would A.A. now be able to take over from the old-timers, from Dr. Bob and from Bill? If so, by what agency, and just how?

For a long time these questions had been asked anxiously, and for over five years solutions for these problems had been eagerly sought, especially by old A.A. hands, people like myself who must soon relinquish their twenty years' guardianship of A.A. and turn over their trust to the vast family now fully reared. The time had come for the answers.

High in the great hall of the Kiel Auditorium there hung a banner on which everyone could see the new symbol for Alcoholics Anonymous, the triangle within the circle. On the stage far beneath the banner, at four o'clock on Sunday, our society was to be declared come of age. Its elected Service Conference, taking over the guardianship of our Traditions and the custody of our World Services, would then become the successor to the founders of Alcoholics Anonymous. The thousands of us were united in one spirit and in a great expectation as we sat waiting for the opening of this last meeting. What we thought and felt is hard to tell, hard especially for one person. It would help if someone could speak for all of us, and perhaps in a way this is possible. . . .

Each day at the Convention I had spoken with many A.A.'s, folks of every description and persuasion: plainsmen and mountain people, city dwellers and townsmen, workmen and businessmen, school-teachers and professors, clergymen and doctors, ad men and journalists, artists and builders, clerks and bankers, socialites and skid-rowers, career girls and housewives, people from other lands speaking in strange accents and tongues, Catholics and Protestants and Jews and men and women of no religion.

Of many of these people I asked the same questions: "What do you think of this Convention?" and "What do you think of A.A.'s future?" Each of course reacted according to his or her own viewpoint, but I was astonished when I sensed the unanimity of feeling and opinion that ran through all. I felt and still feel this so strongly that I believe it may be permissible here to introduce a spokesman for the whole Convention itself, a sort of composite character who nevertheless may truly portray what practically everybody at St. Louis really saw, really heard, and really felt. Let's call our anonymous spokesman Mr. Grassroots. He hails from Centerville, U.S.A., and this is what he has to say:

"I went to the Kiel," says Mr. Grassroots, "ahead of time for that last meeting. While I was waiting I thought of all that had happened to me in three days. I come from the small town of Centerville. I was born and raised there, did my drinking and got into my trouble there, and was about ready to throw in the sponge when A.A. came to town. Several years back a traveling chap tossed us the idea, and since then about a dozen of us alkies in Centerville have grabbed the life-line.

"The groups in my state are pretty small and scattered, and so we do not see much of each other. We've never had a state get-together. Our Centerville group has been just about all of A.A. for me. Good A.A., too. Of course we've had the Big Book and some pamphlets and the *Grapevine,* and now and then a traveler told us something about A.A. in other places. It was fine to know that other people like us were getting their chance, too. But our main interest was in each other and in the Centerville drunks that had not yet sobered up. The rest of A.A. seemed a long way off. There did not seem to be much that we could do about it anyhow, even if we wanted to. This was how it was with me before St. Louis.

"This Convention has been a terrific experience. I ran into hundreds of A.A.'s and their families charging around in the hotels. Then I saw thousands in the big Auditorium. I am sort of shy, but I got over that. I got mixed in with people who were having the time of their lives, people who came from five hundred, a thousand, maybe five thousand miles away—from places I'd only read about in the papers. Pretty soon I was telling them about A.A. in Centerville, rattling on as happy as anybody.

"These people were not strangers to me at all; it seems as if I had known and trusted and loved them all my life. I had felt that way about my A.A. group at home, but now I felt the same way about every A.A. and all of A.A. I can't tell you what this meant. To me it was big. This was real brotherhood. These were my people, my kin and my kind. I belonged to them and they belonged to me. Every barrier, every thought of race, creed, or nationality dropped out of my mind. This tremendous thing happened to me in only a few hours.

"I took in every meeting I could. I heard those doctors tell how much their profession was for us. I went to an Al-Anon meeting and realized for the first time that A.A. is for the whole family, too. The sessions on prisons and mental institutions convinced me that as a drinker I had been a piker and that almost no alcoholic disaster was too tough for A.A. to help. At other meetings I saw that A.A. had been facing and solving a lot of problems I never knew we had; problems in the big cities and all over the world. I saw that we still had plenty wrong with us as a fellowship, but I was sure that our present troubles would iron out as well as the others had.

"On Friday night I heard how A.A. started—how many people, nonalcoholic friends as well as ourselves, had been required to do the job—at how many points we could have run off the road for a complete smashup, yet how we had never yet overskidded a curve or failed to take the right turn. The hand of a higher Power had been on the wheel all the time.

"On Saturday night I felt like getting worried all over again as Bill told us how he and Dr. Bob had wondered all the way from 1939 to 1945 if A.A. was going to hang together after all, what with the troubles of members, groups, and new beginnings in foreign countries. I got a jolt when I heard that the A.A. book and the New York Headquarters had once been the source of the most hair-raising squabbles of all. Maybe this kind of thing could get going again someday. But I calmed down when it was made clear that all this old-time grief and uproar had actually been very good for us and that without this experience A.A.'s Twelve Traditions could never have been written. And I felt still better when I heard that by 1950 most of those woes were things of the past and that the Twelve Traditions had been adopted unanimously at the International Convention in Cleveland in 1950 when Dr. Bob made his final appearance and spoke so confidently of his faith in A.A.'s future.

"On Sunday morning—the last day of the Convention—I found those Twelve Traditions still on my mind. Each of them I saw is an exercise in humility that can guard us in everyday A.A. affairs and protect us from ourselves. If A.A. were really guided by the Twelve Traditions, we could not possibly be split apart by politics, religion, money, or by any old-timers who might take a notion to be big shots. With none of us throwing our weight around in public, nobody could possibly exploit A.A. for personal advantage, that is sure. For the first time I saw A.A.'s anonymity for *what it really is*. It isn't just something to save us from alcoholic shame and stigma; its deeper purpose is actually to keep those fool egos of ours from running hog wild after money and public fame at A.A.'s expense. It really means personal and group sacrifice for the benefit of all A.A. Right then I resolved to learn our Twelve Traditions by heart, just as I had learned the Twelve Steps. If every A.A. did the same thing and really soaked up these principles we drunks could hang together forever.

"I watched as the big hall of the Kiel Auditorium filled up. Thousands of my new-found friends were pouring in for the final windup. I caught sight of Father Ed as he eased himself into a seat across the aisle. He was a wonderful reminder of our morning session on the spiritual part of the program. In that session something happened to me I'll never forget.

"I had always carried a certain amount of prejudice against churches and clergymen and their concepts of God. Like many A.A.'s, my ideas about God were still mighty vague.

"But as these two spoke, it had loomed up on me that most of A.A.'s spiritual principles had come to us through clergymen. Without clergymen, A.A. could never have started in the first place. While I had been nursing my grudges against religion, Father Ed and Dr. Sam had been going all out for us. This was a brand-new revelation. Suddenly I realized that it was high time I began to love them, even as they had loved me and the rest of my kind.

"When I knew that I could now do this, I commenced to feel warm clear through. The conviction spread in me that love is a mighty personal thing. Then came the feeling that maybe my Creator really did know me and love me. So I could now begin to love Him, too. This was one of the best things that happened to me at St. Louis, and there must have been a lot of others there who had the same experience.

"Our last meeting finally began, and it opened with a silence that was charged with confident hope and faith. We knew that ours was a fellowship of the Spirit and that the grace of God was there."

Although these are only words put into the mouth of our created character Mr. Grassroots, they do represent much of the spirit and the truth that lived in the heart of many an A.A. as the St. Louis Convention moved toward its culmination.

From the Kiel stage I looked out upon the sea of faces gathered there, and I was powerfully stirred by the wonder of all that had happened in the incredible twenty years now coming to a climax. Had this meeting place been a hundred times larger, it still could not have held all of A.A.'s members and their families and friends.

Who could render an account of all the miseries that had once been ours, and who could estimate the release and joy that these last years had brought to us? Who could possibly tell the vast consequences of what God's work through A.A. had already set in motion? And who could penetrate the deeper mystery of our wholesale deliverance from slavery, a bondage to a most hopeless and fatal obsession which for centuries had possessed the minds and bodies of men and women like ourselves?

It may be possible to find explanations of spiritual experiences such as ours, but I have often tried to explain my own and have succeeded only in giving the story of it. I know the feeling it gave me and the results it has brought, but I realize I will never fully understand its deeper why and how.

We A.A.'s had tried out a radical and old-time formula, one rather out of fashion nowadays, and it had worked. "We admitted that we were powerless—that our lives had become unmanageable" and "we made a decision to turn our wills and our lives over to God *as we understood Him.*" Every one of us who could make and fairly well maintain this humbling admission and sweeping decision had found relief from obsession and had begun to grow into a totally and wonderfully different mental, physical, and spiritual existence.

The thought of Dr. Foster Kennedy crossed my mind. Years ago this noted physician had asked if one of A.A.'s early friends of psychiatry would come to the New York Academy of Medicine to explain A.A. to its neurological section. Since several doctors publicly had endorsed us, some in the *Saturday Evening Post* article of 1941, I thought there would be no difficulty about this. But every one of these medical friends of ours rejected the unusual opportunity.

In substance, this was what they said: "In A.A. we see an unusual number of social and psychological forces working together on the alcoholic problem. Yet fully allowing for this new advantage, we still cannot explain the *speed* of the results. A.A. does in weeks or months what should take years. Not only does drinking stop abruptly but great changes in the alcoholic's motivation follow in a few weeks or months. There is something at work in A.A. which we do not understand. We call this 'the X factor.' You people call it God. You can't explain God and neither can we—especially at the New York Academy of Medicine."

Such is the paradox of A.A. regeneration: strength arising out of complete defeat and weakness, the loss of one's old life as a condition for finding a new one. But we of A.A. do not have to understand this paradox; we have only to be grateful for it.

My mother was there on the auditorium stage, she who had brought me into life fifty-nine years before and who had waited a long anxious time for a happy fulfillment to my failure-ridden years. Beside her was my wife Lois, the one who held steadfast when hope had gone, who had attended my second birth, and who in full partnership had shared with me the pains and joys of our exciting life for the past twenty years.

And there sat my sponsor Ebby, who had first brought the word that lifted me out of the alcoholic pit.[11] With the whole convention I rejoiced that he could be with us. And I thought of many non-alcoholic friends of the very early days. Without them there could have been no A.A. at all. They had set us wonderful examples of unselfish devotion. They were the prototypes of thousands of men and women of good will who have since helped make our society what it is.

One after another I looked at my friends and fellow workers in A.A.'s Headquarters—trustees, directors, staff members—whose dedicated labor had been given for years to perfect the structure that would now be given into the final keeping of our fellowship itself.

Among the crowd in the great Kiel hall I could see many an old-timer. This had been indeed a reunion of the veterans. They had carried the very first torches, and I could feel the deep kinship that will always be something very special among us. I remembered, too, how their ranks had already thinned, and I reflected that in a little more time all of us who had been pioneers of A.A. would belong to its past. Suddenly I was seized with a desire to turn the clock back. I felt a nostalgia for the old days blending strangely with my gratitude for the great day in which I was now living.

11 Ebby died in 1966.

Bernard Smith, [12] our chairman, presently summoned me to speak. I recounted and relived the seventeen-year story of the building of A.A.'s World Service structure. This talk together with a full account of our subsequent proceedings on this historic day may be read farther on in this book.

The full attendance of thousands of A.A.'s at St. Louis, representing an accurate cross section of A.A. opinion, now sat in convention before us. On the auditorium stage was the Service Conference of Alcoholics Anonymous, about a hundred men and women who were the named and chosen representatives of the whole fellowship. The Conference, having completed the fifth year of its experimental period with a record of high success, was no longer an experiment. It was the instrument destined to become the heart of A.A.'s Third Legacy of Service and the whole of A.A.'s conscience, world-wide.

In the simple ceremony that followed, I offered a resolution to the effect that our society should now take its affairs into its own hands and that its Conference ought to become the permanent successor to the founders of Alcoholics Anonymous.

Amid a roar of acclamation from the floor, the Convention carried that resolution. There was silence, and then we heard chairman Smith offer the resolution to the Conference for its confirmation. A simple show of hands expressed the consent of the Conference and marked the exact moment when A.A. came of age. It was four o'clock.

An address was then given by Bernard Smith. It had been his skill and devotion that had tipped the scales of opinion among A.A.'s Trustees—nearly all of whom had had grave doubts—in favor of proposing the Conference in the first place. And so we knew that this was as wonderful a day in Bern Smith's life as it was in ours.

And now the history-making hours had almost run their course. It remained only for Lois and me to say brief words of farewell.

The Convention listened affectionately as Lois highlighted some of her memories of other days and gave thanks for the blessings that the years had brought to us and to her. To all present she was a symbol of what every family under the lash of Barleycorn had suffered, and

[12] Bernard Smith died in 1970.

she was also a symbol of what every united A.A. family has since found and has become. Lois made us all feel good clear through.

Standing before the Convention for the last time, I felt as all parents do when sons and daughters must begin to make their own decisions and live their own lives. No more would I act for, decide for, or protect Alcoholics Anonymous. I saw that well-meaning parents who cling to their authority and overstay their time can do much damage. We old-timers must never do this to the A.A. family. When in the future they might ask us, we would gladly help them in the pinches. But that would be all. This new relationship was indeed the central meaning of what had just taken place.

Like most parents at such an anxious time, I could not resist a few admonitions, which can be read in Part III of this book.

As I spoke I again felt the tug of that desire to set back the clock, and for a moment I dreaded the coming change as much as anyone. But this mood quickly passed, and I knew that all worrying concern as a parent was now at an end. The conscience of Alcoholics Anonymous as moved by the guidance of God could be depended upon to insure A.A.'s future. Clearly my job henceforth was to *let go* and *let God*. Alcoholics Anonymous was at last safe—even from me.

II

The Three Legacies of Alcoholics Anonymous

THE chief inheritances of the first twenty years of Alcoholics Anonymous are the Legacies of Recovery, of Unity, and of Service. By the first we recover from alcoholism; by the second we stay together in unity; and by the third our society functions and serves its primary purpose of carrying the A.A. message to all who need it and want it.[1]

The next section of this volume is based upon three talks given by Bill, a co-founder, at A.A.'s twentieth anniversary celebration. The first tells the story of the people and the streams of influence that made A.A. *Recovery* possible. The second shows the experience out of which the traditions of Alcoholics Anonymous were formed, the traditions that today hold A.A. together in *Unity*. The third tells how Alcoholics Anonymous developed the *Services* that carry its message to the far corners of the earth.

[1] See: Recovery, p. 51; Unity, p. 79; Service, p. 139.

THE TWELVE STEPS

Step One: We admitted that we were powerless over alcohol—that our lives had become unmanageable.

Step Two: Came to believe that a Power greater than ourselves could restore us to sanity.

Step Three: Made a decision to turn our will and our lives over to the care of God *as we understood Him.*

Step Four: Made a searching and fearless moral inventory of ourselves.

Step Five: Admitted to God, to ourselves, and to another human being the exact nature of our wrongs.

Step Six: Were entirely ready to have God remove all these defects of character.

Step Seven: Humbly asked Him to remove our shortcomings.

Step Eight: Made a list of all persons we had harmed, and became willing to make amends to them all.

Step Nine: Made direct amends to such people whenever possible, except when to do so would injure them or others.

Step Ten: Continued to take personal inventory and when we were wrong promptly admitted it.

Step Eleven: Sought through prayer and meditation to improve our conscious contact with God *as we understood Him,* praying only for knowledge of His will for us and the power to carry that out.

Step Twelve: Having had a spiritual awakening as the result of these steps, we tried to carry this message to alcoholics, and to practice these principles in all our affairs.

RECOVERY: THE FIRST LEGACY

We are gathered here in St. Louis to celebrate A.A.'s twentieth anniversary. We have come to thank God that He has delivered great numbers of us out of our bondage. We are here to tell A.A.'s innumerable friends of our gratitude for all that they have done to help in this wholesale miracle of recovery, and to share with them and with each other the sure evidence of God's grace among us.

Close by many of us this evening are wives, husbands, mothers, fathers, sons, and daughters—those who lived through the dark night of alcoholism with us, those who waited with devotion and hope for a brighter morning to come. Their faith and fidelity at last have been justified, indeed have made this occasion possible. Our gratitude is something none of us can put into words, but we hope all these near and dear ones will realize the full measure of thanksgiving that is in our hearts.

We wish to pay tribute to our friends of medicine and religion whose knowledge, faith, and help without stint were invested in the formation of our society and in its growth in the twenty years just concluded.

And we can never forget those couriers for A.A., the men and women of the press and of all kinds of communication, who have carried A.A.'s message to alcoholic sufferers and their families. Only God knows the immense amount of misery and death they have averted by telling the story of A.A. to the world.

We are gathered in St. Louis for yet another purpose, which is to declare that A.A. has come of age. We are not claiming that we have finally grown up! But we are here to consider what our twenty years of experience has taught us, what are the legacies of this experience, and what are the responsibilities toward the preservation of this treasured inheritance. We are here to review the knowledge we have gained of how to recover from our illness, how to stay together in unity, and how to serve by carrying the A.A. message to all those who still suffer this strange and deadly malady of alcoholism.

It is traditional in Alcoholics Anonymous that we do not make speeches; we just talk about our own experiences and about the experiences of those around us. My talk will be no exception.

About the middle of the summer of 1934, I lay in Charles B. Towns Hospital on Central Park West. I had been there before. I had met dear old Dr. Silkworth. He had thought at one time that I might recover. But I had gone steadily downhill, and now I lay upstairs in the hospital, knowing for the first time that I was utterly hopeless.

Lois was downstairs, and this kind old doctor was trying in his gentle way to tell her the bad news that so many wives and husbands have received. He was trying to tell her what was wrong with me and that I *was* hopeless. And Lois was exclaiming, "But Bill has a tremendous amount of will power. You never saw such an obstinate man when he sets his heart on something. He has tried desperately to get well. We have tried everything. Doctor, *why* can't he stop?" The gentle little man explained that my drinking, once a habit, had become an obsession, a true insanity that condemned me to drink against my will. And she said, "Doctor, what can we do?" So he had to tell her that I would have to be locked up or go mad or die.

Upstairs, I knew the story. It was the end of a long road. For the benefit of our friends who may not yet know how alcoholics get that way, let me go back to the time when I was a child, the time when I acquired some of the traits that had a lot to do with my insatiable craving for alcohol.

I was brought up in a little Yankee town of about fifty houses, East Dorset, Vermont. I was born under the shadow of a mountain there called Mount Aeolus. An early recollection is one of looking up and seeing that vast and mysterious mountain and wondering what it was and whether I would ever climb that high. But I was presently distracted by my aunt who, as a fourth-birthday present, made me a plate of fudge. For the next thirty-five years I pursued the fudge of life and quite forgot about the mountain.

When I was ten I went to live with my grandfather and grandmother. They were wonderful old-fashioned Yankees, a breed nearly extinct today. I was tall and gawky, and I felt pretty bad about it because the smaller kids could push me around in quarrels. I remember being very depressed for a year or more, and then I began to develop a fierce resolve to win. I resolved to be a Number One man.

My grandfather came along one day with a book, and he said, "This is all about Australia. It says that nobody but an Australian bushman knows how to make and throw the boomerang." "Oh," I thought to myself, "here's my chance. I will be the first man in America to make and throw a boomerang." Well, any kid could have a notion like that. It might have lasted two or three days or two or three weeks. But mine was a power drive that kept on for six months, and I did nothing else during all that time but whittle on those infernal boomerangs. I sawed the headboard out of my bed to get just the right piece of wood, and out in the old workshop at night by the light of the lantern I whittled away. And finally, sure enough, I made a boomerang that swung around the churchyard in front of the house and almost hit my grandfather in the head when it came back.

Emotionally I had begun the fashioning of another sort of boomerang, one that almost killed me later on. In that early period I had to be an athlete because I was not an athlete. I had to be a musician because I could not carry a tune. I had to be the president of my class in boarding school. I had to be first in everything because in my perverse heart I felt myself the least of God's creatures. I could not accept this deep sense of inferiority, and so I did become captain of the baseball team, and I did learn to play the fiddle well enough to lead the high-school orchestra, even though it was a terribly bad band. I was the leader and lead I must—or else. So it went. All or nothing. I must be Number One.

Then the scene changed. In boarding school I was very successful.

I felt secure with grandfather's liberal allowance and with the love and respect of my schoolmates. I was somebody, substantial and real, and life lacked only one ingredient: romance. Then came the minister's daughter, and in spite of my awkward adolescence things were complete. I had romance, security, and applause. I was ecstatically happy.

Then one morning the school principal appeared with a sad face and announced that my girl had died suddenly the night before. I dropped into a depression that lasted for three solid years. I did not graduate from school. I was unable to finish because I could not accept the loss of any part of what I thought belonged to me. The healthy kid would have felt badly, but he would never have sunk so deep or stayed submerged for so long.

Then along came Lois, and I was suddenly alive again, a going concern once more. We married during the World War when I was a young officer at New Bedford. There we were projected among the society folk of the town. For the first time in my life I saw a butler. Again came that terrible feeling of inadequacy, that shy inability to speak more than two or three words in a row. It was overwhelming. But one night someone handed me a Bronx cocktail. Liquor had killed off a lot of my relatives and I had been repeatedly warned against it. Still I took this first drink, and then another, and another. Ah, what magic! I had found the elixir of life! Down went that strange barrier that had always stood between me and people around me. My new companions drew near to me and I drew near to them. I was part of life at last. I could talk easily, I could communicate. Here was the missing link!

When the war was over, I returned from France and Lois and I lived in the city. I, the former officer, had to go to work as a clerk. But that only spurred the same old power drive. Although I was only a clerk for the New York Central Railroad, I set my sights to become president of a steel corporation. When the railroad fired me because I was such a bad clerk, I vowed I would show that railroad and everybody else, too.

Finally I got into Wall Street, that famous short cut to wealth and power—or poverty. In a few years' time I made far too much money for one so young. I was not disturbed about my drinking, although Lois had become increasingly concerned. In this period I was drinking to dream great dreams of greater power. I wanted to be a director of many large enterprises; indeed I was on the point of realizing my ambitions at the time of the 1929 crash when everything melted away. Although I had gone many thousands of dollars into debt, my arrogance was supreme. I looked with disgust upon the bankrupt people who were then jumping from the high buildings. I said and believed, "I can build all this up once more. I've done it once; I can do it again."

But I did not do it again. My alcoholic obsession had already condemned me; I no longer had the capacity to hold even the first rung on any comeback ladder. So I began sinking. I could not get a toe hold any more and became a hanger-on in Wall Street. Without money or sobriety I was discredited everywhere. People knew all too well what I was becoming. Finally I slid down into a state where I was not drinking to dream dreams of power; I was drinking to numb the pain, to forget.

All at once, at the very bottom of the depression, there came a business opportunity that might have meant millions for Lois and me. But I had to sign a contract which bound me legally not to drink. During the life of the agreement, which might be long, I committed myself not to drink at all. This opportunity was colossal from any Wall Street point of view. I said to myself, "I'll soon have Lois out of that department store where she's supporting me and I'll make more money than I ever did. This time we are really going to arrive!"

We Vermonters set great store by our contracts. I really meant to keep my agreement, and for two or three months I did stay absolutely sober. The new business operation began, and I went on a trip to look over an industry.

One night a few engineers and I were sitting in a hotel room. They produced a jug. With great relief, I found that I could easily say

"No." I could think of my contract. I could think of Lois. But as the evening wore on I began to be bored. The jug kept going around and finally someone said, "Bill, this is applejack, Jersey Lightning. Better have one." I suddenly realized that in all my drinking career I had never had any Jersey Lightning. I said, "Boys, *one little shot won't hurt me.*" Inexplicably, both Lois and my business promise faded. I could think only of the applejack. In that moment my insane obsession seized me once again. There followed three days of complete oblivion; then my new business partners called me on the phone and told me that the deal was off.

And now I really began to lose hope. My mental disintegration proceeded rapidly and implacably. Soon I was in a hospital, the first of many such "cures" during the next two years. But it wasn't until that fateful night in September, 1934, that Lois and I learned from the doctor what my score really was.

After leaving the hospital in that month, I kept sober for a while on stark fear and constant vigilance. November came and I still had not had a drink. This was unheard of. The fear of getting drunk was getting hazier now. I did not have to exert myself so much to resist. I actually began to talk to people about alcoholism. When I was offered drinks, I would volunteer the information I had acquired about the nature of my disease. I found this a defense against taking anything and also a justification for my former condition. Confidence was beginning to grow fast and my fear left me. Somehow I managed to pick up a few dollars. Perhaps I was not such a serious case after all. I was proving I could stop. I had learned how.

Armistice Day, 1934, rolled around. Lois had to go to the Brooklyn department store where she worked. Wall Street was closed down and I began to wonder what I would do. I thought of golf. I had not played in a long time. The family purse was slender, so I suggested to Lois that I might go over to Staten Island where there was a public course. She could not quite conceal her apprehension, but she managed to say cheerfully, "Oh, please do. That would be wonderful."

I crossed on the ferry and took a bus. I found myself seated beside a man with a target rifle. That brought back memories of the Remington single-shot piece grandfather had given me when I was eleven years old. We got to talking about shooting.

Suddenly our bus collided with the bus ahead of us. There was little shock or damage. My friend and I alighted on the pavement to wait for the next bus to come along. Still talking about shooting irons, we noticed something that looked like a speakeasy. He said to me, "What about a little nip?" I said, "Fine, let's go." We walked into the place. He ordered a Scotch and I ordered a ginger ale. "Don't you drink?" he said. "No," I said, "I'm one of those people who can't manage it." And then I dwelt on the allergy and the obsession and the whole business of alcoholism. I told him about the terrible time I had had with liquor and how I was through with it forever. I carefully explained the whole illness to him.

We got onto another bus and presently found ourselves in front of a country inn well down on the Island. I was to go to the golf course nearby, and my new friend was to take another bus to his rifle range. But it was noontime and he said, "Let's go in and have a sandwich. Besides, I'd like to have another drink." We sat at the bar this time. As I have said, it was Armistice Day. The place was filling up and so were the customers. There was the familiar buzz which arises from drinking crowds. My friend and I continued to talk, still on the subject of shooting. Sandwiches and another drink for him, sandwiches and ginger ale for me.

My mind turned again to Armistice Day in France, to all the joy of those hours, to the great celebration. I no longer heard what my friend was saying. Suddenly the big Irish bartender came up to us, beaming. In each hand he held a drink. "Have one on the house, boys!" he cried. "It's Armistice Day!" Without an instant's hesitation, I picked up the liquor and drank it. My friend looked at me aghast. "My God!" he cried. "Is it possible that you can take a drink after what you just told me? You must be crazy!" And my reply was, "I am."

The next morning about five o'clock Lois found me unconscious in the areaway of our house. I had fallen against the iron grating and was bleeding from a bad scalp wound. My hand still clutched the strap of my golf bag. When I regained consciousness nothing much was said. Indeed, there was nothing much to say. We both hit an all-time low. I went back to drinking—one, two, three bottles of bathtub gin a day. I could not stop, and I knew it.

Then one afternoon the telephone rang. It was my old boarding-school friend and drinking companion, Ebby. Even over the phone I somehow knew that he was sober. I could not remember a time when he had been sober in New York City. Long ago I had marked him for a hopeless case. I had heard in fact that they were going to put him away because of alcoholic insanity. Eagerly I said, "Come right on over. We'll talk about the good old days." Now why did I say that? It was because my present was unbearable and I knew there was to be no future. Soon Ebby stood beaming in the doorway. Then he was sitting across the kitchen from me. There was a big crock of gin and pineapple juice between us.

Immediately I felt that there was something different about Ebby. It was not only that he was sober. I could not put a finger on what it was. I offered him a drink and he refused. Then I asked him, "What's this all about? You say you aren't drinking. But you also say you aren't on the water wagon, either. What's up?"

"Well," said Ebby, "I've got religion."

What a crusher that was—Ebby and religion! Maybe his alcoholic insanity had become religious insanity. It was an awful letdown. I had been educated at a wonderful engineering college where somehow I had gathered the impression that man was God. But I had to be polite, so I said, "What brand of religion have you got, Ebby?" "Oh," he said, "I don't think it has got any special brand name. I just fell in with a group of people, the Oxford Groups. I don't go along with all their teachings by any means. But those folks have given me some wonderful ideas. I learned that I had to admit I was licked; I learned that I ought to take stock of myself and confess my defects to another person in confidence; I learned that I needed to make restitution for the harm I had done others. I was told that I ought to practice the kind of giving that has no price tag on it, the giving of yourself to somebody. Now," he added, "I know you are going to gag on this, but they taught me that I should try to pray to whatever God I thought there was for the power to carry out these simple precepts. And if I did not believe there was any God, then I had better try the experiment of praying to whatever God there *might* be. And you know, Bill, it's a queer thing, but even before I had done all this, just as soon as I decided that I would try with an open mind, it seemed to me that my drinking problem was lifted right out of me. It wasn't like the water wagon business at all. This time I felt completely released of the desire, and I have not had a drink for months."

Ebby didn't try to pressure or evangelize me, and pretty soon he left. For several days I went on drinking. But in no waking hour was the thought of my friend absent from my mind. I could not forget what he had said. In the kinship of common suffering, *one alcoholic had been talking to another.*

My mood swings continued from rebellion against God to hope and then back again. One day while pretty maudlin I got a great idea. I figured it was time I did some religious investigation on my own hook. Remembering that Sam Shoemaker's Calvary Church had a mission where Ebby's Oxford Group friends had lodged him, I thought I would go and see what they did down there. I left the subway at Fourth Avenue and Twenty-third Street. It was a good long walk along Twenty-third Street, so I began stopping in bars. I spent most of the afternoon in the bars and forgot all about the mission. At nightfall I found myself in excited conversation in a bar with a Finn named Alec. He said he had been a sailmaker and a fisherman in the old country. Somehow that word "fisherman" clicked. I thought again of the mission. Over there I would find fishers of men. Oddly enough it seemed like a wonderful idea.

I sold Alec on coming along, and soon we reeled in the front door of the mission. Tex Francisco, an ex-alky in charge, was right there to meet us. He not only ran the place; he proposed to run us out of it. This made us quite sore as we thought of our good intentions.

Just then Ebby turned up, grinning. He said, "What about a plate of beans?" After the food, Alec and I had slightly clearer heads. Ebby told us there would be a meeting in the mission pretty soon. Would we like to go? Certainly we would go; that's why we were there. The three of us were soon sitting on one of those hard wooden benches that filled the place. I had never seen a mission before and I shivered a little as I looked at the derelict audience. There was a smell of sweat and alcohol. I could well imagine how much suffering was represented in this gathering.

There were some hymns and prayers. Then Tex, the leader, exhorted us. Only Jesus could save, he said. Somehow this statement did not jar me. Certain men got up and made testimonials. Numb as I was I felt interest and excitement rising. Then came the call. Some men were starting forward to the rail. Unaccountably impelled, I started too, dragging Alec with me. Ebby reached for my coattails, but it was too late. I knelt among the shaking penitents. Maybe then and there, for the very first time, I was penitent, too. Something touched me. I guess it was more than that. I was hit. I felt a wild impulse to talk. Jumping to my feet, I began.

Afterward I could never remember what I said. I only knew that I was really in earnest and that people seemed to pay attention. Ebby, who at first had been embarrassed to death, told me with relief that I had done all right and had "given my life to God."

Upstairs after the meeting I saw the dormitory where the derelicts slept. I met a few who had made good recoveries. Some were living at the mission, working outside by day. Eagerly I listened to their stories. I sobered up very fast and the dead weight on me seemed to go on lifting. With a qualm I remembered Lois. I had not phoned her and she would be worried. I must tell her all about this. It was good to hear her sigh of relief at the other end of the wire.

Slowly and quite confidently I made my way up Twenty-third Street to the subway. As I went down the stairs it was startling to realize that I hadn't thought of looking in any of the bars. This was something new, very new. Had I too been released?

Before going to bed, Lois and I had a long talk. There was hope in every word. Without an ounce of gin I slept like a child. I was due for a terrible hangover the next morning, but I had almost none at all. Yet that small hangover was my undoing once more. I felt I would be more comfortable watching the sun come up if I had a drink. Just one or two, maybe. Saying nothing to Lois, I took a couple aboard and followed them up with mouthwash. She noticed nothing and I felt fine.

After she left for work the hangover got very troublesome again. This was to be the last one. Rationalizing as usual, I felt justified in tapering off. As always of course I tapered on instead of off, and at six o'clock poor Lois found me upstairs on the bed dead drunk.

Yet I had seen some kind of light, and although I drank on for three days, I kept pondering that mission experience. Sometimes it seemed real; then again I would brush it away, charging it off to an alcohol-fired imagination.

On the morning of the third day my wandering thoughts gathered into a sharp focus. I remember comparing myself to a cancer victim. If I had cancer, I would do anything to get well, would I not? Yes, anything whatever. Would I sit home and put cold cream on the affected parts? No, of course not. What would I do? I would head for the best physician in the business and beg him to destroy or cut away those consuming cells. I would have to depend on him, my God of medicine, to save me. My dependence would be absolute; for myself I could do nothing.

Alcoholism, not cancer, was my illness, but what was the difference? Was not alcoholism also a consumer of body and mind? Alcoholism took longer to do its killing, but the result was the same. So if there *was* a great Physician who could cure the alcoholic sickness, I had better seek Him now, at once. I had better find what my friend had found. Would I, like the cancer sufferer, do anything to get well? If getting well required me to pray at high noon in the public square with the other sufferers, would I swallow my pride and do that? Maybe I would. Meanwhile, though, I would go back to Towns

Hospital where Dr. Silkworth would sober me up again. Then I could look clear-eyed at Ebby's formula for sobriety. Perhaps I would not need an emotional conversion. Maybe a conservative doubter like me could get by without anything like that. Anyhow, I started for the hospital.

Walking up Clinton Street to the subway, I fished six cents out of my pocket. A nickel would get me to the hospital. But hadn't I forgotten something? Here I was on my way to be cured. Typical alcoholic that I was, I figured I might as well be comfortable until the hospital took over. So I stepped into a grocery store where I had a slim credit. I remember explaining to the clerk that I was an alcoholic on my way to be cured. Could I have four bottles of beer on the cuff?

I drank one bottle on the street and another in the subway. My spirits rose as I offered the third to a passenger. He turned down my refreshment, so I drained that bottle on the station platform near the hospital. Holding the last bottle by the neck, I walked into Towns, where Dr. Silkworth met me in the hall.

Now in very high spirits, I waved the bottle and shouted, "At last, Doc, I've found something!" Even through my haze I could see the good old man's face fall. I now know how much he loved me. This fresh outburst really hurt him. I tried to explain the new thing I thought I had found. He looked at me, shaking his head, and after a while he quietly said, "Well, my boy, isn't it time you went upstairs and went to bed?"

I was not in too awful a condition. In three or four days I was free of what little sedative they gave me, but I was very depressed. I was still choking on the God business. Bright and early one morning friend Ebby showed up and stood in the doorway, smiling broadly. I didn't see what was so funny. Then I had a suspicion: maybe this is the day he is going to evangelize me; maybe he is going to pour on the sweetness and light. But no, he made me wait until I asked him. "Well," said I, "what is your neat little formula once more?" In perfectly good humor, he handed it out again: You admit you are licked; you get honest with yourself; you talk it out with somebody else; you make restitution to the people you have harmed; you try to give of yourself without stint, with no demand for reward; and you pray to whatever God you think there is, even as an experiment. It was as simple and yet as mysterious as that. After some small talk he was gone.

My depression deepened unbearably and finally it seemed to me as though I were at the very bottom of the pit. I still gagged badly on the notion of a Power greater than myself, but finally, just for the moment, the last vestige of my proud obstinacy was crushed. All at once I found myself crying out, "If there is a God, let Him show Himself! I am ready to do anything, anything!"

Suddenly the room lit up with a great white light. I was caught up into an ecstasy which there are no words to describe. It seemed to me, in the mind's eye, that I was on a mountain and that a wind not of air but of spirit was blowing. And then it burst upon me that I was a free man. Slowly the ecstasy subsided. I lay on the bed, but now for a time I was in another world, a new world of consciousness. All about me and through me there was a wonderful feeling of Presence, and I thought to myself, "So this is the God of the preachers!" A great peace stole over me and I thought, "No matter how wrong things seem to be, they are still all right. Things are all right with God and His world."

Then, little by little, I began to be frightened. My modern education crawled back and said to me, "You are hallucinating. You had better get the doctor." Dr. Silkworth asked me a lot of questions. After a while he said, "No, Bill, you are not crazy. There has been some basic psychological or spiritual event here. I've read about these things in the books. Sometimes spiritual experiences do release people from alcoholism." Immensely relieved, I fell again to wondering what actually had happened.[2]

[2] Nearly every A.A. has a spiritual experience that quite transforms his outlook and attitudes. Ordinarily, such occurrences are gradual and may take place over periods of months or even years.

A considerable number of A.A.'s, including Bill, who have had the sudden variety of spiritual experience see no great difference so far as the practical result is concerned between their quick illumination and the slower, more typical kinds of spiritual awakening.

More light on this came the next day. It was Ebby, I think, who brought me a copy of William James' *Varieties of Religious Experience*. It was rather difficult reading for me, but I devoured it from cover to cover. Spiritual experiences, James thought, could have objective reality; almost like gifts from the blue, they could transform people. Some were sudden brilliant illuminations; others came on very gradually. Some flowed out of religious channels; others did not. But nearly all had the great common denominators of pain, suffering, calamity. Complete hopelessness and deflation at depth were almost always required to make the recipient ready. The significance of all this burst upon me. *Deflation at depth*—yes, that was *it*. Exactly that had happened to me. Dr. Carl Jung had told an Oxford group friend of Ebby's how hopeless his alcoholism was and Dr. Silkworth had passed the same sentence upon me. Then Ebby, also an alcoholic, had handed me the identical dose. On Dr. Silkworth's say-so alone maybe I would never have completely accepted the verdict, but when Ebby came along and one alcoholic began to talk to another, that clinched it.

My thoughts began to race as I envisioned a chain reaction among alcoholics, one carrying this message and these principles to the next. More than I could ever want anything else, I now knew that I wanted to work with other alcoholics.

As soon as I was discharged from the hospital, I associated myself with the Oxford Groups. We worked at Sam Shoemaker's Calvary Mission and also at Towns Hospital. Ebby came to live with Lois and me in Brooklyn. I started out after drunks on jet propulsion.

My sudden spiritual experience, however, had its disadvantages. I was soon heard to say that I was going to fix up all the drunks in the world, even though the batting average on them had been virtually nil for the last 5,000 years. The Oxford Groupers had tried, had mostly failed, and were fed up. Sam Shoemaker in fact had just had a run of bad luck. He had housed a batch of drunks in an apartment near his church, and one of them, still resisting salvation, had peevishly thrown a shoe through a fine stained-glass window in Sam's church.

No wonder my Oxford Group friends felt that I had better forget about alcoholics. But I was still mighty cocksure and I ignored their advice. Mine was a kind of twin-engine power drive consisting of one part of genuine spirituality and one part of my old desire to be a Number One man. This posture didn't pan out well at all. At the end of six months nobody had sobered up. And, believe me, I had tried them by the score. They would clear up for a little while and then flop dismally. Naturally the Oxford Groupers became very cool indeed toward my drunk-fixing.

Lois meanwhile was still working in the department store, and folks were beginning to say, "Is this fellow Bill going to be a missionary for life? Why doesn't he go to work?" Even to me, this began to look like a good idea. I began to hang around Wall Street again and, through a chance acquaintance I had scraped up in a brokerage shop, I insinuated myself into a proxy row that involved control of a little machine tool company in Akron, Ohio. In May of 1935 a party of us went out to Akron, fighting for control of the company. I could already see myself as its new president. But when the chips were down the other side had more proxies and our side got licked. My new-found acquaintances were discouraged, and they left me in Akron's Mayflower Hotel with only about ten dollars in my pocket.

They departed on Friday. On Saturday, Mother's Day eve, I was pacing up and down the hotel lobby, wondering what I could do. The bar at one end of my beat was filling up rapidly. I could hear the familiar buzz of conversation in there. Down at the other end of the lobby I found myself pausing before a church directory. Then I was seized with a thought: I am going to get drunk. Or no, maybe I won't get drunk; maybe I'll just go into that bar and drink some ginger ale and scrape up an acquaintance. Then I panicked. That was really a gift! I had never panicked before at the threat of alcohol. Maybe this meant that my sanity *had* been restored. I remembered that in trying to help other people, I had stayed sober myself. For the first time I *deeply* realized it. I thought, "You need another alcoholic to talk to. You need another alcoholic just as much as he needs you!"

Then followed a strange chain of consequences. Choosing at random from the church directory, I called up an Episcopal padre by the name of Walter Tunks, a great friend of A.A. to this day. In frantic eagerness I poured out my tale to him. I asked if maybe he knew some people who could put me in touch with another alcoholic. I thought he might know some of the Oxford Groupers around Akron. When the good man learned that I was an alcoholic looking for another alcoholic to work on, he at first apparently envisioned two people drunk instead of one, but he finally got the point and gave me a list of about ten people who might be able to direct me.

I immediately began calling them up. It was Saturday afternoon. People were not at home. Others were not interested and made excuses. The list quickly dwindled until it came down to one name at the very end. That name was Henrietta Seiberling. I had a vague recollection from my Wall Street days of meeting an elderly Mr. Seiberling, one-time founder and president of Goodyear Rubber. I could hardly imagine calling up his wife and telling her that I was a drunk from New York looking for another drunk to work on. So I went back downstairs and walked up and down the lobby some more. But something kept saying to me, "You'd better call her." So I finally rang up. Unexpectedly, a young Southern voice came over the wire, which turned out to be that of a Seiberling daughter-in-law. I explained that I was an alcoholic from the New York Oxford Groups who needed to help another drunk in order to stay sober himself. Very quickly she got the drift of what I was saying. She said, "I'm no alcoholic, but I've had my difficulties. When you talk about spiritual matters, I think I understand. I know someone you might help. Won't you come out here right away? I live in the gatehouse of the Seiberling place."

When I got there I found a person of charm and understanding. She said she had worked through many a hard problem and had found her answers in the Oxford Groups. She understood deep suffering. When I had told my story she said, "I know just the man for you. He is a doctor. We all call him 'Dr. Bob.' His wife, Anne, is a grand person. Bob has tried so hard; I know he wants to stop. He has tried medical cures, he has tried various religious approaches, including the Oxford Groups. He has tried with all his will, but somehow he cannot seem to do it. So how would you like to talk with Dr. Bob and Anne?"

Soon Anne S. was on the phone—A.A.'s much-loved Anne. Quickly Henrietta told her about me, an alcoholic from New York who wanted to talk about his drinking problem. Could she and Dr. Bob come over? Anne said, "I'm sorry, Henrietta. I don't think we can make it today. Bob always makes a great fuss over me on Mother's Day. He has just come home, bringing a big potted plant." What Anne didn't say was that the plant was on a table and that Bob was under the table, so potted that he couldn't get up. Henrietta said, "What about tomorrow? Why can't both of you come over to dinner?" Anne said they would try to make it.

Next afternoon at five o'clock that wonderful couple, Dr. Bob and Anne, stood at Henrietta's open door.

This was the man who was to be my partner and founder of Akron's Group Number One. With the remarkable Sister Ignatia, he was to care for 5,000 cases of alcoholism in the time when A.A. was still very young. This was the wonderful friend with whom I was never to have a hard word. This was Dr. Bob, A.A.'s co-founder-to-be.

But at five o'clock that Sunday afternoon Bob did not look much like a founder. He was shaking badly. Uneasily he told us that he could stay only about fifteen minutes. Though embarrassed, he brightened a little when I said I thought he needed a drink. After dinner, which he did not eat, Henrietta discreetly put us off in her little library. There Bob and I talked until eleven o'clock.

Just before leaving for Akron, Dr. Silkworth had given me a great piece of advice. Without it, A.A. might never have been born. "Look, Bill," he had said, "you're having nothing but failure because you are preaching at these alcoholics. You are talking to them about the

Oxford Group precepts of being absolutely honest, absolutely pure, absolutely unselfish, and absolutely loving. This is a very big order. Then you top it off by harping on this mysterious spiritual experience of yours. No wonder they point their finger to their heads and go out and get drunk. Why don't you turn your strategy the other way around? Aren't you the very fellow who once showed me that book by the psychologist James which says that deflation at great depth is the foundation of most spiritual experiences? Have you forgotten all about that? Have you also forgotten that Dr. Carl Jung in Zurich told a certain alcoholic, the one who later helped sober up your friend Ebby, that his only hope of salvation was a spiritual experience? No, Bill, you've got the cart before the horse. You've got to deflate these people first. So give them the medical business, and give it to them hard. Pour it right into them about the obsession that condemns them to drink and the physical sensitivity or allergy of the body that condemns them to go mad or die if they keep on drinking. Coming from another alcoholic, one alcoholic talking to another, maybe that will crack those tough egos deep down. Only then can you begin to try out your other medicine, the ethical principles you have picked up from the Oxford Groups."

Now—talking with Dr. Bob—I remembered all that Dr. Silkworth had said. So I went very slowly on the fireworks of religious experience. I just talked away about my own case until he got a good identification with me, until he began to say, "Yes, that's me, I'm like that."

In turn, Dr. Bob talked to me about himself as he had never talked before. He too was a Vermonter. His father had been a stern but deeply respected judge in St. Johnsbury. Also, as in my case, Dr. Bob's drinking proclivities had shown up early. In fact, he had busted out of Dartmouth College for this reason. Somehow he had wormed his way through medical school and internship in Chicago. Despite his drinking, he had shown a talented flair for surgery. After his marriage to Anne, they had settled in Akron where in due course young Bob was born and a daughter, sister Sue, was adopted.

Dr. Bob at the time of our first meeting was fifty-five, some fifteen years older than I. He must have had an iron constitution. He said that all through the years his drinking had been practically continuous. When he got too jittery to operate or to see patients, he sedated himself heavily. When this recourse sometimes failed, he would steal away for a week or so to a drying-out place so that he could start the same cycle all over again. In those rare moments when he got thoroughly sober, the insatiable craving for alcohol never let up. This was a physical phenomenon which bedeviled even his first years in A.A., a time when only days and nights of carrying the message to other alcoholics could cause him to forget about it. Although this craving was hard to withstand, it doubtless created some part of the intense incentive and energy that went into forming Akron's Group Number One. Bob's spiritual release did not come easily; it was to be painfully slow. It always entailed the hardest kind of work and the sharpest vigilance. Yet he seemed to have no serious neurotic difficulties. As he often put it, "I just loved my grog."

By the time I met him this compelling love had almost done him in. His surgical skill was still recognized, but few colleagues or patients dared to trust him. He had lost his post on the staff of Akron's City Hospital and barely existed through a precarious and dwindling general practice. In debt up to his ears, he was only one jump ahead of the sheriff and his mortgage payments. Anne verged on a nervous crack-up, and their two children of course were greatly upset. Such was the pay-off of twenty-five years of alcoholism. Hope was a word they had come to avoid.

In our first conversation I bore down heavily on the medical hopelessness of Dr. Bob's case, freely using Dr. Silkworth's words describing the alcoholic's dilemma, the "obsession plus allergy" theme. Though Bob was a doctor, this was news to him, bad news. Always better versed in spiritual matters than I, he had paid little attention to that aspect of my story. Even though he could not make them work, he already knew what the spiritual answers were. What really did hit him hard was the medical business, the verdict of inevitable annihilation. And the fact that I was an alcoholic and knew what I was talking about from personal experience made the blow a shattering one.

In Dr. Bob's story as afterwards written for the A.A. book, and years later in his last full-length talk at Detroit, he made this point very clear: it was not any spiritual teaching of mine, rather it was those twin ogres of madness and death, the allergy plus the obsession, that triggered him into a new life. It was Dr. Silkworth's idea, confirmed by William James, that struck him at great depth.

You see, our talk was a completely *mutual* thing. I had quit preaching. I knew that I needed this alcoholic as much as he needed me. *This was it*. And this mutual give-and-take is at the very heart of all of A.A.'s Twelfth Step work today. This was how to carry the message. The final missing link was located right there in my first talk with Dr. Bob.

Unexpectedly I got a little fresh financing from my New York business associates, so I stayed on in Akron that summer of 1935 to continue the proxy fight. Still worried about Dr. Bob, Anne invited me to come over and live with them at their home at 855 Ardmore Avenue. How well I remember our morning meditation, when Anne would sit in the corner by the fireplace and read from the Bible, and then we would huddle together in stillness, awaiting inspiration and guidance.

Three or four weeks after the Mother's Day debacle, Dr. Bob looked at me one morning and said, "Bill, for a number of years I have had to go down to Atlantic City to our medical convention. I haven't missed one in a long time. Don't you think I had better go?" Very frightened, Anne said, "Oh, no, no!" But seeing that he had to face the music sometime, I replied, "Well, why don't you go? After all, we must learn to live in a world that's full of alcohol." And slowly Bob said, "I guess maybe you're right."

So he went to the Atlantic City medical convention and nothing was heard of him for several days. Then one morning his office nurse called up and said, "He is over here at my place. My husband and I picked him off the railroad station platform at about four A.M. Please come over and see what you can do."

We got Bob back home and into bed, and right then we made an alarming discovery. He had to perform a certain operation that only he could do. The deadline was just three days away; he simply had to do the job himself; and here he was, shaking like a leaf. Could we get him sober in time? Anne and I took turns around the clock trying to taper the old boy off. Early on the morning of the operation he was almost sober. I had slept in the room with him. Glancing across toward his bed, I saw that he was wide awake but still shaking. I'll never forget the look he gave me as he said, "Bill, I am going to go through with it." I thought he meant the operation. "No," he said, "I mean this thing we've been talking about."

Anne and I drove him to the hospital at nine o'clock. I handed him a bottle of beer to steady his nerves so he could hold the knife, and he went in. We returned to the house and sat down to wait. After what seemed an endless time, he phoned; all had gone well. But after that he didn't come home for hours. Despite the awful strain, he had left the hospital, got into his car, and commenced to visit creditors and others he had harmed by his behavior. That was June 10, 1935. To the time of his death fifteen years later, Dr. Bob never took another drink of alcohol.

Next day he said, "Bill, don't you think that working on other alcoholics is terribly important? We'd be much safer if we got active, wouldn't we?" I said, "Yes, that would be just the thing. But where can we find any alcoholics?" He said, "They always have a batch down at the Akron City Hospital. I'll call them up and see what they've got." Getting hold of a nurse friend of his on the receiving ward of the hospital, Dr. Bob explained that a man from New York had just found a new cure for alcoholism. (We called it a cure in those days.) But the nurse knew Dr. Bob of old. So she retorted, "Is that so, Dr. Bob? You don't mean to tell me you've tried it on yourself!" "Yes," he said, "I sure have."

The new customer was in no shape to be seen. But two days later,

Dr. Bob and I were looking into the face of the first "man on the bed." It was old Bill D., A.A. number three, whose story you can read in the second edition of the Big Book. Bill was still pretty glassy-eyed. When Dr. Bob and I gave him the medical bad news about the allergy and the obsession, old Bill showed a startled interest. But when we began to describe our spiritual approach, Bill shook his head and said, "No, I'm too far gone for that. I've always believed in God. I used to be a deacon in the church. But, boys, I've been in and out of this place six times in the last four months. This time in d.t.'s I badly beat up one of the nurses. I know I can't even get home from here sober. I'm afraid to go out. No, it's too late for me. I still believe in God all right, but I know mighty well that He doesn't believe in me any more."

"Well, Bill," we said, "can we come back and see you tomorrow?" "Yes," he replied, "you fellows really understand. Sure, I'd like to see you." So the next day we came back and found him talking to his wife, Henrietta. Bill pointed to us and said, "These are the fellows I was telling you about. They are the ones that know. They understand what this thing is all about."

Then Bill told us how, during the night, hope had dawned on him. If Bob and I could do it, he could do it. Maybe we could all do together what we could not do separately. Two days later Bill suddenly said, "Henrietta, fetch me my clothes, I'm going to get up and get out of here." Bill walked out of that hospital a free man and he never took a drink again. The spark that was to flare into the first A.A. group had been struck.

Dr. Bob and Bill D. and I went frantically to work with more of those alcoholic characters at the City Hospital. We had a long string of failures. Notable among these had been Eddie. In fact, Dr. Bob and I had tackled him just before our first visit with Bill D. Every time Eddie got drunk he wanted to jump off the Cleveland docks. Once when angered he had tried to emphasize a point by waving a knife at Anne and me. He finally did make the grade and recently wrote me that he has been sober for seven wonderful years. So Eddie, our first "failure," so-called, is today a success.

Then from another quarter we turned up with a prize. I guess this was the beginning of A.A.'s young people's department. This new one, Ernie, had been a terribly wild case, yet he caught on very quickly to become A.A. number four. As I remember it, we straightened up only two more during that whole summer in Akron. By September, my proxy fight backers had got tired again. I had to go home to New York.

Right here I want to set on record the timeless gratitude that A.A.'s will always have for Henrietta Seiberling, she who first brought Dr. Bob and me together. Of the ten people to whom I had been directed by Clergyman Walter Tunks, Henrietta was the only one who had understood enough and cared enough. And this had been only the beginning of her mission. During that first summer at Akron she affectionately counseled many an alcoholic's family, just as Anne was doing. Despite the fact that she had no direct experience of alcoholism, Henrietta had a rare capacity for identification with us. Therefore she was eagerly sought out for her great spiritual insight and the help she could give. What Alcoholics Anonymous owes to her will always be beyond anybody's reckoning. And Dr. Bob's debt and mine are the greatest of all.

By the time I got home I was endowed with a little more humility, a little more understanding, and considerably more experience. Very slowly a group began to take shape in New York. Lois, not content with nursing me all those years, thought it would be wonderful if we filled the old family house in Clinton Street with alcoholics. Her mother had passed away and her father, a doctor, had moved elsewhere. So why not? We thought we could feed our charges at low cost and pick up a lot of knowledge about alcoholism. As it turned out, we did not sober up a single one. But we *did* pick up a lot of knowledge. We used to have as many as five in the house at a time, and sometimes they would all be drunk at once. One day we came home to find a drunk swinging a piece of two-by-four on another down in the cellar. I don't remember what their resentment was. On another occasion we had been away for a week, leaving only one problem drinker alone in the house, and we came back to find him dead, a suicide.

We continued our work on alcoholics, some of them in Sam Shoemaker's Oxford Group, some at Calvary Mission, some at Charlie Towns' hospital, where good old Dr. Silkworth risked his reputation by letting us see them. Lois and I continued to find, however, that if we permitted alcoholics to become too dependent on us they were apt to stay drunk. In that fall of 1935, a weekly meeting took shape in our Brooklyn parlor. In spite of much failure, a really solid group finally developed. There was first Henry P., and there was Fitz M., both out of Towns Hospital. Following them, more began to make real recoveries.

Until the middle of 1937 we in New York had been working alongside the Oxford Groups. But in the latter part of that year we most reluctantly parted company with these great friends. Naturally enough, they did not think too highly of our objective, limited as it was to alcoholics. From our point of view, we felt very sure we couldn't do much about helping the Oxford Groups to save the whole world. But we were becoming more certain every day that we might be able to sober up many alcoholics.

The Oxford Groupers had clearly shown us what to do. And, just as importantly, we had also learned from them *what not to do* as far as alcoholics were concerned. We had found that certain of their ideas and attitudes simply could not be sold to alcoholics. For example, drinkers would not take pressure in any form, excepting from John Barleycorn himself. They always had to be led, not pushed. They would not stand for the rather aggressive evangelism of the Oxford Groups. And they would not accept the principle of "team guidance" for their own personal lives. It was too authoritarian for them. In other respects, too, we found we had to make haste slowly. When first contacted, most alcoholics just wanted to find sobriety, nothing else. They clung to their other defects, letting go only little by little. They simply did not want to get "too good too soon." The Oxford Groups' absolute concepts—absolute purity, absolute honesty, absolute unselfishness, and absolute love—were frequently too much for the drunks. These ideas had to be fed with teaspoons rather than by buckets.

Besides, the Oxford Groups' "absolutes" were expressions peculiar to them. This was a terminology which might continue to identify us in the public mind with the Oxford Groupers, even though we had completely withdrawn from their fellowship.

There was yet another difficulty. Because of the stigma then attached to the condition, most alcoholics wanted to be anonymous. We were afraid also of developing erratic public characters who, through broken anonymity, might get drunk in public and so destroy confidence in us. The Oxford Groups, on the contrary, depended very much upon the use of prominent names—something that was doubtless all right for them but mighty hazardous for us. Our debt to them, nevertheless, was and is immense, and so the final breakaway was very painful.

Out in Akron wonderful friends continued to show up. In the forefront of these was T. Henry Williams and his wife Clarace, Oxford Groupers also. They and Henrietta had repeatedly tried to help Dr. Bob. On several occasions they had gone far in discussing their own personal defects with him in order to get some kind of closer identification with him. This had impressed him a great deal and had doubtless made him far more ready to work with me when I showed up. I had met T. Henry at the time of the proxy fight, and as a result of the shake-up he had lost a fine job. He was bighearted enough, nevertheless, to let us alcoholics come to his house for meetings along with his Oxford Group friends. I am afraid those early problem drinkers often gave the Williamses a bad time, ranging from jarring glimpses of life in the raw to cigarette burns on their carpets.

But T. Henry and Clarace always treated us with great generosity and kindness, and none of us can ever forget the inspirational atmosphere of their home and their spiritual influence on that first frightened little group of Akron alcoholics, each wondering who might slip next. It was not until later, and well after the A.A. book was published, that our Akron members withdrew from the Oxford Groups and finally from the home which had sheltered them so well. T. Henry and Clarace Williams will always be counted in the front rank of A.A.'s pioneers.

Gradually the New York and Akron groups began to multiply. From New York we began to reach out toward Philadelphia and Washington. In Akron they began to have visitors from Cleveland: Clarence and Dorothy and Abby and all those grand folks. The A.A. ferment had begun to work and spread.

In 1937 I went back to Wall Street for a brief stretch. In the fall of that year another depression hit the U.S. and I was suddenly out of a job. I went west, where I tried Detroit and Cleveland for another position in the financial business. Nothing turned up, but this trip gave me a much needed chance to visit Dr. Bob in Akron. It was on a November day in that year when Dr. Bob and I sat in his living room, counting the noses of our recoveries. There had been failures galore, but now we could see some startling successes too. A hard core of very grim, last-gasp cases had by then been sober a couple of years, an unheard-of development. There were twenty or more such people. All told we figured that upwards of forty alcoholics were staying bone dry.

As we carefully rechecked this score, it suddenly burst upon us that a new light was shining into the dark world of the alcoholic. Despite the fact that Ebby had slipped, a benign chain reaction, one alcoholic carrying the good news to the next, had started outward from Dr. Bob and me. Conceivably it could one day circle the whole world. What a tremendous thing that realization was! At last we were sure. There would be no more flying totally blind. We actually wept for joy, and Bob and Anne and I bowed our heads in silent thanks.

Then came a mighty sobering thought. This knowledge, this precious know-how, was still in the hands of too few of us. Must every alcoholic come to New York or Akron in order to get well? No, that would never do; that would be impossible. How, then, could we spread our message? Ruefully we remembered that alcoholics even when sober are far from being grown-up people. All of us could still be terribly erratic characters. Would the forces that everywhere divide society finally invade and smash us up just as they had invaded and destroyed the promising Washingtonian group movement among alcoholics a century before? How could we possibly hang together and cling to our new life line, this line whose strands were woven of medicine and of religion and of our own experience? Could we carry the message to the distant alcoholic? Could we grow rapidly and soundly?

We saw that we had a grave responsibility. Fortunately we found we had great faith, too—faith that we could go farther, perhaps much farther. But I must confess that as we sat there that afternoon in Dr. Bob's living room we could not see at all how these riddles might actually be answered. Yet tonight, only eighteen years later, thousands of us in this vast auditorium can see and hear and touch one another. Bound in the unbreakable kinship of a common suffering and a common world-wide deliverance, we know at last that Alcoholics Anonymous is safe. Even this great gathering is only a token representation of us all—of A.A.'s thousands of groups, of our 200,000 members in seventy U.S. possessions and foreign countries. This host, we think, is but the first fraction of multitudes still to come.

Would that tonight Dr. Bob could stand here among us to voice all that we now feel so deeply. Indeed, we who know him well can almost see and hear him now. With us, we know that he is exclaiming: "What hath God wrought!"

THE TWELVE TRADITIONS

One: Our common welfare should come first; personal recovery depends upon A.A. unity.

Two: For our group purpose there is but one ultimate authority—a loving God as He may express Himself in our group conscience. Our leaders are but trusted servants; they do not govern.

Three: The only requirement for A.A. membership is a sincere desire to stop drinking.

Four: Each group should be autonomous, except in matters affecting other groups or A.A. as a whole.

Five: Each group has but one primary purpose—to carry its message to the alcoholic who still suffers.

Six: An A.A. group ought never endorse, finance, or lend the A.A. name to any related facility or outside enterprise, lest problems of money, property, and prestige divert us from our primary purpose.

Seven: Every A.A. group ought to be fully self-supporting, declining outside contributions.

Eight: Alcoholics Anonymous should remain forever nonprofessional, but our service centers may employ special workers.

Nine: A.A., as such, ought never to be organized; but we may create service boards or committees directly responsible to those they serve.

Ten: Alcoholics Anonymous has no opinion on outside issues; hence the A.A. name ought never to be drawn into public controversy.

Eleven: Our public relations policy is based on attraction rather than promotion; we need always maintain personal anonymity at the level of press, radio, and films.

Twelve: Anonymity is the spiritual foundation of all our Traditions, ever reminding us to place principles before personalities.

UNITY: THE SECOND LEGACY

Today we in A.A. are together, and we know we are going to stay together. We are at peace with each other and with the world around us. So many of our conflicts are resolved that our destiny seems secure. The problems of yesterday have produced the blessings of today.

Ours is not the usual success story; rather it is the story of how, under God's grace, an unsuspected strength has arisen out of great weakness; of how, under threats of disunity and collapse, world-wide unity and brotherhood have been forged. In the course of this experience we have evolved a set of traditional principles by which we live and work together and relate ourselves as a fellowship to the world around us. These principles are called the Twelve Traditions of Alcoholics Anonymous. They represent the distilled experience of our past, and we rely on them to carry us in unity through the challenges and dangers which the future may bring.

It was not always so. In the early days we saw that it was one thing for a few alcoholics to get well, but the problem of living and working together was something else. Therefore it was into an uncharted future that we looked from the window of Dr. Bob's living room in 1937 when we first realized that alcoholics might be able to get well in large numbers. The world around us, the world of more normal people, was being torn apart. Could we recovered alcoholics hold together? Could we carry A.A.'s message? Could we function as groups and as a whole? No one could say. Our friends the psychiatrists, with some reason, had begun to warn: "This fellowship of alcoholics is emotional dynamite. Its neurotic content can blow it to bits." When drinking we were certainly explosive enough. Now that we were sober, would dry benders and emotional jags blow us up?

When I think of explosions I always think of my friend Icky. Down in Houston, Texas, they call him the "Dynamite Man." Icky is an expert on explosives, on demolition. He was in the rear of the Russian retreat blowing up bridges during the war. After the war he started to ply his trade again, and I guess he fell into the same error that a poor fellow in London did the other day. This alcoholic Londoner turned up before a magistrate. He had been picked up stiff drunk. His bottle was empty. The magistrate said, "Did you drink it all?" "Oh, yes." "Why did you drink it all?" "Because I lost the cork." Down there in Houston, it must have been one of those days when our friend Icky lost his cork. Icky was commissioned to blow up a certain pier in Houston Harbor, and he blew up the wrong one!

The great question in the early days was this: would we blow up or could we stay together? Today we have the answers. This anniversary meeting in St. Louis is a vast testament to the fact that we *have* held together.

Pioneering in A.A. of course has not stopped. I hope it never will. We feel secure here today, but there are still places out on the A.A. front in distant lands where right now they are going through all the pains and trials of our early days. For example, the New York office recently received a letter written by a Jesuit priest in India. It told the story of a Hindu schoolteacher who owned a cow and a tiny plot of ground. His wife was stone deaf and he had a sister who, like himself, drank like a fish. His salary as a teacher was about fifty cents a day. The Jesuit translated A.A.'s Twelve Steps for him. And—in spite of his poverty, in spite of his wife's deafness, in spite of his domineering and drunker sister, he was staying sober. We know that this lone Hindu is probably feeling just the same worries that Dr. Bob and I did back there in the living room in Akron. This Hindu pioneer is probably asking, "Can I hang together myself? Can I carry this message? Will I be able to form a group?" Yes, he is asking those very questions. But he will soon be in communication with our world office and we can send solid assurance to that distant outpost that we are with him, all of us, and that our experience is his to draw on.[3]

Almost in the same mail a letter came from a Presbyterian minister out on another A.A. front. He said, "For a long time I've been trying to get a group started here in Thailand. Recently a highly educated Thai, speaking fluent English, came along. He was a terrible case of alcoholism, and he desperately wanted to get well. Now he has had a promising period of sobriety and is eager to translate the entire A.A. literature into Siamese. He and I are already at work, starting groups. Can you give us a hand?" The minister continued, "We took A.A.'s Twelve Steps over to the largest Buddhist monastery in this province. We showed them to the priest at the head of it. After he had finished looking over the Twelve Steps, the monk said, 'Why, these are fine! Since we as Buddhists don't understand God just as you do, it might be slightly more acceptable if you inserted the word 'good' in your Steps instead of 'God.' Nevertheless, you say in these Steps that it is God *as you understand Him*. That clears up the point for us. Yes, A.A.'s Twelve Steps will certainly be accepted by the Buddhists around here.' "

To some of us, the idea of substituting "good" for "God" in the Twelve Steps may seem like a watering down of A.A.'s message. But here we must remember that A.A.'s Steps are suggestions only. A belief in them as they stand is not at all a requirement for membership among us. This liberty has made A.A. available to thousands who never would have tried at all had we insisted on the Twelve Steps just as written. But changes in them seldom last; the original version usually wins out. What has proved so true here in America will probably prove true in many a far-off land. Alcoholics may be led to believe in God, but none can be forced.

Now what does this all mean? It means that there are going to be A.A. groups in India and in Thailand and in many other faraway places where alcoholics dwell. They are going to be plagued by our early fears, but we can help them and reassure them.

[3] As of 1977, there were over 570 A.A. members in India.

Speaking of fears, a story turned up at the office. It seems that A.A. had made a start in Tokyo. As usual it began among the American drunks, but then it spread out to the Japanese. Soon there was quite a Japanese contingent, of which we heard very good reports. Then one day a Japanese appeared at the New York Office. He had heard that his fellows in the homeland now had A.A. groups and had begun to write to them to get the inside track. Now, in a state of great alarm, he said, "Awful things are going on over there in Japan! Did you know that they have two kinds of A.A.'s over there? Of course they have the Twelve Steps just as we have them here, but there is now another A.A. leader who has written Ten Steps and they are charging 100 yen to attend his meetings!"

Once upon a time that sort of heresy would have scared us to death. Today it is only amusing. We know that they will soon be infiltrated by common sense and experience. They will find that nobody can professionalize A.A.'s Twelfth Step and the elder who means well and does badly will mend his ways. He will finally see that alcoholism is a quest for survival in which the good is sometimes the enemy of the best, and that only the best can bring the true good.

Very much more could be told about A.A. out on its distant reaches, its pioneering fronts. For example, there is an A.A. night-and-day radio communication that passes from tankers on the Atlantic over to the Pacific. There is good old Captain Jack on a Standard Oil tanker plying the world ports; he leaves A.A. literature when he goes ashore, and he looks up bartenders, doctors, and preachers, asking them for prospects. An A.A. group just recently started in Florence, Italy, because an A.A. sailor came ashore and got a prospect from a bartender. Many a group starts in such an improbable and fantastic way. It has become almost literally true that where two or three of us are gathered together in His name, there a group will form.

Let me tell you the wonderful legend about that A.A. group way up toward Point Barrow in Alaska. A couple of prospectors went out and got themselves a cabin and a case of Scotch. The weather turned bitter, fifty below, and they got so drunk they let the fire go out.

Barely escaping death by freezing, one of them woke up in time to rekindle the fire. He was prowling around outside for fuel, and he looked into an empty oil drum filled with frozen water. Down in the ice cake he saw a reddish-yellow object. They thawed it out, and it turned out to be an A.A. book. One of the pair read the book and sobered up. The legend has it that he became the founder of one of our farthest north groups, perhaps the one in which we now have plenty of Eskimos. The last I heard about those Alaskan groups was that they were in communication by radio every day with the A.A. group that functions on the north end of the Greenland icecap among the men at our air base there.

Alcoholics Anonymous got started in Ireland in 1946 when Connor F., an A.A. tavern owner from Philadelphia, decided to go on a vacation with his wife to the Emerald Isle. When they got to Dublin they both said, "Never mind the vacation; let's start a group here." So they made their way to a local mental hospital, the one endowed by the author-clergyman Swift, and there they found their first man, Richard P. And so A.A. began to take root in Ireland. The Dublin group, by the way, has achieved a special renown because of its world correspondent, Sackville M., the group's honorable secretary. When it comes to helping alcoholics by mail, he is no doubt the world's champion.

The beginning of A.A. in England in early 1947 was a striking one. Some years ago Bob B., a Canadian mining engineer, went to London, where he met up with Bill H., an alcoholic greengrocer. By correspondence with New York two or three of the English were already struggling for sobriety. But the appearance of these two upon the scene soon resulted in an active A.A. group. As a result London and indeed all England is today sprawling with groups. At first, however, they met such resistance in Britain that at one time only the *Financial Chronicle* would publish an advertisement about A.A. All the other English papers were afraid that it was a fraud.

The reverse process was seen when a Scottish nobleman, Philip, journeyed to America. He came over to have a look at the International Christian Leadership Movement, where he met with a group of businessmen who were interested in bringing God into industry through the medium of breakfast clubs for prayer and planning. Philip thought that maybe he could introduce the breakfast club idea to Scotland, and he hoped that such a good work would loosen his fatal attachment to the bottle. At the very first session he met an old-time Philadelphia A.A., George R., who gave him A.A. right off the spiritual main line. The head of one of Scotland's most ancient clans sobered up on the spot. He took A.A. back to his native heath, and soon alcoholic Scots were drying up all the way from Glasgow ship chandlers to society folks in Edinburgh.

Canadian A.A., too, is of the very best. Sometime in 1940 a temperance worker at Toronto showed the A.A. book to an alcoholic who had resisted all other attempts at rescue. Again the A.A. book turned the trick, and together these two exposed many a Toronto problem drinker to the A.A. contagion, and the process of multiplication set in which eventually carried A.A. to about every city and town in the Province of Ontario. This good friend, George Little, a minister as well as a temperance worker, was not a little disappointed that his strange new flock showed no interest whatever in getting everybody bone dry. They insisted they were concerned only with local imbibers who wanted A.A. Here it was definitely proved for the first time that A.A. could never become a dry crusade, a fact which has since puzzled many a worker in the dry cause. This first crossing of the border was followed in 1941 by another, when Windsor, Ontario, just across the river from Detroit, began to harbor Canada's group number two.[4]

In Vancouver, British Columbia, a nonalcoholic was also paired with an alcoholic from the very start. This time it was a public-spirited candy manufacturer who passed the book on to Charlie B., a real-estate broker. Inspired with the message and full of energy, this pair canvassed the city of Victoria and half the Province in a hurry, and soon B.C.'s Alcoholics Anonymous was a reality. After a time the message spread eastward over the prairies of Alberta, Saskatchewan, and Manitoba.

4 Though some meetings were held in 1941-42, start of Windsor group dates from Oct. 1943.

Montreal meanwhile had begun to simmer. Dave B., the Montreal group's founder and a marathon Twelfth Stepper, had sobered up on reading an A.A. book sent him by his sister. Here we saw A.A.'s very first French members. I shall forever remember that early bilingual Provincial meeting where I first heard the Lord's Prayer in French. In due course, solid A.A. began to flourish in Newfoundland and the Maritime Provinces, and of course it was only a question of time when Quebec City and Trois-Rivières, thus flanked on both sides, would have their own groups. The Quebec clergy, at first doubtful, are today among A.A.'s most ardent well-wishers. So are many public officials. We can never forget the party that Montreal's Mayor Houde once threw for us. It was probably the first *official* reception that any A.A. group ever had.

As we know, A.A. literature has a way of turning up in most surprising places. A broker of Johannesburg, South Africa, read an article in the *Reader's Digest* about us and sent to New York for a pamphlet, which so excited him that he fell like a buzz saw on the derelict drunks of his city. He had a calling to scrape the bottom of the barrel. As an extra inducement he offered his clients a certain amount of "rehabilitation" money. Naturally he was flooded by swarms of eager aspirants, who, it soon appeared, were far more interested in handouts than they were in sobriety. Verging on complete wreck, this enterprise was saved by the timely arrival of another drinker, Val D., who had just obtained a copy of the A.A. book, one reading of which had struck him cold sober. Almost at the same time, another South African, a native of Perth, had sobered up through the book and had gone right to work on the alcoholics in his own town. Through the more orthodox methods of these two devotees of A.A.'s Big Book, and with reinforcing letters from General Headquarters, things began to hum in South Africa. A whole volume could now be written about our progress down there, telling how A.A. has grown from these very fragile beginnings.

In the latter part of 1942 we began to get our first letters from Australia: from S. J. Minogue, a psychiatrist, associated with Rydalmere Mental Hospital in Sydney, and from a priest, Father Dunlea, at the same institution. We furnished them with literature, including the A.A. book, and a correspondence started with Dr. Minogue which has lasted ever since.

Month after month the doctor and the priest labored with their grim cases and were aided by an attendant named Mr. Arch McKinnon. Letter after letter from Dr. Minogue reported no results at all; indeed, it took over two years to produce anything like an A.A. group. These nonalcoholics had great difficulty in getting the proper identification with their patients, but late in 1944 they finally had success with two of them, Ben and Rex, the latter becoming Australia's first A.A. secretary.

In March, 1945, Rex wrote Bobbie at the New York office in substance as follows: "Dear Secretary: Dr. Minogue has handed over all of the correspondence to me, he being too fully occupied as Superintendent at Rydalmere to answer it himself. It must not be thought, however, that the Doctor's interest is flagging for the contrary is the case. You will be pleased to know that a group has now been formed in Sydney. Our address is above. The movement here was started by Dr. Minogue, Father Dunlea, and Mr. McKinnon, a hospital attendant. They are not alcoholics, but they have gathered around themselves seven or eight real ones, including myself, and we are 'netting' new recruits every day. We feel that the movement is gathering momentum in Australia . . . so we now want a formal affiliation with Alcoholics Anonymous. . . . Sincerely yours, Rex A., Secretary."

The Aussies were indeed on their way. Australia now has its thousands of members in all walks of life, and on all sides they enjoy the warmest public blessing. The Australia development will certainly be remembered as a seldom matched example of pioneering fortitude and faith.

These glimpses of A.A. world-wide reveal the incredible distance that A.A. has come since that fall day in 1937 when Dr. Bob and I looked apprehensively toward the future. Then we had only the word-of-mouth program, the substance of the formula for sobriety that

Ebby had given me. A.A.'s Twelve Steps had not yet been written, and the A.A. book was scarcely an idea. World-wide service and unity were only dreams.

A.A.'s first national development of consequence came in 1939. In September that year, Fulton Oursler, then editor of *Liberty* magazine, published a piece called "Alcoholics and God," written by Morris Markey. About 800 frantic inquiries descended upon us immediately and we wrote to them all.

Then came Mr. Rockefeller's dinner in 1940. It was followed by another large number of letters pleading for help. But the really big flood came in March 1941, when Jack Alexander's feature article appeared in the *Saturday Evening Post*. A real Niagara then broke loose, and we were deluged with letters and with alcoholics by the thousands.

This sudden growth ushered in a period of awful uncertainty. The big test of A.A.'s unity began in earnest. We were operating with only the benefit of casual contacts, travelers going from one place to another, letters from the office, one pamphlet, and one book. Could we, on that slender basis, form ourselves into groups that could function and hang together? We simply did not know. Alcoholics in twos and threes were tough enough, but if they were gathered in much larger groups, what then? There had already been an ominous foretaste of the problems of mushrooming groups; quarrels over leadership, money, membership, clubs, exploitation of A.A.'s name, panhandling, and even romancing. As the *Saturday Evening Post* crop of alcoholics tried to form themselves into hundreds of new groups, the specters of disunity and collapse grew to frightening proportions. We could only do our best, and leave the rest to God.

Just before the big test fell upon us, one of our New York members named Ray W., went to San Francisco in 1940 to take a sales course. This was another one of those improbable beginnings. Ray had been an atheist and he still stuck to it. Nevertheless, he had been sober a couple of years and was broad-minded enough to take the A.A. book to San Francisco with him. We handed him a list of inquiries from that area which had been contacted by mail only. When he got to

San Francisco Ray began calling up these people, and a few of them gathered at his hotel. He said to them, "Now, boys, this A.A. is great stuff. It really saved my life. But there's one feature of it I don't like. I mean this God business. So when you read this book, you can skip that part of it." Ten days later, Ray was on his way back East, leaving a shivering and divided group in his wake.

But they soon found two wonderful friends, Mrs. Gordon Oram and Dr. Percy Poliak, a psychiatrist who had been impressed with A.A. as he had seen it at work in Bellevue Hospital in New York. Now at the San Francisco County Hospital, Dr. Poliak gave the group his full support, and he continued it ever afterward. Mrs. Oram had a boarder, Ted, for whom she had already obtained the A.A. book. She opened her flat for the first A.A. meeting late in 1939, where salesman Ray's contacts foregathered with Ted.

Ted never made the grade. But one John C. did, and he has stayed in the clear ever since. Soon these were joined by Fred and Amy C. and a little bit later by King, Ned, and others. At this stage there was plenty of slipping and backsliding. But, encouraged by Mrs. Oram and Dr. Poliak, the group somehow held together.

From New York we began writing letters to San Francisco, but the replies were sketchy and uncertain. At the end of a year an alky lady appeared at our New York office on Vesey Street. She was a little tight, and crying. Though of course she exaggerated a bit, she said, "Bill, we've been going a whole year in San Francisco and do you know that at Christmas time we were all drunk."

Only a few years later, in 1951, the Lasker Award was given to Alcoholics Anonymous in the San Francisco Opera House. On the night following the award presentation there was an A.A. meeting and the huge place was packed. Sober alcoholics were practically hanging from the rafters. What once looked like a mighty poor acorn had produced a great oak.

As early as 1941 the group had picked up steady wheel horses like Nic N., Ray H., and Warren T. Other starts had been made in the

Bay area, notably by Nic at Oakland and by Vic M. and Dr. P. at Sacramento.

This readied the area for the impact of Jack Alexander's piece in the *Saturday Evening Post*. It saw Warren at work in the Kaiser shipyard, where he became the first A.A. member to be employed as an alcoholic specialist by industry. And perhaps even more importantly, Warren and the others [5] were able to start the first penitentiary group at San Quentin Prison.

By the time of the Lasker Award, the inspiring account of the founding of the first A.A. group behind the prison walls of San Quentin was a familiar story to most of our members.

San Quentin's enlightened and liberal warden, Clinton T. Duffy, had, prior to 1942, given much thought to the urgent and pressing problem of prison reform, including the special needs of the inmates imprisoned for crimes committed while drinking. As Warden Duffy said, the program he now proposed "would include education, vocational training, medicine, psychiatry, and religion. But the alcoholic did not seem to fit *completely* into this program . . . all the rest would not help him if the problems which drove him to drink were not solved. If every offender were to receive full advantage of the new program, then the alcoholic too must receive the assistance and understanding of all available knowledge and procedures. And in line with this new approach to rehabilitation, I looked upon Alcoholics Anonymous as a tool to help us rebuild lives." [6]

To Warden Duffy's aid came Warren and other members in the San Francisco area and thus began the pioneering of A.A.'s first prison group in 1942. As Warden Duffy has since said, "Had it not been for the regular help and understanding given by our A.A. friends outside, the San Quentin chapter of Alcoholics Anonymous would most assuredly have failed. And by the same token, if it had not been for the persistence of that first group of alcoholic inmates who realized their

[5] Leo F., of the Los Angeles Group, was particularly instrumental in bringing A.A. to San Quentin, together with other devoted A.A. members of the San Francisco Group. Also, Ricardo, an inmate, was continuously helpful from the beginning.

[6] Warden Clinton T. Duffy, "San Quentin Prison and Alcoholics Anonymous," 1950.

serious problem and their need for help, we could never have continued beyond the first few meetings." [7]

But even with such enthusiasm and willingness, there were formidable problems to solve. The establishment of regular A.A. meetings would mean carloads of A.A.'s from the outside running in and out of prison. It would probably draw the ridicule of other prisoners. Those penologists who still thought hard-boiled methods to be the only way and those skeptics who thought A.A. only a "useless fad" would shake their heads. It would mean large gatherings of prisoners unattended by guards. The risks were great, but Warden Duffy took them, and his faith was justified. A.A. soon won the respect of other prisoners, and many of them, although nonalcoholic, wanted to join up anyhow. The morale of what was now a really progressive institution hit a new high. A.A.'s came and went freely. The meetings had only one guard, stationed outside the meeting room, who was there mainly to care for the needs of the outside A.A. visitors at the meeting.

When the parole figures on alcoholic prisoners suddenly dropped from the usual 80 per cent return to prison to a spectacular 20 per cent, and held that way, skeptics were everywhere convinced. This piece of pioneering made A.A. history. More than 300 prison groups have since been established behind prison walls. We know for sure that thousands of former inmates are today making the grade on the outside.

Warren, just mentioned as one of the originators of the first prison group, was also the earliest pioneer of A.A. in industry. At the time of the prison venture, he was employed at the nearby Kaiser shipyards to look after the alcohol problem there. Though his success was notable, it was only a starter. A few years later he and his A.A. wife Alice had persuaded the top management of one of America's leading railroads that something could be done in their offices and out on the lines for afflicted workers. This was perhaps the understatement of the year. Still on the job today, Warren[8] and Alice can count recoveries among their railroad friends by the hundreds and it is surely no co-

---

[7] *Ibid.*

[8] Warren died soon after the 1957 publication of this volume.

incidence that this road has meanwhile achieved an unsurpassed safety record. It is certain that other carriers will one day make use of this outstanding model for the rehabilitation of their alcoholic workers.

Before returning to the aftermath of the *Saturday Evening Post* piece, let's journey down the coast to Los Angeles. Just before the Big Book came out in 1939, we had made a prepublication mimeographed copy of it. Four hundred of the books in this form were circulated among all kinds of people so that we could correct errors and get suggestions for improvement. Late in that year I made a business trip to Cleveland and handed one of these mimeographs to a friend who was an attorney. He happened to be the attorney for a wealthy young Clevelander who then lived on the coast, where he had been drinking himself into one dilemma after another.

My lawyer friend sent him the prepublication copy of the Big Book, and he gobbled it up. He insisted on going straight to Akron, where he placed himself under the tutelage of Dr. Bob and the benign influence of Wally G., in whose home he lived for a time. His ex-wife Kaye M. was not an alcoholic, but she turned up in New York, full of enthusiasm about A.A. for itself. She was inspired with the same spirit which is found in the Family Groups of today.

She took a boat to the west coast and presently landed at Los Angeles, and the next thing we knew she had looked up Johnny Howe of the city's Probation Department. He had plenty of drunks on his hands, both hospital inmates and parolees. Johnny had been laboring hard with his charges, but to little avail. When he was shown the book *Alcoholics Anonymous* and was told what Kaye had seen at the twin Meccas of Akron and New York, he became more hopeful and asked Kaye to join forces with him, but with certain reservations. Johnny had been running instruction classes for his alcoholic customers on a strictly psychological basis. "Know yourself and be free" was the idea. The A.A. book was a revelation to him, but it was a revelation he did not much like at first. He could not go for that "surrender to the higher Power" business. The spiritual side of A.A. simply was not for Johnny.

Legend has it that he and Kaye compromised. Johnny would continue his lectures to inmates as before. But he and Kaye would try out certain A.A. ideas on some of the parolees. The prospects were told that they could try Kaye's ideas, or Johnny's, or both. Of course this sort of approach was not exactly orthodox A.A. Nevertheless it produced some results. For example, certain well-known residents of Los Angeles and vicinity because of their drinking had fallen into the hands of the law, and thence into Johnny's hands. On parole, some of them began to take notice of the new dispensation as offered by Kaye and Johnny. Hal S. was the very first. He was later to become the founder of the San Diego group. Others who came in the same way were Marshall B., Barney B., and Dr. Forrist H., the latter to become a marathon Twelfth Stepper around Los Angeles in after years. With this much accomplished, Kaye and Johnny had made a definite start in Los Angeles, and we want to record our thanks to these two non-alcoholics for all they did for us.

Meanwhile, the New York office notified the coast of the coming of Chuck, an artist, and his wife Lee, who at that time was the A.A. member of the family, the first alcoholic to arrive from the East. Lee was a real eager beaver. She and Chuck came to Los Angeles just in time to attend the first of the so-called "home" meetings. This particular gathering was held at Kaye's place on Benecia Avenue on December 19, 1939. It included Kaye and Johnny, Lee and Chuck, and a number of prospects. Lee agreed with Kaye on stressing the spiritual aspects of the A.A. program, so a chapter from the A.A. book was read at this meeting. Johnny gave his lecture and delivered a medical paper on alcoholism.

For the next few weeks meetings of this character were held in one home after another. Kaye and Lee were for the "higher Power," and Johnny was still for psychology only.

At about this time Lee secured some publicity in the Los Angeles papers which brought in more prospects and finally led to A.A.'s friendship with Ted LeBerthon, a prominent Los Angeles columnist whose subsequent articles did a far-reaching job for us.

As was to be expected, this little pioneering group had many difficulties, both personal and doctrinal. Frantic letters from the several contestants poured into our one-room Headquarters in New York. Finally Lee began to drink. She called upon Johnny to hospitalize her and was out in a few days. This was, however, a very heavy jolt to everyone. But the group nonetheless survived for the time being. Lee and Chuck then returned East to live happily—and both of them soberly—ever since.

While all this was going on a Denver resident named Mort J. had bought the A.A. book in September of 1939. Without even looking through the volume, Mort dropped it into his suitcase and set off on a spree that lasted several weeks. He finally came to himself at Palm Springs and discovered the A.A. book in his luggage. Shaking violently, he began to read. This was sometime in November, 1939, and he has never had a drink since. Mort was a book convert pure and simple.

In March, 1940, Mort moved to Los Angeles. He looked up the Benecia group and found that it had just about fallen apart. Erstwhile stalwarts like Hal and Dr. H. were rarely seen. Kaye was downright discouraged and said she was going to Honolulu. Just as she left she gave Mort a small list of prospects that hadn't yet been visited. That first candle at Los Angeles was flickering, but it never quite went out.

Mort got busy at once on Kaye's list and promptly turned up a customer named Cliff W. This one grabbed for the life line, and he soon sobered up for good.

At his own expense, Mort hired a meeting place at Los Angeles' Cecil Hotel. Right then another book convert, Frank R., put in his appearance. A real sanitarium commuter, Frank had read the A.A. book in Arizona and had, at the suggestion of the New York Headquarters, rushed to Los Angeles to see if what it said was really true.

This founding trio soon enlarged the Cecil meeting. Mort insisted on a reading from Chapter 5 of the A.A. book at the start of every session. This firmly established a custom for which A.A. on the west coast is now notable, and it put the Cecil group on a foursquare A.A.

basis. The debate whether the meeting was to center around "psychology" or around "God as we understand Him" was at an end. The first solid foundation for A.A. in Southern California was thus built. In fact the Cecil Hotel meeting after a while became known as the Los Angeles "Mother Group."

From New York we tried hard to keep Los Angeles in good cheer and advice. The A.A. book became their mainstay, even their bible. They were not to see a sober, experienced A.A. member from outside their area for a long while to come. Once they plaintively wrote us, "Well, we've got a lot of people sober out here. But we do sometimes wonder if anybody is sober east of the Rocky Mountains. We haven't seen a single Easterner who is really dry. They've all been drunk, every one of them."

Led by Mort, the three elders continued to push on. And so did their wives. Mort's wife Frances backstopped the huge amount of Twelfth Step work that Mort began to do. Frank was at times laid low by a recurring fever and his wife Eleanor would take over his prospects and carry on his large correspondence with the New York office. When in the following year the *Saturday Evening Post* article appeared, Cliff had a telephone installed in his home under the A.A. name in order to handle the enormous demand for quick help. Cliff's wife Dorothy carried this load of work to a point of her complete exhaustion. The efforts of these six will always be well remembered in the annals of Alcoholics Anonymous.

The *Saturday Evening Post* piece not only brought in large numbers of new members; it also added several scores of magnificent workers of all kinds and conditions. Never could Los Angeles have prospered as it did without their labors over the years to follow. It is regrettable that in the limited range of this book we cannot detail all their wonderful services.

Now let us return once more to the aftermath of the *Saturday Evening Post* article. Lois and I visited Los Angeles sometime in 1943, and the groups called a meeting in the American Legion Hall. When I peered out from behind the curtain, I saw a thousand people sitting there. It was incredible. Here was evidence that A.A. could cross the seas and mountains pretty much on its own. In the future no alcoholic messenger-in-the-flesh might be needed at all.

The rush and resulting growing pains in Los Angeles had been appalling. It seemed impossible that they could have stood the confusion and the pace. Before this first visit was over, I began to wonder if they could continue to bear up under it. Yet in 1950, only seven years later, I spoke to an A.A. audience in the Shrine Auditorium, where 7,000 members and their families were gathered. By then, Los Angeles County represented the most densely populated A.A. region in our whole fellowship. Today it harbors 14,000 members and they are as solid as Gibraltar.

On that first 1943 trip to the coast Lois and I also looked in on Doc H., an Oregon chiropractor who was struggling with the alkies in Portland. And in Seattle, Washington, we first met businessman Dale A., who with real valor was trying hard to hold a small band together there. This he was able to do, and they went on to real success.

Meanwhile, Minneapolis got under way. Chicago's Chan F. and Bill Y. were pinned down there by a 1940 blizzard, and they took time out to carry the message to an alcoholic named Pat C. Pat took on the hectic job of trying to start an A.A. group and a club at the same time. He persuaded one of the city's flour barons to sell the A.A.'s his former town house on a shoestring. Today there is no more club-minded group in all of A.A. than this one. The A.A. life of the town still gathers around that pioneering monument. And, believe it or not, those Minneapolis alkies burned the mortgage on that clubhouse in just three years' time.

As I remember it, Buffalo and Pittsburgh started up not much later. And right out in the middle of the country that most loved salesman, Johnny P. had put in an appearance to plant A.A. in Kansas City, Missouri. This touched off another group right across the river in Kansas City, Kansas. It was sparked by one of A.A.'s first doctor-members, Miles N., who was later to become a prodigious A.A. worker and a national authority on the chemistry of drunks.

In these same years, the Boston Irish had joined forces with certain Back Bayers and had grabbed the A.A. life line with a will, forming that wonderful nucleus from which so much of A.A. in New England later stemmed. The Boston group provided us with a fresh wonder and a big heartbreak, too. Its founder could never get sober himself and he finally died of alcoholism. Paddy was just too sick to make it. Slip followed slip, but he came back each time to carry A.A.'s message, at which he was amazingly successful. Time after time the group nursed him back to life. Then came the last bender, and that was it. This very sick man left behind him a great group and a triple-A rating for valor. His first two successes, Bert C. and Jennie B., carry on to this day.

Such was our adolescence. I hope that some day many more of its wonderful stories can be told. This was the welter of exciting and fearsome experience out of which A.A.'s Twelve Traditions were drawn and first put to paper in 1946. Against this background we shall now consider those Twelve Traditions, the vital principles upon which the survival of Alcoholics Anonymous so heavily depends.

Implicit throughout A.A.'s Traditions is the confession that our fellowship has its sins. We confess that we have character defects as a society and that these defects threaten us continually. Our Traditions are a guide to better ways of working and living, and they are also an antidote for our various maladies. The Twelve Traditions are to group survival and harmony what A.A.'s Twelve Steps are to each member's sobriety and peace of mind.

But the Twelve Traditions also point straight at many of our individual defects. By implication they ask each of us to lay aside pride and resentment. They ask for personal as well as group sacrifice. They ask us never to use the A.A. name in any quest for personal power or distinction or money. The Traditions guarantee the equality of all members and the independence of all groups. They show how we may best relate ourselves to each other and to the world outside. They indicate how we can best function in harmony as a great whole. For the sake of the welfare of our entire society, the Traditions ask that every individual and every group and every area in A.A. shall lay aside all desires, ambitions, and untoward actions that could bring serious division among us or lose for us the confidence of the world at large.

The Twelve Traditions of Alcoholics Anonymous symbolize the sacrificial character of our life together and they are the greatest force for unity that we know.[9]

Take Tradition One. It says that *"Our common welfare should come first; personal recovery depends upon A.A. unity."* Probably no society sets a higher value on the personal welfare of the individual member than does A.A. But long ago we found that the common welfare had to come first; without it there could be mighty little personal welfare. In the beginning we felt very much like Eddie Rickenbacker and his company when their plane crashed in the Pacific. They had been saved from death but found themselves still floating upon a dangerous sea. There was no doubt in their minds that the common welfare came first. Nobody dared rock that raft, lest they all perish. Bread and water were shared equally; there were no gluttons.

Our case was something like that. But some of our sick and careless members did rock the raft, and that scared us to death. Some of those early fears are today almost amusing. The first big one was that of slips or relapses. At first nearly every alcoholic we approached began to slip, if indeed he sobered up at all. Others would stay dry six months or maybe a year and then take a skid. This was always a genuine catastrophe. We would all look at each other and say, "Who next?" We were afraid that alcohol might completely undo us. But today we see tens of thousands of members completely sober for five, ten, fifteen, or even twenty years. Slips are a very serious difficulty, but as a group we take them in stride. Fear has evaporated. Alcohol always threatens the individual, but we know that it cannot destroy the common welfare.

The next big scare was the out-of-bounds romance, the well-known triangle. In the cases of more than half of our membership the family relation had been distorted. Drinking had turned the husband into the household's bad boy and the wife into his protective and possessive

[9] See A.A.'s Twelve Traditions, p. 78.

mother. When this relation persisted after A.A., the husband sometimes got the wandering eye. Alcoholic women whose husbands had
long since cast them off put in an appearance. Here and there we
began to witness explosions gathering around these situations. People
violently took sides. Whole groups got into uproars, and a number of
people got drunk. There was some throwing of rocks at the sinners.
We trembled for A.A.'s reputation and for its survival. But at last we
woke up to the fact that we were not having any more sex difficulties
than other societies, and possibly less. We found that these situations
would often right themselves if they were treated with patience and
kindness. The sinners and the self-righteous eventually saw the folly
of their ways. Most alcoholics whose wives had seen them through
their terrible days returned to the straight and narrow. The Al-Anon
Family Groups put in an appearance and did wonders for A.A.'s
domestic relations. So these experiences all conspired toward a good
end. A.A.'s present divorce rate is among the lowest in the whole
world. It became apparent that the relationship between the sexes was
not going to do us in after all, and our fears in this area subsided.

But like other societies, we soon found that there were forces among
us that could threaten us in ways that alcohol and sex could not.
These were the desires for power, for domination, for glory, and for
money. They were all the more dangerous because they were invaria-
bly powered by self-righteousness, self-justification, and the destructive power of anger, usually masquerading as righteous indignation.

Pride and fear and anger—these are the prime enemies of our common welfare. True brotherhood, harmony, and love, fortified by clear
insights and right practices, are the only answers. And the purpose
of A.A.'s traditional principles is to bring these forces to the top and
keep them there. Only then can our common welfare be served; only
then can A.A.'s unity become permanent.

Now let us think about Tradition Two: *"For our group purpose
there is but one ultimate authority—a loving God as He may express
Himself in our group conscience. Our leaders are but trusted servants;
they do not govern."* We A.A.'s have learned this principle the hard

way. Few obstacles have been tougher to remove than those which blocked the way to realization that A.A.'s group conscience can be the only ultimate authority in our affairs.

I expect that many an old-timer still does not believe this proposition. He feels that he is older and more experienced than recent generations of A.A.'s and that it was his guidance and leadership that brought them into the new life. We oldsters often construed our longer experience as a sort of vested right, even an unlimited license, to run A.A. indefinitely. Whenever we got sick, tired, or old, we naturally thought ourselves entitled to hand-pick our own successors. Who could know better than we?

But with the passage of time most of us came up against some hard facts of A.A. life. We ruefully discovered that the groups, no matter how much they liked and respected us, simply did not want us to be the self-appointed managers of their service and policy affairs forever. Neither would they let us pick our own successors to do the job for them. They wanted to name their own service committees. Again and again they showed us that the ultimate authority must speak through the groups. For some of us this was tough to take.

Harder still to accept was the now proven fact that the conscience of the group, when properly informed of the facts and issues and principles involved, was often wiser than any leader, self-appointed or not. We slowly realized that the old-timer frequently was faulty in judgment. Because of his position of assumed authority, he was too often influenced by personal prejudices and interests. With all his experience and good works, there was still nothing infallible about him at all.

Does this mean that as old-timers our usefulness is over? No. Once we old-timers have surrendered to the group conscience we are pleasantly surprised to find that the groups, when in deep difficulty, will again turn to us for the kind of guidance that only our longer experience can give.

I well remember when I had to swallow my first dose of this hard but healthy doctrine.

In 1937 the financial going was rough at 182 Clinton Street. Several alkies were living with us, most of them paying no board. Lois was still in the department store and her pay was just about all the money we had. Meanwhile, many of the sober members coming to our weekly meetings were back on their feet and earning good money.

One day at Charlie Towns' hospital, Charlie beckoned me into his office for one of his Dutch-uncle talks. "Look here, Bill," said he, "I've got a hunch that this A.A. business of yours is someday going to fill Madison Square Garden. Now I am not a religious man and you must know that I was mighty skeptical of this business when it first came in here. Silkworth really scared me by his co-operation with you. But that is all changed. I believe in you people. Your methods are going to work." And he said, "Look, Bill, don't you see you're getting the bad end of this deal? You are starving to death, and your wife is working at that store. All around you, these drunks are getting well and making money, but you're giving this work full time, and still you're broke. It isn't fair."

Charlie fished in his desk and came up with an old financial statement. Handing it to me, he continued, "This shows the kind of money this hospital used to make back in the 1930's. Thousands of dollars a month. It should be doing just as well now, and it would—if only you'd help it. So why don't you move your work in here? I'll give you an office, a decent drawing account, and a very healthy slice of the profits. What I propose is perfectly ethical. You can become a lay therapist, and more successful than anybody in the business."

I was bowled over. There were a few twinges of conscience until I saw how really ethical Charlie's proposal was. There was nothing wrong whatever with becoming a lay therapist. I thought of Lois coming home exhausted from the department store each day, only to cook a supper for a houseful of drunks who were not paying board. I thought of the large sum of money I still owed my Wall Street creditors. I thought of some of my alcoholic friends who were making as much money as they ever did. Why shouldn't I do as well as they?

Although I asked Charlie for a little time to consider it, my own mind was about made up. Going back to Brooklyn on the subway, I had a flash of seeming divine guidance. It was only a single sentence, but it was most convincing. In fact, it came right out of the Bible. A voice kept saying to me, "The laborer is worthy of his hire."

At home I found Lois cooking as usual, while three drunks looked hungrily on from the kitchen door. I drew her aside and told her the glorious news. She looked interested, but not as excited as I thought she should be.

It was meeting night. Although few of the alcoholics we boarded seemed to get sober, some others had. With their wives, they crowded into our downstairs parlor. At once I burst into the story of my opportunity. I never shall forget their impassive faces and the steady gazes they focused on me. With waning enthusiasm, my story trailed off to the end. There was a long silence.

Almost timidly, one of my friends began to speak. "We know how hard up you are, Bill," he said. "It bothers us a lot. We've often wondered what we might do about it. But I think I speak for everyone here when I say that what you now propose bothers us an awful lot more." The speaker's voice grew more confident. "Don't you realize," he went on, "that you can never become a professional? As generous as Charlie has been to us, don't you see that we can't tie this thing up with his hospital or any other? You tell us that Charlie's proposal is ethical. Sure, it's ethical. But what we've got won't run on ethics only; it has to be better. Sure, Charlie's idea is good, but it isn't good enough. This is a matter of life and death, Bill, and nothing but the very best will do." My friends looked at me challengingly as their spokesman continued. "Bill, haven't you often said right here in this meeting that sometimes the good is the enemy of the best? Well, this is a plain case of it. You can't do this thing to us."

Thus spoke the group conscience. The group was right and I was wrong; the voice on the subway was not the voice of God. Here was the true voice welling up out of my friends. I listened and—thank God—I obeyed.

Three blows, well and truly struck, had fallen on the anvil of group experience. They rang in my consciousness. "The common welfare must come first," "A.A. cannot have a class of professional therapists," and "God, speaking in the group conscience, is to be our final authority." Clearly implied in these three embryo principles of tradition was a fourth: "Our leaders are but trusted servants; they do not govern."

Tradition Three for a long time was a puzzler, too: *"The only requirement for A.A. membership is a sincere desire to stop drinking."* We worried a lot about membership. In fact, when heavy publicity first came our way, we were scared witless. We said to ourselves, "Won't all kinds of odd people show up? Complications, you know; alcohol mixed with other things." In those days we were always talking about the mythical character called the pure alcoholic; no complications, you understand, just a guzzler. We actually thought we were like that ourselves! Hence, when members began pouring in, our worry mounted. "Won't there be mighty queer people? Won't there be criminals? Won't there be social undesirables?" we asked. Mixed with a certain amount of snobbishness and smugness, this was downright fear. We simply did not know what or who would turn up.

Since that early time literally all kinds of people have found their way into Alcoholics Anonymous. Our inclusiveness is now very broad indeed. For example, not too long ago I sat talking in my office with a member who bears a title of Countess. That same night I went to an A.A. meeting. It was a winter night and there was a mild-looking little gent taking the coats. He was not charging anything, either. He was just doing it to be obliging. I said, "Who's that little guy?" And somebody answered, "Oh, he's been around for a long time. Everybody likes him. He used to be one of Al Capone's mob." That's how universal A.A. is today.

But it took us a long, long time to become really democratic. There used to be so many membership rules out among the groups that if they were all enforced at once nobody—actually *nobody*—could have joined Alcoholics Anonymous. But as our fears subsided we finally said to ourselves, "Who are we to keep anybody out? To many a desperate drunk A.A. is the court of his last appeal. How can we slam the door on anybody who stands outside?" No, we must never do that. We must always take the risk, no matter who comes in. Maybe our public relations will be damaged because a few strange characters are among us. Of course our public relations are important, but is not the real character of this society still more important? Who of us dares to say, "No, you can't come in," thereby setting himself up as judge, jury, and perhaps executioner of his brother alcoholic? So the experience through the years, now distilled into Tradition Three, says, "You are an A.A. member if you say so. No matter what you have done, or still will do, you are an A.A. member as long as *you* say so."

Now here comes Tradition Four. It declares that *"Each group should be autonomous, except in matters affecting other groups or A.A. as a whole."*

As one of the people who helped start this movement, I thought for a long time that I ought to be able to manage it from New York. But I soon found that I could do no such thing. Neither could anybody else at A.A.'s Headquarters. The groups said to us, "We like what you are doing. Sometimes your suggestions and advice are good. But whether to take you or leave you alone is going to be *our* decision. Out in the groups, we are going to run our own show. We are not going to have a personal government in New York, or anywhere else. Services, yes. But government, no."

Hence, A.A.'s Tradition of group autonomy. It didn't take long to formulate that one. They told us just what they wanted, and that included the right to be wrong.

To illustrate: Years ago in a certain town a super-promoter got sobered up in A.A. At once he got very big ideas, all for the good of A.A. of course. As he saw it, the right setup would require a very big building and would take an awful lot of money. On one floor there would be a club. On the next floor there would be a meeting room. On the next, a clinic and rehabilitation center. Upstairs, there surely would have to be a loan agency where the indigent alcoholic could borrow a little spare cash. Such was his vision of the new center! He was some promoter, this one, and he actually sold the townspeople on his idea. He, naturally, was to become the general manager. His blueprint involved three separate corporations, one for the club, one for the clinic, and one for the loan department. Altogether, he wrote sixty-one rules, regulations, and by-laws to make these corporations do their good work.

With the exception of a few diehards, his fellow A.A.'s were sold. He was the man of the hour. He applied to New York for a supercharter. Hearing of this, some of the dissenters wrote us. We had to tell them that each A.A. group could manage its own affairs as it liked, provided it did not harm surrounding groups. But as strongly as we dared, we did point out that even less grandiose schemes of a like character had failed everywhere before. As it had a right to, this very autonomous group ignored our warnings.

Maybe you can guess what happened. After many a rumbling, the crash came. It was like a boiler explosion in a clapboard factory. The thump of colliding egos could be heard and felt for miles.

But of course things quieted down, and after a long interval we heard from the promoter. He wrote, "You told us that outside enterprises can be fine and very helpful. But you also said that they could not be mixed with A.A. I figured that they could be, and should be. Well, you folks at Headquarters were right and I was wrong."

With his letter, the promoter sent us a card, which he had already mailed to every group in the United States. It was folded like a golf score card, and on the outside was printed, "Group so-and-so, place so-and-so. Rule No. 62." When the card was unfolded a single pungent sentence met the eye: "Don't take yourself too damned seriously."

Thus, under Tradition Four, an A.A. group had exercised its right to be wrong. Moreover, it had performed a great service for Alcoholics Anonymous, because it had been humbly willing to apply the lessons it had learned. It had picked itself up with a laugh and had gone on to better things. Even the chief architect, standing in the ruins of his dream, could laugh at himself—and that is the acme of humility.

Some may think that we have carried the principle of group autonomy to extremes. For example, in its original "long form," Tradition Four declares: "Any two or three gathered together for sobriety may call themselves an A.A. group, provided that as a group they have no other affiliation." This means that these two or three alcoholics could try for sobriety in any way they liked. They could disagree with any or all of A.A.'s principles and still call themselves an A.A. group.

But this ultra-liberty is not so risky as it looks. In the end the innovators would have to adopt A.A. principles—at least some of them—in order to remain sober at all. If, on the other hand, they found something better than A.A., or if they were able to improve on our methods, then in all probability we would adopt what they discovered for general use everywhere. This sort of liberty also prevents A.A. from becoming a frozen set of dogmatic principles that could not be changed even when obviously wrong. Healthy trial and error always have their day and place in A.A. Of course any dissident group is urged—though never commanded—not to make any other affiliation. Obviously we could not very well have Catholic A.A. groups, Protestant A.A. groups, Republican A.A. groups, Democratic A.A. groups, or Communist A.A. groups. Nor should an A.A. group ally itself with any particular brand of medical or psychiatric treatment. We can co-operate with anyone. But the name "Alcoholics Anonymous" must be reserved for us only.

Many people wonder how A.A. can function under such a seeming anarchy. Other societies have to have law and force and sanction and punishment, administered by authorized people. Happily for us, we found we need no human authority whatever. We have two authorities which are far more effective. One is benign, the other malign. There is God, our Father, who very simply says, "I am waiting for you to do my will." The other authority is named John Barleycorn, and he says, "You had better do God's will or I will kill you." And sometimes he does kill. So, when all the chips are down, we conform to God's will or perish. At this level, the death sentence hangs over the A.A. member, his group, and A.A. as a whole. Therefore we have the full benefits of the murderous political dictatorships of today but none of their liabilities. So there is authority enough, love enough, and punishment enough, all without any human being clutching the handles of power. Such is A.A.'s backstop against dissolution, and its final guarantee of survival under any conditions. For us, it is do or die.

But this is not the whole story. As our individual and group development progresses, we begin to obey the A.A. Traditions for other reasons. We begin to obey them because we think they are right for us. We obey these principles because we think they are good principles, even though we still resist somewhat. Then comes the final level of obedience, the best of all. We obey A.A.'s Steps and Traditions because we really want them for ourselves. It is no longer a question of good or evil; we conform because we genuinely want to conform. Such is our process of growth in unity and in function. Such is the evidence of God's grace and love among us.

Much of our discussion so far leads straight to Tradition Five, which states: *"Each group has but one primary purpose—to carry its message to the alcoholic who still suffers."*

We think we should do one thing well rather than many things to which we are not called. That is the central idea of this Tradition. Our society gathers in unity around this concept. The very life of our fellowship requires its preservation. "Shoemaker, stick to thy last" is no dull cliché for Alcoholics Anonymous. Together we have found a substantial remedy for a terrible malady. Of course we might interest ourselves in fields of education, research, neurosis, and the like. But, as a society, should we? Our experience says that we definitely should not. We can and we do help, as individuals, in those fields. That is good. But, as a fellowship, we know that we must not be diverted. It is our experience as alcoholics that makes us of unique value on our sector of the total alcoholic front. We can approach sufferers as no one else can. Therefore, the strongest kind of moral and ethical compulsion is upon us to do this and nothing more. If we had discovered a widely applicable cancer cure, we would be begged to attend to that and that only. We would not try to look after all tumors and branch out into tuberculosis and tapeworms besides. In such a case we would certainly stick to cancer. Though A.A. is obligated to both medicine and religion, we cannot become experts in either. We know that theology is for clergymen and that the practice of medicine and psychiatry is for doctors. Certain that we can do together what we cannot do separately, we shall always co-operate but never compete. We shall direct our energies where they count most.

Most emphatically, then, A.A. has but one single purpose: *to carry its message to the alcoholic who still suffers.* That is our basic objective, our real reason for existence.

A logical outgrowth of Tradition Five, Tradition Six reads: *"An A.A. group ought never endorse, finance, or lend the A.A. name to any related facility or outside enterprise, lest problems of money, property, and prestige divert us from our primary purpose."*

In the old days our Foundation (now the General Service Board) was originally chartered to do everything but lobby for Prohibition. We were chartered for education; we were chartered for research; we could do almost anything. And we used to think we wanted a lot of money to do a lot of things. Out in the groups the same ideas often prevailed.

At that time hospitals did not want us, so we thought we would build and operate our own. People needed to be told what alcoholism was, so we thought we would educate the public, perhaps rewrite school and medical textbooks. We thought we would revise the laws of the land and have it declared that alcoholics are sick people. We would carry A.A. into the dark regions of dope addiction and criminality. We would form groups for depressive and paranoid folks, and the deeper the neurosis the better we would like it.

If alcoholism could be licked, so could any problem! A.A.'s uncompromising honesty might soon clean up politics. In the factories it could cause laborers and capitalists to love each other. Having learned to live so happily, we would show everybody else how. We thought our society of Alcoholics Anonymous might prove to be the spearhead of a new spiritual advance. Our principles might transform the world!

Yes, we did dream those dreams. How natural that was, since most alcoholics are bankrupt idealists. Nearly every one of us had wished to do great good, perform great deeds that embodied great ideals. We were perfectionists who, failing to attain perfection, had gone to the other extreme and settled for the bottle and the blackout. Providence through A.A. had brought us within reach of our highest expectations. So why shouldn't we share our way of life with everyone?

Well, we tried A.A. hospitals. And they all bogged down because you cannot put an A.A. group into business; too many busybody cooks always spoil the broth. A.A. groups had their fling at education and when they began publicly to whoop up the merits of this or that brand of education, people became confused. Did A.A. fix alcoholics, or was it an educational project? Was A.A. spiritual or was it medical? Was it a reform movement? In consternation, we saw ourselves getting married to all kinds of enterprises, some good and some not so good.

When we saw alcoholics committed willy-nilly to prisons and asylums, we began to say, "There ought to be a law." In full public view, some A.A.'s commenced to thump tables in legislative committee rooms and to agitate for legal reform. That made good newspaper copy but little else. We saw that we would soon be mired in politics. We found it imperative even inside A.A. to remove the A.A. name from clubs and Twelfth Step Houses. These strenuous adventures implanted the deep-rooted conviction that in no circumstances could we endorse any related enterprise, no matter how good. We of Alcoholics Anonymous could not be all things to all men, and we should not try to be. The moment we lent the A.A. name to any outside enterprise, we got into trouble, sometimes very serious trouble.

At one time we nearly got embroiled in the "wet-dry" controversy. A liquor trade association wanted to hire an A.A. member as an educator. Its members wanted to teach that too much grog is bad for everybody and that alcoholics cannot drink at all. So far, so good. But it further appeared that in all their publicity, they wished to stress the fact that their educator, Mr. X, was a member of Alcoholics Anonymous. That was something else again. The public would at once think that Alcoholics Anonymous had gone into the field of education, via the liquor industry. If that happened, the "drys" would instantly hire another A.A. member for "educational purposes." This would land us, of course, smack in the middle of endless controversy. We simply could not take sides in this fight and do business with sick alcoholics too.

The would-be educator showed up at the New York office, asking for advice. Of course we told him that we thought factual education to be a very good thing and that as a public relations expert and as a citizen he certainly had a perfect right to take the job. But did he think that he should advertise his A.A. membership at the same time?

Our member got the point. He said, "Alcoholics Anonymous saved my life. It comes first. I certainly won't be the guy to land A.A. in big-time trouble, and this might really do it." Our friend had summed up the whole endorsement problem. We saw as never before that we could not lend the A.A. name to any cause other than our own.

Long afterward we saw something else. We saw that the more A.A. minded its own business the greater its general influence would become. Medicine and religion and psychiatry began to borrow some of our ideas and experience. So did research, rehabilitation, and education. All sorts of therapeutic groups began to spring up. They dealt with gambling, divorce, delinquency, dope addiction, mental illness, and the like. They, too, borrowed from A.A., but they made their own adaptations. They worked their own fields, and we did not have to endorse them or tell them how to live.

Our influence has not been confined just to these fields. It is beginning now to be general. It crops out in political and business life. People who know alcoholics and their families are deeply affected. The very developments that we once wanted to force have begun to take place of themselves.

Today we understand and accept this paradox: The more A.A. sticks to its primary purpose, the greater will be its helpful influence everywhere.

Let us now talk about money and A.A.'s attitude toward it. Wealth had ruined many men and nations. So would it ruin us? Especially in America, money was the symbol of prestige and power and comfort. Money can do a lot of good, yet there is practically no evil which it cannot arouse. Would A.A.'s brand of spirituality mix with any money at all? Or, on the other hand, should we have a *lot* of money, the better to do good works? This was the age-old dilemma and the temptation that faced us.

The conservatives said, "Why tempt ourselves with money? We don't need it. We can meet in homes and no group will have to have a treasury. Why do we need books and offices and world services? One alcoholic carries the message to another. Let's keep it that simple and stay out of money trouble." The radicals thought otherwise: "Not only do we need essential services, we need plenty more. We need hospitals, paid therapists, traveling lecturers, rehabilitation centers, and heaven knows what else. It is going to take millions. And where will we get all this money? Well, we will get it from the public, just as most other good works do."

After a while we awoke to the pleasant fact that A.A. as such was not going to require much money after all. When we got rid of our grandiose ideas about hospitals, research, rehabilitation, and education, not much of a bill was left to pay. Other enterprises needed large sums, but we did not. We could be spared that headache.

A big factor in our thinking at the time was the philosophy of St. Francis of Assisi. His also began as a lay movement, one man carrying the good news to the next. In his day it was common enough for individuals to pledge themselves to poverty. But it was unusual, if not unique, for a whole organization or fellowship to do the same thing. For the purpose of his society Francis thought corporate poverty to be fundamental. The less money and property they had to quarrel about, the less would be the diversion from their primary purpose. And just like A.A. today, his outfit did not need much money to accomplish its mission. Why be tempted and diverted when there was no need for it?

Therefore A.A. adopted the wisdom of Francis as its own. Not only would we have the least possible service organization; we would use the least possible money. For us this does not mean no money at all. But it does mean the least possible money to do the job well. It is in this sense that A.A. has declared for the principle of corporate poverty. It is a chief safeguard of our future.

Despite our early Tradition of keeping A.A. poor for its own safety, we were still to have temptations. There were three of them.

The first came when we met with Mr. John D. Rockefeller, Jr., and his friends in the fall of 1937. At that time the possibility of unlimited financial backing pretty much dimmed our sharing of the vision of St. Francis. Dr. Bob and I, and indeed most of us, were awfully broke. Ideas of comfortable and well-paid jobs, chains of A.A. hospitals, and tons of free literature for suffering alkies seized our imagination. But Mr. Rockefeller had other ideas. He said, "I think money will spoil this." He acted accordingly, and A.A. stayed poor. St. Francis had given us the idea, but John D. wisely forced us to live up to it. This was the oddly assorted pair who were really responsible for A.A.'s Tradition on money. Thank God for them both!

The second temptation veered to the other extreme. We got so scared of money that we went tightwad, half-refusing to support A.A.'s simple but essential area-and-over-all services, without which we would fail to function and grow. Even now we haven't quite surmounted this one. We still drag our heels when the hat is passed to support local Intergroup offices and General Headquarters. And this holding back is not for lack of folding money either. The collective income of A.A.'s membership—the sum of our wages, salaries, and other emoluments—will presently reach a total of a billion dollars yearly. When sober and working, few alcoholics have any money trouble. Our earning power as individuals may actually be double the average. The material pay-off, as well as the spiritual pay-off, of A.A.'s way of life is downright incredible. Nevertheless, we still balk a bit when it comes to paying A.A.'s very reasonable service bills. Sometimes I think this may be all to the good. There is not the slightest danger that A.A. is ever going to get too rich from the voluntary contributions of its own members!

There is a funny but revealing story about this. And the joke is on me. It was in 1941, just after the *Saturday Evening Post* story broke. The income from the A.A. book would not pay for answering the thousands of inquiries, and we had set up a dollar-a-year per member as the measuring stick for voluntary contributions that might meet the bill. It was the first time A.A. Headquarters had asked groups for any help.

At the time, Lois and I were receiving thirty dollars a week as the result of Mr. Rockefeller's dinner. We were living in a little room in the Twenty-Fourth Street club. Our household furniture was still in storage and we were mighty hard up. One morning a bleary-eyed friend just off a bender stuck his head into the little Vesey Street office. I was pacing up and down, cussing out the drunks for being so slow in sending in their buck apiece. I was in a really mean mood, so I gave my bleary-eyed friend a big gripe on how stingy drunks were. Naturally, he agreed. Just to make myself generous I pulled out a five-dollar bill and handed it to him. It was money that Lois needed for the groceries, and I knew very well that he would go out and drink it up. But this grandiose act made me feel good. I, poor I, could give five dollars when those guys out there couldn't even send in one dollar!

Distinctly satisfied with myself, I went to the meeting that night in the club. The club was behind with its rent. In those days, you could not mix the material with the spiritual at all. Money was a subject you could hardly mention. But the landlord was not getting his rent, so it *had* to be mentioned. At intermission, my old friend Tom B., who led the meeting that night, timidly said, "Now, folks, can't you go a little heavy on the hat tonight? We're kind of behind with the rent." Such was his apologetic announcement. I was sitting on the stairs with some new convert. Nevertheless I heard him and I knew the club was behind. Finally the hat came up the stairs where we were, and I reached in my pocket and got a coin. When I fished it out, it was half a dollar. Scarcely thinking, I dropped that half-dollar back into my pocket and produced a dime that clinked thinly in the hat. A minute later I woke up. I who had boasted of my generosity that morning was treating my own club worse than the alcoholics who had forgotten to send the Foundation their dollars. I realized that my five-dollar gift to the backslider was an ego-feeding act, bad for him and bad for me. There *was* a place in A.A. where spirituality and money would mix, and that was in the hat. I never since have criticized anybody for failing to send a dollar or so to Headquarters.

Our third money temptation was the greatest peril of all three.

One night the Trustees of our Foundation were having their quarterly meeting. The agenda included a crucial question: A certain lady had died, and when her will was read, it was discovered that she had left to Alcoholics Anonymous, in trust with the Foundation, a sum of $10,000. The question was, should A.A. take the gift?

What a debate we had on that one! The Foundation was really hard up just then; the groups were not sending in enough money for the support of the office; we had been tossing in all the book income, and even that had not been enough; the reserve fund was melting like snow in springtime. We badly needed that $10,000. "Maybe," some said, "the groups will never fully support the office. We can't let it shut down; it is far too vital. Yes, let's take the money. Let's take all such donations in the future. We're going to need them."

Then came the opposition. They pointed out that the Foundation Board already knew of a total of half a million dollars set aside for A.A. in the wills of people still alive. Heaven only knew how much we had *not* heard about. If outside donations were not declined, not absolutely cut off, the Foundation would one day become rich. Moreover, at the slightest intimation to the general public from our Trustees that we needed money, we could become immensely rich. Compared to this prospect the $10,000 under consideration was not much, but like the alcoholic's first drink, it would, if taken, inevitably set up a disastrous chain reaction. Where would that land us? Whoever pays the piper is apt to call the tune, and if the A.A. Foundation obtained money from outside sources, its Trustees might be tempted to run things without reference to the wishes of A.A. as a whole. Every alcoholic, feeling relieved of responsibility, would shrug and say, "Oh, the Foundation is wealthy! Why should I bother?" The pressure of that fat treasury would surely tempt the Board to invent all kinds of schemes to do good with such funds, and so divert A.A. from its primary purpose. The moment that happened, our fellowship's confidence would be shaken. The Board might be isolated and might fall under heavy attack and criticism from both A.A. and the public. These were the possibilities pro and con.

Then our Trustees wrote a bright page of A.A. history. They declared for the principle that A.A. must always stay poor. Reasonable running expenses plus a prudent reserve would henceforth be the Foundation's financial policy. Regardless of current needs, the Trustees officially declined that $10,000 and adopted a formal, airtight resolution that all such future gifts would be similarly declined. At that moment, the principle of corporate poverty was firmly and finally imbedded in A.A. tradition.

When the newspapers got hold of these facts, there was a profound reaction. To people familiar with endless drives for charitable funds, A.A. presented a strange and refreshing spectacle. Approving editorials here and abroad generated a great new wave of confidence in the integrity of Alcoholics Anonymous. They pointed out that the irresponsible had become responsible, and that by making financial independence part of its tradition, Alcoholics Anonymous had revived an ideal that this era had almost forgotten. This is why A.A.'s Tradition Seven now reads: "*Every A.A. Group ought to be fully self-supporting, declining outside contributions.*"

Tradition Eight says that "*Alcoholics Anonymous should remain forever nonprofessional, but our service centers may employ special workers.*"

Alcoholics Anonymous will never have a professional therapeutic class. We have gained some understanding of the ancient words

People and places . . .

A.A.'s first friend of medicine, William Duncan Silkworth, M.D. This is the doctor who treated Bill in the beginning and was with him during his experience in Towns Hospital. "Silky" had greater faith in our Society than we did ourselves at first. He encouraged us and endorsed us openly when we were almost unknown. He gave us knowledge of the nature of our disease: "physical allergy plus mental obsession." He made indispensable contributions to the development of the A.A. program of recovery. During his lifetime "the kindly little doctor" treated 40,000 alcoholics. Dr. Silkworth epitomizes the great understanding and help that Alcoholics Anonymous has received from the medical profession. (See pages 13, 52, 63, 67.)

"The incomparable Sister Ignatia," Dr. Bob's partner in pioneering the hospitalization of prospective A.A. members. "The ministry of Dr. Bob, his wife Anne, Sister Ignatia, and Akron's early timers set an example for the practice of A.A.'s Twelfth Step that will remain for all time." (See pages 7, 8, 143, 206.)

Historic decision for A.A.'s future was made at this spot in the lobby of the Mayflower Hotel in Akron. Here one co-founder turned away from the first drink to make a phone call that led to the other co-founder—and to the chain of recovery that now extends around the world. (See pages 65, 66.)

First psychiatrist to recognize the work of Alcoholics Anonymous and to use A.A. principles in his own practice was Dr. Harry Tiebout (left). Since his first exposure to our fellowship in 1939, Dr. Harry has continued to endorse A.A. to the psychiatric profession. Together with Drs. Kirby Collier, Foster Kennedy, A. Wiese Hammer, Dudley Saul, and others, Dr. Tiebout has hastened and deepened the world-wide acceptance of A.A. among men of medicine. (See pages 2, 205, 235 *et seq.,* 309.)

Symbol of approval of A.A. by the medical profession is the Lasker Award (above), presented to Alcoholics Anonymous in San Francisco in 1951, the gift of Albert and Mary Lasker, and the recommendation of the twelve thousand physicians of the American Public Health Association. (See pages 4, 301.)

This is where it all started. The house
(right) where Dr. Bob and Anne lived
in Akron, where Bill and Dr. Bob applied
the first principles of recovery, where Lois
and Anne laid the groundwork of what
would one day be called the Family Groups.
The actual coffee pot that Anne used to make
the first A.A. coffee is shown above.
Dr. Bob's and Bill's very first get-together
took place in the gatehouse of the Seiberling
estate (below) in Akron. (See pages 6,
19, 32, 33, 67.)

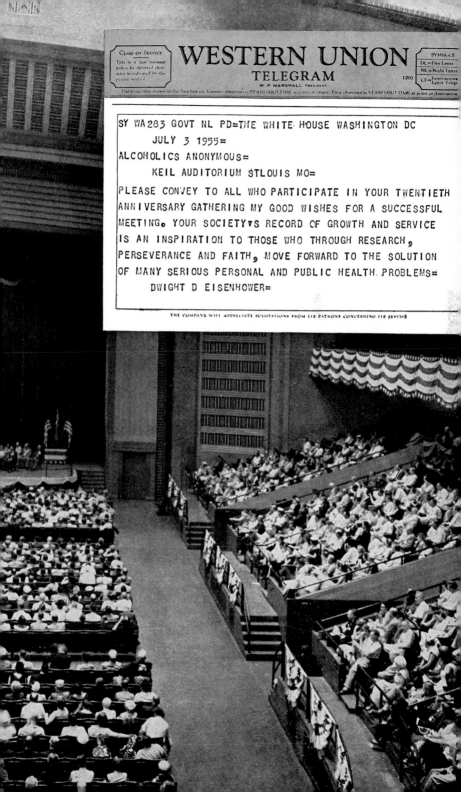

WESTERN UNION
TELEGRAM

SY WA283 GOVT NL PD=THE WHITE HOUSE WASHINGTON DC
JULY 3 1955=
ALCOHOLICS ANONYMOUS=
KEIL AUDITORIUM STLOUIS MO=
PLEASE CONVEY TO ALL WHO PARTICIPATE IN YOUR TWENTIETH
ANNIVERSARY GATHERING MY GOOD WISHES FOR A SUCCESSFUL
MEETING. YOUR SOCIETYⱽS RECORD OF GROWTH AND SERVICE
IS AN INSPIRATION TO THOSE WHO THROUGH RESEARCH,
PERSEVERANCE AND FAITH, MOVE FORWARD TO THE SOLUTION
OF MANY SERIOUS PERSONAL AND PUBLIC HEALTH PROBLEMS=
DWIGHT D EISENHOWER=

The house in Clinton Street, Brooklyn (right). In the basement stood the famous kitchen table across which Ebby brought the message to Bill. Here the first meetings in New York were held. This was Bill and Lois' home, from which they were evicted when the mortgage was foreclosed. They now live in a home that thousands of A.A.'s have visited in Bedford Hills, New York (above). Nearby is "the shack" where Bill works at the desk shown below. (See pages 10, 99, 173.)

This is Sam Shoemaker, the Episcopal clergyman whose teaching inspired the co-founders and early members of A.A. Bill says "Sam's utter honesty, his forthrightness, his almost terrible sincerity, struck me deep. It was from him that Dr. Bob and I in the beginning absorbed most of the principles that were afterward embodied in the Twelve Steps. . . . Sam Shoemaker gave us concrete knowledge of what we could do about our illness . . . he passed on the spiritual keys by which we were liberated." (See pages 38, 64, 261.)

In the days of Sam's greatest help to A.A., meetings were often held in the homes of friends, such as T. Henry and Clarace Williams (above) in Akron. The meetings here were the beginning of A. A. Group No. 1. (See page 75.)

This is Father Ed, the Catholic priest whose personal influence and work for A.A. have done so much to make our Society what it is. Father Edward Dowling of the Jesuit Order helped to start the first A.A. group in St. Louis. Friend, adviser, great example—he has been all of these to us, and more. "Whether I was in joy or in pain," one A.A. has written, "he has always brought the same sense of the grace and the presence of God. He is made of the stuff of the saints." Many who meet Ed Dowling experience this touch of the eternal. At the same time he himself has said, "If I ever get to heaven it will be from running away from hell." (See pages 37, 38, 253.)

Below, the Old 24th Street Club House in New York City. This is the famous long entrance corridor leading to the old meeting hall. (See page 180.)

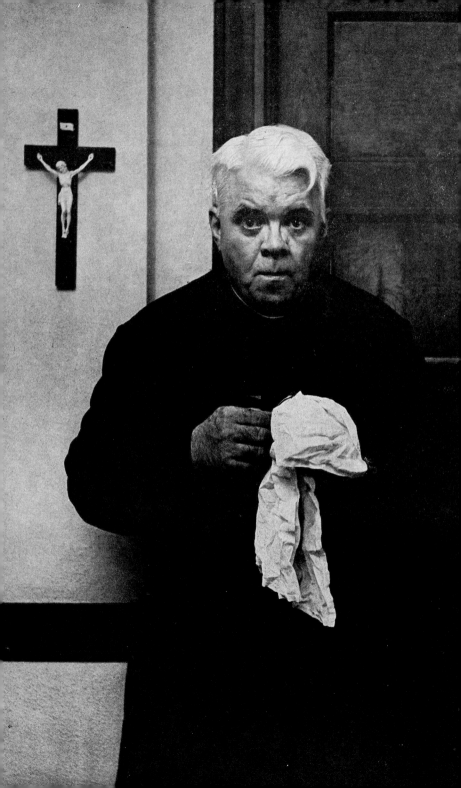

"One of the finest servants of God and man that I shall ever know."
In these terms has Willard Richardson (left) been well described.
"Uncle Dick" Richardson was a key figure in the growth of A.A. and
its Headquarters until his death in 1952. (See pages 14, 147.) He
represents a class of men to whom Alcoholics Anonymous owes much:
enthusiastic and selfless non-alcoholics who have contributed their
interest, support, time, and hard work to our problems and our affairs
from the beginning. There are old-timers like Frank Amos, John D.
Rockefeller, Jr., A. LeRoy Chipman, Dr. Leonard Strong, Jack
Alexander, Leonard Harrison—later friends like Fulton Oursler,
Bernard Smith, Frank Gulden, Dr. Jack Norris—and old friends in
new roles, like Dr. Harry Tiebout who now serves on our Board of
Trustees. In the persons of these non-alcoholic laymen and men of
medicine, religion, and communications—God has greatly blessed and
helped us alcoholics, and we are deeply grateful.

"Freely you have received, freely give." For our purpose, we have discovered that at the point of professionalism money and spirituality do *not* mix. We do not decry professionalism in other fields, but we accept the sober fact that it does not work for us. Every time we have tried to professionalize our Twelfth Step, the result has been exactly the same; our single purpose has been defeated.

You remember how I was told by A.A.'s group conscience that I could not go to work for Charlie Towns as a professional therapist, and that was right. Early in the game we discovered that under no conditions should an A.A. be paid for taking or carrying this message to somebody else, person to person and face to face. That was out. If professionalism ever invaded us at that level, we were doomed.

But the issue of professionalism had other aspects. For years we were trying to figure out what in A.A. was professionalism and what was not. This problem arose out of the need for paid workers in our service centers, the need for people who would do the jobs that volunteers could not or would not do. Were service workers professionals, or were they not? That was the issue.

The first situation of this kind that I can remember came up in the old clubhouse on Twenty-Fourth Street in New York. Volunteers had painted the place and shined it up and were answering the telephone, and that was fine. When they went home they would hand out numerous keys for the benefit of the night owls. But some of the owls had a habit of getting stewed and lying around the place in all conditions and at all hours. That was not good. The volunteers also got very tired of sweeping out the place, so it stayed dirty most of the time. Plainly enough we needed a caretaker.

Well, we approached old Tom, a fireman we had recently sprung out of Rockland asylum. We were shrewd. We already knew that Tom had a pension as a fireman. So we said to him, "How would you like to come over, Tom, and live at the club? Nice room for you there." Tom said, "What's the angle?" "Well, Tom, we'll give you a nice room and you can kind of look after the place." Tom said, "Seven days a week?" "Yeah." "What am I supposed to do?" "Well, Tom, you ought to make the coffee and, you know, lead the drunks out if they're too bad, and sweep the place up." "Do that seven days a week?" said Tom. "What you guys want is a janitor." "All right," we said, "sure, we want a janitor." "Well," said Tom, "ain't you going to pay me nothing?" "Oh, no," we said, "that would make you a professional. This is Alcoholics Anonymous. We must not mix money with spirituality." "Okay," said Tom, "no money, no work. I'm doing my Twelfth Step work free, but if you're going to have me here as a janitor, you're going to pay me, see?" Lots of us were working at that time and earning money. But believe it or not, we actually haggled with that old man to get him down to the last cent we could for doing that grubby job!

But old Tom was right. In order for A.A. to function, we had to hire some help. In all the length and breadth of A.A., among the whole 200,000 or more of us, we have today only two or three hundred hired help all around. That includes cooks frying hamburgers in clubs, janitors sweeping out the places, and women answering telephones in our central offices. It also includes me. I once wrote some literature for you, so I am paid a royalty for being a writer. That is where the line finally fell: For face-to-face treatment of a drunk, no money, ever. But A.A. does have to hire people so that it can function where there are legitimate jobs to be done.

Even after A.A.'s Tradition Eight was thus established in principle, it took still more years to work out the applications. There were all sorts of borderline cases, always in hot debate.

For example, no A.A.'s have been more buffeted by such emotional gusts than those bold enough to accept employment with outside agencies dealing with the alcohol problem. A university wanted an A.A. member to educate the public on alcoholism. A corporation wanted a personnel man familiar with the subject. A state drunk farm wanted a manager who could really handle inebriates. A city wanted an experienced social worker who understood what alcohol could do to a family. A state alcohol commission wanted a paid researcher. These are only a few of the jobs which A.A. members as individuals are filling today. Now and then A.A. members have bought farms or rest homes where badly beat-up topers could find needed care. The question was, are such activities to be branded as professionalism under A.A. tradition?

Our years of experience tell us that the answer is "No." Members who select such full-time careers do not professionalize A.A.'s Twelfth Step. The road to this conclusion was long and rocky. At first, we could not see the real issue involved. In former days, the moment an A.A. hired out to such enterprises he was immediately tempted to use the name Alcoholics Anonymous for publicity or money-raising purposes. Drunk farms, educational ventures, state legislatures and commissions advertised the fact that A.A. members served them. Unthinkingly, A.A.'s who were so employed recklessly broke their anonymity to thump the tub for their pet enterprises. For this reason, some very good causes and everything connected with them suffered unjust criticism from A.A. groups. There were cries of, "Professionalism! That guy is making money out of A.A.!" Yet not a single one of them had been hired to do A.A.'s Twelfth Step work.

The violation in these instances was not professionalism at all; it was breaking anonymity. A.A.'s sole purpose was being compromised and the name of Alcoholics Anonymous was being misused.

It is significant now that almost no A.A. in our fellowship breaks anonymity at the general public level, and so nearly all of these fears have subsided. We see that we have no right or need to discourage A.A.'s who wish to work as individuals in these wider fields. It would be actually antisocial were we to discourage them. We cannot declare A.A. such a closed corporation that we keep our knowledge and experience top secret. If an A.A. member, acting as a citizen, can become a better researcher, educator, or personnel officer, why not? Everybody gains, and we have lost nothing. True, some of the projects to which A.A.'s have attached themselves have been ill conceived, but that makes not the slightest difference in the principle involved.

This is the exciting chain of events that finally cast up A.A.'s tradition of nonprofessionalism. Our Twelfth Step—carrying the message

—is never to be paid for. But those who labor in service for us are worthy of their hire.

Tradition Nine states: "*A.A., as such, ought never to be organized, but we may create service boards or committees directly responsible to those they serve.*" This one still puzzles a lot of people. How can you have a society that is unorganized, and at the same time organize services? Yet A.A. does it.

When Tradition Nine was first written it said, "Alcoholics Anonymous needs the least possible organization." In the years since then, we have changed our minds about that. Today we are able to say with assurance that Alcoholics Anonymous—A.A. as a whole—should never be organized at all. Then, in seeming contradiction we proceed to create special boards and committees which in themselves are organized. How can we have an unorganized movement which can and does create a service organization for itself? Scanning this puzzler, people say, "What do they mean, no organization?"

What we really mean, of course, is that A.A. can never have an organized direction or government. To amplify this: Did anyone ever hear of a nation, a church, a political party, even a benevolent association that had no membership rules? Did anyone ever hear of a society that could not somehow discipline its members and enforce obedience to necessary rules and regulations? Does not nearly every society on earth give authority to some of its members to impose obedience upon the rest and to punish or expel offenders? Therefore, every nation, in fact every form of society, has to be a government administered by human beings. Power to direct and govern is the essence of organization everywhere.

To this rule Alcoholics Anonymous is a complete exception. It does not at any point conform to the pattern of a government. Neither its General Service Conference, its General Service Board, nor the humblest group committee can issue a single directive to an A.A. member and make it stick, let alone hand out any punishment. We have tried it lots of times, but failure is always the result. Groups have tried to expel members, but the banished have come back to sit in the meeting place, saying, "This is life for us; you can't keep us out." Committees have instructed many an A.A. to stop working on a chronic backslider, only to be told: "How I do my Twelfth Step work is my business. Who are you to judge?" An A.A. may take advice or suggestions from more experienced members, but he surely will not take orders. Who is less popular than the old-time A.A., full of wisdom, who moves to another area and tries to tell the group there how to run its business? He and all like him who "view with alarm for the good of A.A." meet with stubborn resistance, or worse still, laughter. In fact, A.A. is so unorganized that someone once suggested we put up a sign in each A.A. club saying: "Anything goes here, folks, except you mustn't smoke opium in the elevators!"

One would think that A.A.'s Headquarters and General Service Conference would be exceptions. Surely the people there would have to have some authority. But long ago Trustees and staff members alike found they could do no more than make suggestions, and very mild ones at that. They even had to coin a couple of sentences which still go into half the letters they write: "Of course you are at perfect liberty to handle this matter any way you please. But the majority experience in A.A. does seem to suggest . . ." Now, that attitude is far removed from central government, isn't it? We recognize that we cannot dictate to fellow members, individually or collectively.

At this juncture we can hear a church man exclaim, "They are making disobedience a virtue!" He is joined by the psychiatrist who says, "Defiant brats! They won't grow up and conform to social usage." The man in the street says, "I don't understand it. They must be nuts." But all these observers have overlooked one very unusual condition in Alcoholics Anonymous: Unless each A.A. member follows to the best of his ability our suggested Twelve Steps of recovery, he almost certainly signs his own death warrant. Drunkenness and disintegration are not penalties inflicted by people in authority; they are results of personal disobedience to spiritual principles. We *must* obey certain principles, or we die.

The same stern threat applies to the group itself. Unless there is approximate conformity to A.A.'s Twelve Traditions, the group too can deteriorate and die. So we of A.A. do obey spiritual principles, first because we must and ultimately because we love the kind of life such obedience brings. Great suffering and great love are A.A.'s disciplinarians; we have no others.

Therefore it is now clear that we ought never to name boards to govern us. It is equally clear, however, that we shall always need to authorize workers to serve us. Here we discriminate between the spirit of vested authority and the spirit of service, concepts which are sometimes poles apart. It is in this spirit of service that we elect the A.A. groups' informal rotating committees, the Intergroup Associations of the area, and the General Service Conference for A.A. as a whole. Even our Trustees, once an independent body, are today directly accountable to our fellowship. They are the caretakers and expediters of our world services.

Just as the aim of each A.A. member is personal sobriety, so the aim of our services is to bring sobriety within reach of all who want it. If nobody did the group's chores, if the area's telephone rang unanswered, if we did not reply to our mail, then A.A. as we know it would stop. Our communication lines with those who need our help would be broken.

While A.A. has to function, it must at the same time avoid wealth, prestige, and power, three great dangers which necessarily tempt nearly all human societies. Though Tradition Nine at first sight seems to deal with purely practical matters, it embodies a deep spirituality in its actual operation. A.A. is a society without organization, animated only by the spirit of service—a true fellowship.

How this unique situation developed is seen in the following example: Joe Doe goes to Middletown, U.S.A. He is an A.A. member in good standing from another city. In Middletown there is no A.A. group. Joe feels lonesome and a little frightened. He also wants to carry the message. So maybe he puts an ad in the paper, saying that A.A. has come to town. Maybe he goes to the preachers and the doctors and bartenders and scrapes himself up a few prospects. Pretty soon there is a little group. At first Joe is the dictator and these first members are his hierarchy, literally. They have all the authority there is. This local founder and his friends teach A.A. principles and make all the group's arrangements. The group goes on growing broader and broader at the base. For a while they accept all that Joe and his friends say; they take directions, quite rightly, because at this stage there is no other way.

But by and by something happens. Maybe Joe and his friends have a falling out, or maybe some power-driver down in the base of the triangle begins to murmur, "How long are these old-timers going to keep running this thing?"

Meanwhile the founder and his friends bask a little in glory. They say to one another, "Perhaps it would be a good idea if we continue to keep a firm hand on A.A. in this town. After all, we are experienced. Besides, look at all the good we have done those drunks. They should be grateful." True, founders and their friends are sometimes wiser and more humble than this. But often at this stage they are not.

Growing pains now beset the group. Panhandlers panhandle. Lonely hearts pine. Problems descend. Murmurs are again heard in the body politic which swell into a loud cry: "Do these old-timers think they can run this thing forever? Let's have an election." The founder and his friends are hurt and depressed. They rush from crisis to crisis and from member to member, pleading. But it is no use. The revolution is on. The group is about to take over. If the founder and his friends serve well, they may, to their surprise, be reinstated for a time. If, however, they have heavily resisted the rising tide of democracy, they may be summarily beached. In either case, the group now has a so-called rotating committee, very sharply limited in its authority. In no sense whatever can its members govern or direct the group. Theirs is sometimes a thankless privilege of doing the group's chores. This committee can only make the necessary service arrangements by which the group can function. It can give no spiritual advice, judge no one's conduct, issue no orders. Any committee member may be promptly eliminated at the next election if he tries to throw his weight around.

The members fully realize that they are actually servants, not senators. These are universal A.A. experiences. Thus throughout our fellowship does the group conscience decree the terms upon which its leaders shall serve.

This brings us straight to the question, "Does A.A. have a real leadership?" The answer is, "Yes, notwithstanding the apparent lack of it." Let's turn again to the deposed founder and his friends. What becomes of them? As their grief and anxiety wear away, a subtle change begins. Ultimately they divide into two classes known in A.A. slang as "elder statesmen" and "bleeding deacons." The elder statesman is one who sees the wisdom of the group's decision, who holds no resentment over his reduced status, whose judgment, fortified by considerable experience, is sound, and who is willing to sit quietly on the side lines patiently awaiting developments. The bleeding deacon is one who remains convinced that the group cannot get along without him, who constantly connives for re-election to office, and who continues to be consumed with self-pity. A few deacons hemorrhage so badly that they become drained of all A.A. spirit and principles and get drunk. At times the A.A. landscape seems to be littered with bleeding forms. Nearly every old-timer in our society has gone through this process in some degree. I have myself. Happily most of them survive and live to become elder statesmen. This is the real and enduring leadership of A.A. Theirs is the quiet opinion, the sure knowledge, and the humble example that resolves a crisis. When sorely perplexed, the group inevitably turns to them for advice. They become the voice of the group conscience. They are, in fact, the true voice of Alcoholics Anonymous. They do not drive by mandate; they lead by example. This is how Tradition Nine was evolved. This is why A.A. can never be organized under any known form of government.

But it also remains abundantly clear that we can, and must, create service boards or committees to be directly responsible to those they serve.

Tomorrow afternoon, in this auditorium, the same drama of A.A.

leadership will be re-enacted for A.A. as a whole. The group conscience of Alcoholics Anonymous, as represented by your named and
chosen General Service Conference, will take over the permanent care
and custody of the organized world service of this entire fellowship.
And in the spirit of Tradition Nine, we old-timers will step aside,
leaving with you only the offer of our advice if and when you want
it. We shall no longer direct or govern, nor will anybody else. A.A. as
such should always remain unorganized. It will fall then to your lot
to guard this treasured principle.

We think the future safety of Alcoholics Anonymous greatly depends upon Tradition Ten, A.A.'s principle of no controversy at the
public level. This Tradition reads as follows: *"Alcoholics Anonymous
has no opinion on outside issues; hence the A.A. name ought never be
drawn into public controversy."*

Since it began Alcoholics Anonymous never has been divided by a
major controversial issue. Our fellowship never has taken sides publicly on any question in this embattled world. This has been no earned
virtue. It could almost be said that we were born with it, for as one
old-timer recently declared, "Practically never have I heard a heated
religious, political, or reform argument among A.A. members. So
long as we don't argue these matters privately, it's a cinch we never
shall argue them publicly."

As by some deep instinct, we have known from the very beginning
that, no matter what the provocation, we must never publicly take
sides, *as A.A.'s,* in any fight, even a worthy one. All history affords us
the spectacle of striving nations and groups finally torn asunder because they were designed for, or tempted into, controversy. Others fell
apart because of sheer self-righteousness while trying to force upon the
rest of mankind some millennium of their own specification. In our
own times we have seen millions die in political and economic wars
often spurred by religious and racial differences. We live in the imminent possibility of a fresh holocaust to determine how men shall be
governed and how the products of nature and toil shall be divided

among them. That is the spiritual climate in which A.A. was born and by God's grace has flourished nevertheless.

Let us re-emphasize that this reluctance to fight one another or anybody else is not counted as some special virtue which makes us feel superior to other people. Nor does it mean that the members of Alcoholics Anonymous, now restored as citizens of the world, are going to back away from their individual responsibilities to act as they see the right upon issues of our time. But when it comes to A.A. as a whole, that is a different matter. *As A.A.'s* we do not enter into public controversy, because we know that our fellowship will perish if we do. We conceive the survival and spread of Alcoholics Anonymous to be something of greater importance than any weight we could collectively throw back of other causes. Recovery from alcoholism is life itself to us, and we wish to preserve in full strength our means of survival.

Maybe this sounds as though the alcoholics in A.A. had suddenly gone peaceable, and had become one great big happy family. Of course this is not so at all. We are human beings and we squabble. Before we leveled off a bit, A.A. looked more like one prodigious squabble than anything else, at least on the surface. A corporation director who had just voted a company expenditure of a hundred thousand dollars would appear at an A.A. business meeting and blow his top over an outlay of twenty-five dollars' worth of needed postage stamps. Disliking the attempt of some to manage the group, half of its membership might angrily rush off to form another group more to their liking. Elders, temporarily turned pharisee, often sulked. Sometimes bitter attacks have been directed against people suspected of mixed motives. Yet despite their din, our rows have never done A.A. a particle of harm. They were just part and parcel of learning to work and live together. Let it be noted, too, that they were almost always concerned with how to make A.A. more effective, how to do the most good for the most alcoholics.

The Washingtonian Society, a movement among alcoholics which started in Baltimore a century ago, almost discovered the answer to alcoholism. At first the society was composed entirely of alcoholics trying to help one another. The early members foresaw that they should dedicate themselves to this sole aim. In many respects the Washingtonians were akin to A.A. Their membership passed the five hundred thousand mark. Had they stuck to their one goal, they might have found the full answer. Instead, the Washingtonians permitted politicians and reformers, both alcoholic and nonalcoholic, to use the society for their own purposes. Abolition of slavery, for example, was a stormy political issue then. Soon Washingtonian speakers violently and publicly took sides on this question. Maybe the society could have survived the abolition controversy, but it did not have a chance from the moment it determined to reform all America's drinking habits. Some of the Washingtonians became temperance crusaders. Within a very few years they had completely lost their effectiveness in helping alcoholics, and the society collapsed.

The lesson to be learned from the Washingtonians was not overlooked by Alcoholics Anonymous. As we surveyed the wreck of that movement, early A.A. members resolved to keep our society out of public controversy.

Considering how most of us have really loved controversy, this denial of the privilege of attacking something or somebody in public is no small achievement for the naturally aggressive people that we are. To make our survival as a fellowship sure, we have often gone far in the opposite direction. Years ago, for example, we stood in great fear of the misuse of the A.A. name by A.A.'s and outside groups who wanted to use it for their own money-raising, controversial, or publicity purposes. And we reflected that the bigger A.A. grew, the greater this temptation would surely be. Therefore we felt we had to find a way legally to protect the precious name of our society.

Our Trustees were advised that this could be done only by incorporating the name Alcoholics Anonymous in every state of the Union and in all foreign countries. We actually began this tedious, complicated, and expensive task, which finally bogged down in a mass of technicalities, red tape, and charters.

But the issue was revived with a bang when one of the large motion-picture producers suddenly came up with a script for a picture which they were going to call *Mr. and Miss Anonymous.* The proposed portrayal of A.A. seemed pretty lopsided and in rather bad taste. Though they agreed to change the title, the company refused to do much of anything about the objectionable script. What, then, could we do about it?

We concluded that we ought to ask for an injunction against the company for misuse of the A.A. name. This prospect of legal action caused the company to revise the script more to our liking. Otherwise, we might have sued, forgetting all about A.A.'s principle of non-controversy in public. We were that excited.

After this moving-picture incident, our chairman, Bernard Smith, came up with what looked like a wonderful idea. As a lawyer, he thought Alcoholics Anonymous could easily obtain a Congressional Charter, an act of Congress which would protect the A.A. name everywhere. This would put us in the same class as the Red Cross and several other notable organizations. It was thought that the mere existence of such a charter would restrain nearly all those who might be tempted to misuse A.A.'s name. And a legal bludgeon of this size and weight could easily be used on any who might still defy the law. It looked like a grand idea and we at the Headquarters were all for it.

But the conscience of Alcoholics Anonymous, its General Service Conference, had other ideas. The Conference pointed out to us how foolish it would be to incorporate A.A.'s way of life as a legal instrument with which to attack anyone, no matter what the provocation. We would not be content with such an instrument for purposes of pure restraint. Under enough provocation, we would be bound to start public lawsuits and thus enter the field of public controversy. It would be like building a war machine on the theory that it would always stay home and never fight. It would mean the legal organization of a fellowship whose Traditions insisted on its being unorganized. The Conference thought we ought to forget about the questionable advantages of legality and controversy and rely upon group and public opinion for our ultimate protection. After long debate, we at the Headquarters saw that the conscience of Alcoholics Anonymous, acting through the delegates, was wiser than we were. So the Congress of the United States was never asked to incorporate A.A.

The moving resolution by which the Conference took this action ought to be set on the record. It was drawn by delegate Bob T., a Mississippi lawyer. Reporting for his committee, he said:

We have reviewed all of the arguments pro and con on this subject, have discussed it with many members of A.A. within the Conference and outside of it, and we have come to these conclusions:

1. The evils which caused the question to arise have largely abated.
2. A Congressional incorporation would create by law a power to govern which would be contrary to, and violative of, our Traditions.
3. It would implement the spiritual force of A.A. with a legal power, which we believe would tend to weaken its spiritual strength.
4. When we ask for legal rights, enforceable in Courts of law, we by the same act subject ourselves to possible legal regulation.
5. We might well become endlessly entangled in litigation which, together with the incidental expense and publicity, could seriously threaten our very existence.
6. Incorporation of A.A. could conceivably become the opening wedge that might engender politics and a struggle for power within our own ranks.
7. Continuously since its beginning, and today, A.A. has been a fellowship and not an organization. Incorporation necessarily makes it an organization.
8. We believe that "spiritual faith" and a "way of life" cannot be incorporated.
9. A.A. can and will survive so long as it remains a spiritual faith and a way of life open to all men and women who suffer from alcoholism.

Therefore, keeping in mind the high purpose of the General Service Conference as expressed by the Chairman last year when he said, "We seek not compromise but certainty," your Committee unanimously recommends that Alcoholics Anonymous does not incorporate.

Thus the final foundation was laid for Tradition Ten, *"Alcoholics Anonymous has no opinion on outside issues; hence the A.A. name ought never be drawn into public controversy."*

Tradition Eleven grew out of a large and strenuous public relations experience. Today, it reads as follows: *"Our public relations policy is based on attraction rather than promotion; we need always maintain personal anonymity at the level of press, radio, and films."*

Without its legions of well-wishers, A.A. could never have grown as it has. Throughout the world favorable publicity has been the principal means of bringing alcoholics into our fellowship. In A.A. offices, clubs, and homes telephones ring constantly. One voice says, "I read a piece in the newspaper. . . ." Another, "We heard a radio program. . . ." And still another, "We saw a moving picture . . ." or "We saw something about A.A. on television. . . ." It is no exaggeration to say that half of A.A.'s membership has been led to us through channels like these.

The inquiring voices are not all alcoholics or their families. Doctors read medical papers about A.A. and call for more information. Clergymen see articles in their church journals and also make inquiries. Employers learn that great corporations have set their approval upon us and wish to discover what can be done about alcoholism in their own firms.

Therefore the responsibility fell upon us to develop the best possible public relations policy for Alcoholics Anonymous. Through many painful experiences we think we have arrived at what that policy ought to be. It is opposite in many ways to the usual promotional practice. We found that we had to rely upon the principle of attraction rather than promotion.

Let's see how these two contrasting ideas, attraction and promotion, work out. A political party wishes to win an election and so it advertises the virtue of it leadership in order to draw votes. A worthy charity wants to raise money, and so its letterhead shows the names of every distinguished person whose support can be obtained. Much of the political, economic, and religious life of the world is dependent upon publicized leadership. People who symbolize causes and ideas fill a deep human need. We of A.A. do not question that. But we do have to face the fact that being in the public eye is hazardous, especially for us. By temperament many of us had been irresponsible promoters, and the prospect of a society composed largely of promoters was frightening. We knew we *had* to exercise self-restraint.

The way this restraint paid off is interesting. It has resulted in more favorable publicity for Alcoholics Anonymous than could possibly have been obtained through all the arts and abilities of A.A.'s best press agents. Obviously, A.A. had to be publicized somehow, so we resorted to the idea that it would be far better to let our friends do this for us. And they have done it to an amazing extent. Veteran newsmen, trained doubters that they are, have gone all out to carry A.A.'s message. To them we are something more than the source of good stories; on almost every news front men and women of the press have become our friends. In the beginning they could not understand our refusal of all personal publicity. They were genuinely baffled by our insistence upon anonymity. But soon they got the point. Here was something rare in the world: a society which said it wished to publicize its principles and its work but not its individual members. The press was pleased with this attitude, and these friends ever since have reported A.A. with an enthusiasm which the most ardent members themselves could hardly match.

There was actually a time when the press of America thought the anonymity of A.A. was better for us than some of our own members did. At one point about a hundred of our society were breaking anonymity at the public level. With perfectly good intent, these folks declared that the principle of anonymity was horse-and-buggy stuff, something appropriate to A.A.'s pioneering days. They were sure that A.A. could go faster and farther if it availed itself of modern publicity methods. A.A., they pointed out, included many persons of local, national, or international fame. Provided they were willing (and many were), why shouldn't their membership be publicized, thereby encouraging others to join us?

There were plausible arguments, but happily our friends of the writing profession disagreed with them. Years earlier our Headquarters had written letters to practically every news outlet in North America, setting forth our public relations policy of attraction rather than promotion and emphasizing personal anonymity as A.A.'s greatest protection. Since that time editors and rewrite men have repeatedly deleted names and pictures of members from A.A. copy. Frequently they have reminded ambitious individuals of A.A.'s anonymity policy. They have even sacrificed good stories to this end. The force of their co-operation has helped beyond measure. Only a very few A.A. members are left who deliberately break anonymity at the public level.

An old story, revealing several aspects of A.A.'s public relations problem, comes to mind: One of our pioneer members conceived the idea of starting a group in his city by radio. The local station, with a radius of about a hundred miles, offered to help. So our promoter friend constructed a series of "Twelve Lectures on Alcoholics Anonymous." These were a strange mixture of A.A. and his own religious ideas. He soon put them on the air with all the vigor of a Chautauqua orator. Contrary to our expectations, he got a modest result. Inquiries came in and he started a group.

Now flushed with success, he was smitten with a wonderful vision. He wrote Headquarters, telling how a prominent life insurance company would sponsor him on a national network to deliver his "Twelve Lectures." He was going to appear under his own name, as an A.A. member. For doing such a great work, of course, he was to receive a generous fee.

We remonstrated, but it was no use. We advised him that the Trustees felt his message inappropriate for national consumption. So he wrote a hot letter to this effect: "To hell with the trustees, the world is waiting for my message. I've got the right of free speech, and I'm going on the air whether you like it or not."

This ultimatum was an alarming poser. It looked like promotion, professionalism, and anonymity-breaking all in one package. If this sort of venture proved successful, from the promoter's point of view, every ad man and salesman in Alcoholics Anonymous would soon be selling A.A.'s wares, willy-nilly. We would lose all control of our public relations.

So Headquarters took this tack: We assured our well-meaning friend that we would certainly uphold his right of free speech. But we added that he ought to uphold ours, too. We assured him that if his "lectures" went on the air, we would advise every A.A. group of the circumstances and ask them to write strong letters to the sponsoring life insurance company, letters of a kind the sponsor might not like to receive. The broadcast never went on the air. As a result of this incident, A.A.'s Trustees were empowered to conduct our over-all public relations, and the principle of attraction rather than promotion became established as the key to our relation with the world about us. It is no accident that the original "long form" draft of Tradition Eleven carries the statement that "It is better to let our friends recommend us."

This in brief is the process by which A.A.'s Tradition Eleven was developed. To us it represents more than a sound public relations policy. It is more than a denial of self-seeking. Tradition Eleven is certainly a constant reminder that personal ambition has no place in A.A., but it also implies that each member ought to become an active guardian of our fellowship in its relation with the general public.

As we have seen, anonymity is the protective mantle that covers our whole society. But it is more than protection; it has another dimension, a spiritual significance. And this leads to Tradition Twelve, which reads: *"Anonymity is the spiritual foundation of all our Traditions, ever reminding us to place principles before personalities."*

In my belief, the entire future of our fellowship hangs upon this vital principle. If we continue to be filled with the spirit and practice of anonymity, no shoal or reef can wreck us. If we forget this principle, the lid to Pandora's box will be off and the spirits of Money, Power, and Prestige will be loosed among us. Obsessed by these evil genii, we might well founder and break up. I devoutly believe this will never happen. No A.A. principle merits more study and application than this one. I am positive that A.A.'s anonymity is the key to long-time survival.

The spiritual substance of anonymity is sacrifice. Because A.A.'s Twelve Traditions repeatedly ask us to give up personal desires for the common good, we realize that the sacrificial spirit, well symbolized by anonymity, is the foundation of all these Traditions. It is A.A.'s proved willingness to make these sacrifices that gives people high confidence in our future.

But in the beginning anonymity was not born of confidence; it was the child of our early fears. Our first nameless groups of alcoholics were secret societies. New prospects could find us only through a few trusted friends. The bare hint of publicity, even when it was not for ourselves but for our work, shocked us. Although we were no longer drinking, we still thought we had to hide from public distrust and contempt.

When the Big Book appeared in 1939, we called it *Alcoholics Anonymous*. Its original Foreword made this revealing statement: "It is important that we remain anonymous because we are too few, at present, to handle the overwhelming number of personal appeals which may result from this publication. Being mostly business or professional folks, we could not well carry on our occupations in such an event." Between these lines it is easy to read our fear that large numbers of incoming people might break our anonymity wide open.

As the A.A. groups multiplied, so did anonymity problems. Excited over the spectacular recovery of a brother alcoholic, we would sometimes discuss intimate and harrowing aspects of his case that had been meant for his sponsor's ear alone. The aggrieved victim would then rightly declare that his trust had been broken. When reports of such cases got into circulation outside of A.A., the resulting loss of confidence in our anonymity promise was severe. It sometimes turned people from us. Clearly, each A.A. member's name, and his story too, had to be kept confidential, *if he wished it to be*. This was our first lesson in the practical application of anonymity.

On the other hand, however, with characteristically alcoholic intemperance some of our newcomers cared not at all for personal anonymity. They wanted to shout about A.A. from the housetops, and did. Alcoholics barely dry in A.A. rushed about bright-eyed, buttonholing anyone who would listen to their stories. Others hurried to place themselves before microphones and cameras. Sometimes they got drunk and let their groups down with a bang. They had changed from A.A. members into A.A. show-offs.

This phenomenon of contrast on the anonymity issue really set us thinking. Squarely before us was the question, "How anonymous should an A.A. member be?" Our growth made it plain that we could not be a secret society. But it was equally plain that we could not be a vaudeville circuit either. The charting of a safe path between these extremes took a long time.

As a rule, the average newcomer wanted his family to know immediately what he was trying to do. He also wanted to tell others who had tried to help him: his doctor, his minister, and close friends. As he gained confidence, he felt it right to explain his new way of life to his employer and business associates. When opportunities to be helpful came along, he found he could talk easily about A.A. to almost anyone. These quiet disclosures helped him to lose his fear of the alcoholic stigma and to spread the news of A.A.'s existence in his community. Many a new man and woman came to A.A. as a result of such conversations. Though not within the strict letter of anonymity, these communications were well within its spirit.

But it became apparent that the word-of-mouth method of letting people know about A.A. was limited. Our work, as such, needed to be publicized. A.A. groups wanted quickly to reach as many despairing alcoholics as they could. Consequently many groups began to hold meetings which were open to interested friends and to the public, so that the average citizen could see for himself just what A.A. was all about. The response to these meetings was warmly sympathetic. Soon groups began to receive requests for A.A. speakers to appear before civic organizations, church groups, and medical societies. Provided reporters present were cautioned against the use of full names or pictures, the result was fine.

Then came our first few excursions into major publicity, and these were breathtaking. Cleveland's *Plain Dealer* articles about us ran that town's membership from a few dozen into hundreds overnight. The news stories of Mr. Rockefeller's dinner for Alcoholics Anonymous helped double our total membership in a year's time. Jack Alexander's famous *Saturday Evening Post* piece made A.A. a national institution. Such tributes as these brought opportunities for still more recognition. Other newspapers and magazines wanted A.A. stories. Film companies wanted to photograph us. Radio and finally television companies besieged us with requests for co-operation. What should we do?

As this tidal offering of top public approval swept in, we realized that it could do us incalculable good or great harm. Everything would depend upon how it was channeled. We simply could not afford to take the chance of letting self-appointed members present themselves as messiahs representing A.A. before the whole public. The promoter instinct in us might be our undoing. If even one such person publicly got drunk or was lured into using A.A.'s name for his own purposes, the damage might be irreparable. At this altitude (press, radio, films, and television), anonymity—*100 per cent anonymity*—was the only possible answer. Here principles would have to come before personalities, without exception.

These experiences taught us that anonymity is real humility at work. It is an all-pervading spiritual quality which today keynotes A.A. life everywhere. Moved by the spirit of anonymity, we try to give up our natural desires for personal distinction as A.A. members both among fellow alcoholics and before the general public. As we lay aside these very human aspirations, we believe that each of us takes part in the weaving of a protective mantle which covers our whole society and under which we may grow and work in unity.

We are sure that humility, expressed by anonymity, is the greatest safeguard that Alcoholics Anonymous can ever have.

In recent years our awareness of the deep significance of anonymity has grown in a most heartening and wonderful way.[10] At one time many numbers of A.A.'s were breaking anonymity, and I was one of them. Today these numbers are reduced to a mere handful, despite our alcoholic yearnings for vainglory. This is a tremendous guarantee of even finer things to come.

The kind of sacrifice that we shall always need to make is beautifully illustrated by a talk I recently had with a certain Texas lady. Her temptation was extreme because she is in show business and has great national popularity as an entertainer. This is what she told me: "I sing in the best barrooms only, and I have been doing it for fifteen years. Within a year after joining A.A., I lost about ten pounds, the bags came out from under my eyes, and I began to look like a human being. My manager couldn't figure it out, but at last I told him what had happened to me. At once, he said, 'But aren't you and I going to tell the public about this? Why, this would make terrific publicity, both for A.A. and you too.' 'Well,' I said, 'temporarily I know that it would. Other people have proved that. But, please, not for me. Alcoholics Anonymous has a principle called anonymity—no public big shots allowed. We know that A.A. can't be run like show business, no matter what the short-term benefits may be. A.A. saved my life and my career. Therefore the future welfare of Alcoholics Anonymous is more important to me than any publicity that I could get as an A.A. member.'" Then a little wistfully she added, "You know, Bill, I often see drunks in my audience and wonder how I can help them. If only I could tell them from the stage that I am in A.A. But that would only be temporary, wouldn't it? In the long run, we'd all be ruined if everybody did it." I looked at the lady from Texas and was glad, very glad.

Because I myself have always had strong tendencies toward the pursuit of prestige, wealth, and power, all of A.A.'s Traditions have

---

[10] For further information on anonymity, please see the article "Why Alcoholics Anonymous Is Anonymous," Appendix B.

borne down upon me with great force. You will remember that episode back in our living room on Clinton Street. That was the time when my group told me I could never become an A.A. professional. With nearly every Tradition much the same thing has happened. At first, I obeyed because I had to; I would have lost my standing in A.A. if I had not. After a while I began to obey because I saw that the Traditions were wise and right. While I conformed because it was right to do so, I still resisted inwardly.

This was particularly true of anonymity. Today I hope I have come to a time in my A.A. life when I can obey because I really *want* to obey, because I really want the Traditions for myself as well as for A.A. as a whole. Therefore each of our Twelve Traditions is really an expression of the deflation that each of us has to take, of the sacrifice that we shall all have to make in order to live and work together.

Dr. Bob was essentially a far more humble person than I. In some ways he was a sort of spiritual "natural," and this anonymity business came rather easily to him. He could not understand why some people should want so much publicity. In the years before he died, his personal example respecting anonymity did much to help me keep my own lid on. I think of one affecting instance in particular, one that every A.A. ought to know. When it was sure that Dr. Bob was mortally afflicted, some of his friends suggested that there should be a suitable monument or mausoleum erected in honor of him and his wife Anne—something befitting a founder and his lady. Of course this was a very natural and moving tribute. The committee went so far as to show him a sketch of the proposed edifice. Telling me about this, Dr. Bob grinned broadly and said, "God bless 'em. They mean well. But for heaven's sake, Bill, let's you and I get buried just like other folks."

A year after his passing, I visited the Akron cemetery where Dr. Bob and Anne lie. The simple stone says not a word about Alcoholics Anonymous. Some people may think that this wonderful couple carried personal anonymity too far when they so firmly refused to use the words "Alcoholics Anonymous" even on their own burial stone. For one, I do not think so. I think that this moving and final example of self-effacement will prove of more permanent worth to A.A. than any amount of public attention or any great monument.

THE A.A. PRINCIPLES OF SERVICE

(As expressed in the Twelve Traditions and the Twelve Steps)

Each A.A. group has but one primary purpose—to carry its message to the alcoholic who still suffers.

Every A.A. group ought to be fully self-supporting.

Alcoholics Anonymous should remain forever nonprofessional.

A.A. as such ought never be organized, but we may create service boards or committees directly responsible to those they serve.

Our leaders are but trusted servants; they do not govern.

We try to carry this message to alcoholics, and to practice these principles in all our affairs.

Note: The traditional principles of A.A. service stated above have been amplified by Bill W. and made a part of *The A.A. Service Manual* and *Twelve Concepts for World Service.*

SERVICE: THE THIRD LEGACY

We are gathered here for the final hours of A.A.'s twentieth anniversary celebration.

Above us floats a banner on which is inscribed the new symbol for A.A., a circle enclosing a triangle. The circle stands for the whole world of A.A., and the triangle stands for A.A.'s Three Legacies of Recovery, Unity, and Service. Within our wonderful new world, we have found freedom from our fatal obsession. That we have chosen this particular symbol is perhaps no accident. The priests and seers of antiquity regarded the circle enclosing the triangle as a means of warding off spirits of evil, and A.A.'s circle and triangle of Recovery, Unity, and Service has certainly meant all of that to us and much more.

On our first evening together here in St. Louis, we looked at the base of our triangle, A.A.'s First Legacy of Recovery, on which everything rests and depends. During our second evening we contemplated Unity, A.A.'s Second Legacy, and all its vast meaning for our future. Now we want to think about the third side of our triangle, A.A.'s Third Legacy of Service, which in this afternoon's closing hour will be delivered into your hands for all time to come. Then our symbol will be complete, and may Recovery, Unity, and Service, the means by which, under God, our fellowship has been created, be ever at His command for so long as He may use this society.

A.A.'s Twelfth Step, carrying the message, is the basic service that our fellowship gives; it is our principal aim and the main reason for our existence. A.A. is more than a set of principles; it is a society of recovered alcoholics in action. We *must* carry A.A.'s message; otherwise we ourselves may fall into decay and those who have not yet been given the truth may die. This is why we so often say that *action* is the magic word. Action to carry A.A.'s message is therefore the heart of our Third Legacy of Service.

Yet some of us are still a bit confused about A.A.'s Third Legacy. We still ask, "Just what is this Third Legacy business anyhow? And just how much territory does 'service action' take in?"

The answer is simple. An A.A. service is anything whatever that legitimately helps us to reach fellow sufferers. As we have seen, the Twelfth Step call is the greatest of A.A.'s services. But the publicity that caused the prospect to get in touch with us, the car we rode in, the gasoline we paid for, and the cups of coffee we bought him—all of these aids were necessary to make our call possible and effective. And this is only the start. Our services involve meeting places, hospital co-operation, Intergroup offices, and pamphlets and books. Services can require committees, delegates, trustees, and conferences. They include small voluntary money contributions so that the group, the area, and A.A. as a whole can function. They range all the way from the cup of coffee up to A.A.'s General Service Headquarters for national and international action. The sum of *all* these services is A.A.'s Third Legacy. Such services are utterly necessary to A.A.'s existence and growth. Yearning for simplicity, we often wonder if we could not do away with many of A.A.'s present services. Wouldn't it be wonderful to have no bother, no politics, no expense, and no responsibility! But this is only a dream about simplicity; it would not be simplicity in fact. Without its essential services, A.A. would soon become a formless, confused, and irresponsible anarchy.

Regarding any particular service, we need to ask only one question: "Is this or that service *really needed?*" If it is not, then let it be eliminated. But if it *is* needed, then maintain it we must or fail in our mission to those who want and seek A.A. For twenty years now we A.A.'s have been trying to determine what are needed services and what are not. As I tell the story of the growth of A.A.'s services, I hope that the vision of our Third Legacy will come clear.

Let's begin with my own sponsor, Ebby. When Ebby heard how serious my drinking was, he resolved to visit me. He was in New

York; I was in Brooklyn. His resolve was not enough; he had to *take action* and *spend money*. He called me on the phone and then got into the subway; total cost, ten cents. At the level of the telephone booth and subway turnstile, spirituality and money began to mix. One without the other would have amounted to nothing at all. Right then and there, Ebby established the principle that A.A. in action calls for the sacrifice of much time and a little money.

Now let us have a look at one of those little meetings we held during that first summer in Akron. We gathered in Dr. Bob's living room. Anne made her home ready for us, so we had shelter over our heads. There was some expense for coffee, and Dr. Bob paid it. If Anne and Dr. Bob had not given these hospitable services, no meeting could have been held.

As the Akron meeting got larger, it moved over to the house of T. Henry and Clarace Williams. They purchased a lot of extra chairs, served many suppers, and stood for much wear and tear on their house too. We alcoholics did not pay a cent. T. Henry and Clarace sacrificed a great amount of time and some money. If they had not done so, there could not have been any meeting.

In these obvious examples I think we can see what the test of an A.A. service really is. Whether it is a book, a translation, a service conference, or a twentieth anniversary convention, the principle is the same; the test is identical: *Do we need this particular service* or do we not? That is the only question.

As A.A. grew, homes were no longer big enough for meetings. We had to move into hotel parlors and halls. This marked the time when the groups themselves had to begin to pay. Landlords wanted their money, so a collection had to be taken. These collections were voluntary, but great cries went up nevertheless. A.A. was not supposed to cost anything, it was said. We cannot mix this great spiritual idea with landlords' commercialism! But the landlords were not impressed. We had to pay or get out. So we did pay, and voluntary contributions became a fact of A.A. life. We could not function without them. Moreover, somebody had to collect the money and bank it and account for it. This meant the existence of a treasurer. The group soon found, too, that it needed a secretary and sometimes a chairman. Absolutely necessary arrangements had to be made and people had to be appointed or elected to do the jobs. This often brought friction and power-driving, but it was found that the group had to survive and function, no matter what the cost. Means had to be found to keep friction-makers and power-drivers down to their right size. A suitable service committee, considerable mild coercion, coupled with much love and understanding, proved to be the answer. So these sometimes frightening experiences were not bad for us after all. They helped everybody to grow. Meanwhile the group went on functioning because it had to function or fail in its mission.

Cities and areas had their own special service problems. Unable to reach A.A. on the phone, alcoholics and their families got discouraged as they tried to contact us. This caused needless suffering and sometimes loss of life. Hospitals also became tired of slapdash, irresponsible admittance of patients into their institutions. This condition was not simplicity at all; it was complication. Sponsorship into these places and out of them became imperative; otherwise the hospitals might get fed up and quit. Ignoring the cries of "Let us keep it simple," and goaded by the sheer neccessity of the situation, responsible old-timers in such areas would often hire a small office and a paid secretary, and would then act as a management committee for the service center. Next, the old-timers would ask the surrounding groups for voluntary contributions. When these failed to meet the needs of the simple and inexpensive setup, they often went into their own pockets. If the newly hired secretary happened to be an A.A. member, this was a sure-fire cause for trouble. The often frightened little gal soon learned that she was considered a "professional A.A.," making money out of it. Of course this was unfounded because primarily she was doing a secretarial job. Over the years the areas learned the same lessons the groups did. They found what was necessary to make an A.A. area function, and what was not. Out of this long travail and struggle,

A.A.'s present Intergroup or area Central Offices have emerged. In scores of cities they are doing a vitally necessary job.

Meanwhile we found that we needed services that we could not perform ourselves. Chief among these was the right kind of hospitalization. Doctoring and physically caring for the very sick was not and could not be A.A.'s business. Here great friends like Dr. Silkworth and Sister Ignatia came to our aid. An ever growing number of hospitals has since welcomed us into the closest co-operation. Among these pioneers was Charles B. Towns Hospital in New York, St. Thomas Hospital in Akron, St. Vincent Charity Hospital in Cleveland, and Knickerbocker Hospital in New York. These and many others are superb examples of what our friends outside of A.A. have done to help us better to function and to serve.

In addition to these hospitals, we find today an impressive list of drying-out places—farms, state and provincial clinics, and many kinds of civic and professional people and groups—all interested in the solution of the problem of alcoholism. Jurists, penologists, educational committees, psychiatrists, great industrial enterprises—all are helping. What these outside services have meant in terms of aid to A.A. and endorsement of our society is beyond estimate.

The world of religion likewise has come to our aid. We enjoy the blessings of practically all sects and denominations. Any number of us as individuals have been counseled and brought into greater spiritual understanding and growth by the help of devoted clergymen.

Without all this outside help A.A. might never have started in the first place or grown so well since. These were, and still are, indispensable services.

Another great service has been performed by A.A.'s friends of press, radio, and all kinds of communications. These agencies have given A.A. millions of dollars of free publicity. They have brought alcoholics to us by the tens of thousands. And they never have required anything of us except our co-operation in getting the story of A.A. before the world. We know that without the help of these friends our growth would have been slow indeed.

Now we come to the story of A.A.'s world services. Because these activities are so remote from most of us, not many know how A.A.'s over-all service structure was built or what it has accomplished. To those who do know the real story this is one of the most vital and exciting developments in all our history.

When Dr. Bob and I realized on that fall day in 1937 that some two-score of us had recovered from alcoholism, we at once asked ourselves, "How can this experience be shared? How can the word be spread?" Dr. Bob had recovered two and a half years before, and I had been sober three years.

It had taken all this time to perfect the recovery program and to bring sobriety to a handful of sufferers. The number of alcoholics in the world who wanted to get well was reckoned in millions. How could the great chance we had had be brought to them? At the snail's pace we had been going, it was clear that most of them could never be reached.

We could therefore no longer be a seldom heard of secret society. Word-of-mouth communication with the few alcoholics we could contact by our then-current methods would be not only slow but dangerous; dangerous because the recovery message in which we now had such high confidence might soon be garbled and twisted beyond recognition. Clearly our budding society and its message would have to be publicized.

Hardly a fraction of the world's alcoholics could be expected to come to Akron or New York for treatment. Somehow we would have to reach them where they were. Maybe we would have to get some of our members subsidized as missionaries to do this. It was already plain that most hospitals did not want to be bothered with alcoholics. Their beds were filled with people who seemed better subjects for treatment. Perhaps we would need to operate a chain of hospitals, and maybe the proceeds of such a venture would pay the missionaries. Above all, we would have to put our methods down on paper. A book of experience could carry our message to distant places we could never visit ourselves. Moreover, such a book could prevent the otherwise inevitable garble and distortion that would start as soon as publicity came. It would not only guide alcoholics to recovery, but also become the basis for telling our story to the world and therefore a guide to our public relations as well. These were our reflections and speculations.

Dr. Bob very much liked the idea of a book. But when it came to paid missionaries and profit-making hospitals he was frankly dubious. Promoter that I was, I shared few of his fears. I felt that we would have to have money and maybe a lot of it. Neither of us could give the work our full attention unless we were subsidized. And our members could not be expected to throw over their jobs and ignore their families' needs in order to do free missionary work. If we had our own hospitals, we would have to be financed. The book alone would take considerable time and some money. Neither Dr. Bob nor I had money; we had only debts. Every other member was in much the same fix. We would simply have to solicit money or get nowhere. Only half-convinced, Dr. Bob rightly wondered what all these complications might do to the spirit of our undertaking, the carrying of our message to fellow alcoholics with no strings and no money attached. Finally he said, "Why don't we call the Akron boys together and have a meeting at T. Henry's? Let's try these ideas out on them."

At T. Henry's house, eighteen of the Akron alcoholics listened stolidly to our proposals. I kept pouring on my arguments for missionaries, hospitals, and the book as thick as I could. Despite his doubts, Dr. Bob strongly backed me up, especially about the need for a book.

The moment we were through, those alcoholics really did work us over! They rejected the idea of missionaries. Paid workers, they said, would kill our good will with alcoholics; this would be sheer ruin. If we went into the hospital business, everybody would say it was a racket. Many thought we must shun publicity; we would be swamped; we could not handle the traffic. Some turned thumbs down on pamphlets and books. After all, they said, the apostles themselves did not need any printed matter.

Dr. Bob and I returned to the fray and renewed our pressure. But this settled nothing and a vote had to be taken. By the barest majority, and over the most strenuous objections, the Akron meeting finally decided that we ought to go for the whole works—the missionaries, the hospitals, and the book. Even then, no one present volunteered to do much about these things. If a lot of money was needed, I had better go back to New York where there was plenty and raise it myself. Such was the verdict of that meeting, and a mighty close shave it was. In later years, I came to be very thankful for that powerful minority. Their contention that going into big business and hiring paid missionaries would destroy us turned out to be absolutely correct. On the other hand, had the ultraconservatives prevailed, and had we done nothing, A.A. might have got nowhere after all. Though I did not see it then, the group conscience of Alcoholics Anonymous was already at work hammering out right decisions for A.A.'s future. The majority of the meeting had given me permission to do as I wanted, and it was quite easy for the time being to ignore the minority warnings. But that was not the end of the minority, as we shall presently see.

Much elated, I grabbed a train for home. I figured that the new developments would take millions of dollars. Our little New York group gave me more encouragement than had the Akronites. Most of them soon fell in with my grandiose notions. It was felt that raising money for such a noble enterprise should present no difficulties at all. We said to each other, "Why, this is probably one of the greatest medical and spiritual developments of all time. Certainly the rich will help us. How could they do anything else?" Then, too, the New York group had already scraped up a couple of super-salesmen, people who thought exactly as I did. So A.A.'s first (and last) great crusade for money got off to a flying start.

Armed with a list of wealthy prospects, we commenced to solicit funds. To our astonishment we got absolutely nowhere. Some of the wealthy exhibited mild concern and sympathy, but they were not really interested. Almost unanimously they seemed to think that tuberculosis, cancer, and the Red Cross were better charity investments. Why should they try to revive a lot of down-and-out alcoholics who had brought their troubles upon themselves? In great dejection we finally saw that drunks as objects of large charity might never be a popular cause.

I was quite angry and depressed, and in this mood I visited the office of my brother-in-law, Dr. Leonard V. Strong, Jr., to whom I delivered a diatribe on the stinginess and shortsightedness of the rich. Ours was a movement that would doubtless sweep the world. What was the matter with people anyway? Leonard had heard all this before, and somewhat wearily he said, "Years ago, I knew a man called Willard Richardson. As I remember, he had something to do with John D. Rockefeller's charities. I think he used to be very close to the Rockefeller family. If he is still alive I believe he would remember me. Maybe he is still at the Rockefeller offices. I'll call up and find out."

Leonard called, and at once the voice of one of our greatest friends-to-be, Mr. Willard Richardson, came over the wire. He said, "Why, hello, Leonard, where have you been all of these years? I'd love to see you." My brother-in-law replied, "I have with me a relative who has had some success in straightening out alcoholics. Could we come and talk to you about it?" Mr. Richardson said, "Of course you can. How about tomorrow?"

The next morning Leonard and I alighted on the fifty-sixth floor of the RCA building where Mr. John D. Rockefeller, Jr., had his offices. Soon we were shaking hands with Mr. Richardson, an elderly gentleman who had twinkling eyes set in one of the finest faces I have ever seen. He was warmly cordial. He showed the deepest interest as I unfolded the story of our struggling fellowship. After he had heard me out that wonderful gentleman said, "I think we should have another meeting soon. Maybe you and I ought to have lunch together. What about next week?"

In the elevator lobby my brother-in-law ran into a commuter friend, who said, "So you have been in to see Mr. Richardson? If you happen to want anything from Mr. Rockefeller personally, he is certainly your man. He has been in charge of Mr. Rockefeller's private charities for years." This was *terrific!* Here was the inside track! Here was a patron at last! Our money troubles were over! As promoters, we were doing all right after all.

At lunch with Mr. Richardson the following week my expectations were confirmed. He was keenly interested in the story of our society and its needs. He proposed still another meeting, to be held in Mr. Rockefeller's private board room. He would bring with him Mr. Albert Scott, Chairman of the Trustees for Riverside Church, Mr. Frank Amos, an advertising man and close friend, and Mr. A. LeRoy Chipman, an associate who looked after some of Mr. Rockefeller's personal affairs. And, of course, there would be Dr. Strong, who had brought us together. I was to bring Dr. Silkworth and some of the New York alcoholics, along with Dr. Bob and certain members from Akron. I rushed home to Brooklyn and excitedly called Dr. Bob. We were riding high on pink cloud number 17.

The historic evening in December, 1937, finally arrived. We had supper and presently found ourselves in Mr. Rockefeller Jr.'s private board room. My chair at the great table felt warm, and it was explained that Mr. Rockefeller himself had just vacated it. This made the chair feel even warmer; we were certainly getting close now!

There was a rather awkward pause while our friends waited for us to say something. I guess we were a bit awestruck. Then someone suggested that each alcoholic present tell his own story, just as he would at a meeting. As we told our several tales of alcoholic misery and release, we could see that a very deep impression was being made. When we were through, Mr. Scott, who chaired the meeting at the head of the table, exclaimed, "Why, this is first-century Christianity!" And then, still more to the point, he added, "What can we do to help?"

Our big moment had come. I mentioned our need for money, for paid workers, chains of hospitals, and literature. Though we could of course start modestly, these things eventually might require large sums. The need, I ventured, was very urgent. Though the risks of such undertakings might be considerable, the risk of doing nothing whatever would certainly be greater. Dr. Silkworth and the rest of our contingent at the table expressed the same opinion.

Then Mr. Scott posed a question that is still heard in A.A. to this day. "Won't money spoil this thing?" he asked. The discussion became general, and we were bombarded with questions: "Won't money create a professional class?" "Wouldn't professional members spoil the man-to-man approach that is now successful?" "Wouldn't the management of a hospital chain, with all the property and money required, be a fatal diversion?" This barrage of questions was disconcerting. Though they were calm about it, these men sounded for all the world like the vociferous minority out there in Akron. We all realized that, coming from such unbiased friends, these were good questions indeed. We answered that we had already pondered these perils ourselves but had finally concluded that to do nothing at all would be even more perilous. Being deeply convinced that this was true, we earnestly continued to press our case with the same arguments that had been used in Akron. At last impressed with this logic, our new friends began to yield. They admitted that we did need money, at least *some* money.

At this point, Mr. Amos (who was to become a great friend and a long-time Trustee for A.A.) promised to make an investigation of our society which might be the basis for asking Mr. Rockefeller for some funds. Mr. Amos had never laid eyes on us before, and we were deeply moved by this evidence of his interest and generosity.

We suggested that Mr. Amos first look at the Akron group. Akron was our first group and our largest. It worked in a more typical community than New York. If an A.A. hospital were to be put into operation, the Akron location would be better, and Dr. Bob would be available to superintend it. For fear of embarrassing Dr. Bob, there was another reason we did not mention. Though more than two years sober, he had been unable to revive his surgical practice. People were glad for his sobriety, but they still feared the knife in his hands. Each was asking, "What if he gets drunk the morning he cuts *me* up?" We knew Dr. Bob was facing a mortgage foreclosure on his home, and if any money was forthcoming, he needed it more than any of the rest of us.

A week later Frank Amos arrived in Akron and ran a fine-tooth comb through the situation there. He questioned local citizens and certain medical associates of Dr. Bob's. He went to several meetings and talked with each alcoholic member. He also looked at a large vacant residence which might be converted into a hospital where Dr. Bob could work. Frank caught the contagion, and he came back to New York red-hot. At the conclusion of his enthusiastic report he recommended that Mr. Rockefeller grant us $50,000 just as a starter. With this money two or three of us could be subsidized, a down payment on the hospital could be made, and Dr. Bob could be relieved of his mortgage troubles.

Mr. Richardson quickly took the glowing report to his friend, Mr. Rockefeller, who we thought would surely be interested. Here was medicine, here was religion, and here was a great good work, all in one package. Dick Richardson read Frank's report and then added his own account of what he had seen and heard from us. Mr. Rockefeller listened intently. He was tremendously impressed and said so. He has continued to say so ever since and has repeatedly stated that his connection with Alcoholics Anonymous is numbered among the finest and most moving experiences of his life.

Nevertheless, Mr. Rockefeller flatly turned down this plea for a large sum, despite the fact that our project appealed to his every charitable inclination. After a rereading of Frank's report, he said to his old friend, "Dick, I am afraid that money will spoil this thing." When he gave his reasons, they were identical with those advanced by the Akron group's minority. John D. Rockefeller, Jr., was guided then and there to save the A.A. fellowship from itself and from unnecessary hazards of money, property, and professionalism. It was one of the turning points in A.A.'s history. His great wealth could have ruined us.

At this juncture, Dick Richardson described the desperate financial plight of Dr. Bob and myself. On hearing of this, Mr. Rockefeller said, "I will place $5,000 for their use in the treasury of the Riverside Church. You may draw on this as you like. This will give these men some temporary assistance. But this fellowship should soon become self-supporting. If you and the others do not happen to agree, if you really think that the movement needs money, of course you can help them to raise it. But please don't ever ask me for any more."

This was *very* great news for Alcoholics Anonymous, but at the time it seemed like bad news. It was in fact a shattering blow to our hopes. Nevertheless Dr. Bob and I were grateful to get off the hook, even for a little while. The small mortgage on Dr. Bob's place was paid off, and each of us began to receive thirty dollars a week for as long as the money might last. Otherwise, we stood just where we had been all along. The prospect of missionaries and hospitals and the book had gone dim. Uncle Dick Richardson was definitely disappointed, and so were friends Amos, Chipman, and Strong. Seeing that they were not in complete agreement with Mr. Rockefeller, we renewed our pleas for aid. Maybe they would know other men of wealth who might be solicited with more success. To our delight all four thought this possible, and we held frequent meetings to talk about it.

By the spring of 1938 a definite program of action took shape. It was agreed that we needed a tax-free charitable trust or foundation. Wealthy contributors could then deduct gifts from their tax returns. Such a foundation would be a responsible repository for these funds and would guarantee the wise use of all contributions. Messrs. Richardson, Amos, and Chipman agreed to serve as Trustees and so did my brother-in-law, Dr. Strong. These were the first steps in forming the Alcoholic Foundation (recently renamed the General Service Board of Alcoholics Anonymous).

Frank Amos next secured the valuable help of a young friend, John Wood, then a rising junior in one of New York's famous law offices. This gave us the best possible legal talent. John Wood sat in at our meetings, and we commenced our work.

The first move was to choose a name for the new outfit. After long discussion we decided to call it the Alcoholic Foundation. This seemed like a resounding title, one that could create an impression of large importance. Still swayed by big ideas, we thought our trusteeship ought to be chartered to do just about anything within the field of alcohol or alcoholism except lobby for Prohibition. We intended an arrangement by which we could research, educate, and do a lot of other things. Attention to our membership would be only one of many functions. Thus the Alcoholic Foundation got its name and its charter.

Then we ran up against a legal riddle. It was thought that the Board of Trustees should consist of alcoholics and nonalcoholics. The latter were always to be in the majority by a margin of one. This would assure our membership and other contributors that nonalcoholics would be holding the purse strings. Mr. Wood then blandly asked us to define an alcoholic, and then a nonalcoholic. We came up with the definition that the alcoholic was a sick person who couldn't drink at all. The nonalcoholic, we surmised, was a perfectly well man who could drink if he wanted to! This made no legal sense at all, and Mr. Wood, still puzzled, finally gave up the attempt to describe an alcoholic in legal terms. But he soon found a way out of the impasse by suggesting that we write up a simple trust agreement and sign it. This would avoid the whole business of a formalized charter. Soon afterward this document was completed, and the Alcoholic Foundation was in business.

Our first Board consisted of five Trustees. Dick Richardson, Frank Amos, and Dr. Strong were the nonalcoholic members, and we chose Dr. Bob and one of the New York A.A.'s as the alcoholic contingent. The New York member soon got drunk, but this possibility had been foreseen. Drunkenness on the part of an alcoholic Trustee meant immediate resignation. Another alcoholic was named in the drunken brother's place and we proceeded to business. It was May, 1938.

Our friends came up with the promised list of wealthy men who might be solicited, and from early summer to early fall we pounded that list of prospects. With a tax-free Foundation and the kind of friends we now had, we thought our money problems would be a push-over. But the attraction of tax exemptions and responsible Trustees seemed to make no difference. For a while Carlton Sherwood, a friend of Dick Richardson's, lent us a hand. Mr. Sherwood was a very successful money raiser for charities, but he found he could do little for us because we were too uncertain and glum ourselves. So the whole business bogged down and the treasury of our Foundation remained empty. It looked like the end of the line.

Some time in March or April of 1938 I began to work on what was to become the book *Alcoholics Anonymous*. By the time our big money push was under way I had completed my own story and had roughed out what is now the second chapter of the A.A. book. Mimeographed copies of these two chapters were part of the paraphernalia for the money-raising operation, which had now fizzled out.

Anxious to encourage us, our friends insisted on monthly Trustee meetings. For a while nothing happened at them except commiseration for the fact of the Foundation's empty treasury. But at one of these meetings in the early fall of 1938, Frank Amos popped up with an idea which opened the door upon our real future. Frank said, "One of my friends, Eugene Exman, is Religious Editor of Harper. Perhaps he would be interested in your new book. Why don't you go down there and show him the few chapters you have done? I'll fix it up for you."

So down I went to meet Gene Exman, another wonderful friend-to-be of our society. I related the tale of our struggles and handed over to him my first attempt at authorship. While I waited Gene thoughtfully scanned the two chapters. Then he asked, "Could you do a whole book in this style? And how many months would it take you?" I was shaking, but I had an answer ready: "I believe I can do it. It will probably take nine or ten months." Thereupon he made a proposal that was surprising. "If it would help things along," he said, "I think Harper might be willing to advance you $1,500 in royalties. This amount would be deducted from your account when the book is finished in 1939."

Again in the clouds, I left Harper to break the great news to the gang. I first headed for a visit with Frank Amos, but on the way there my elation was disturbed by disquieting thoughts. Suppose our embryo book were someday to become the chief text for our fellowship. Our principal written asset would then be owned by an outside publisher, a fine and conservative one surely, but nevertheless an outsider. So I wondered if our fellowship should own its own book. Then I thought about the $1,500 of advance royalties. When the book was done, I would still owe Harper that sum, and a good many volumes would have to be sold just to get even. And suppose that when the book appeared there were to be heavy publicity, and thousands of cries for help from alcoholics and their families began to pour in. We would not have any money to cope with this quite possible situation.

I kept these misgivings to myself, and it was good to see Frank's face light up as he heard the news. In any case it was fine to know that a firm like Harper wanted the book and that an editor of Gene's caliber believed that it was going to be good. This experience was one of the confidence builders that kept the book project going through thick and thin.

At the next Foundation meeting our friends smiled happily as they heard the details of the Harper project. It was the first ray of hope we had seen in months. The Trustees were unanimous in their opinion that the Harper deal was the answer.

I had shared my doubts with a few New York friends about the Harper proposal, but I had said nothing about them elsewhere. Now very reluctantly I told the Trustees what they were. But our non-alcoholics on the Board were not impressed with my reasons. They pointed to the well-known fact that authors seldom publish their own books and get away with it. The meeting ended on a dismal note. We were a hung jury; no conclusion or verdict was reached.

Soon afterward, one of the most terrific power-drivers I have ever met got into the act. This was my friend Henry P., one-time Standard Oil executive and the very first alcoholic ever to stay sober even a little while in the New York group. He had been a protégé of Dr. Silkworth's and a frequent visitor at Towns Hospital. At this time he had been sober about two years. Henry had red hair, at least one new idea a minute, and energy beyond telling. He was not a Foundation Trustee, and he had no official say at all, but that mattered not a bit. He was a hard-hitting salesman, and he sold his bill of goods. He said, "Look here, Bill, why do we bother any more with those Trustees and that Foundation? Those folks have not raised a cent and they are not going to. Why don't we put this proposed book on a business basis and form a stock company? Let's sell shares to our own folks right here in New York. If we give them a real argument, I'll guarantee they will will get up the dough." I was an ex-Wall Streeter and had already toyed with this notion myself, but Henry had much bigger ideas and he breathed confidence. Our society would organize its own publishing company and maybe we would have to forget about the Foundation. I told him the Trustees would never agree to our scheme, and I did not want to hurt their feelings. But Henry's skin was thicker than mine. He was implacable; he said that it simply had to be done, and I finally agreed.

Still much disturbed about the whole business, I went back to Gene Exman and frankly explained to him what was about to happen. To my utter amazement, he agreed, quite contrary to his own interest, that a society like ours ought to control and publish its own literature. Moreover, he felt that very possibly we could do this with success. Though Gene's opinion did not register at all when it was transmitted to the Trustees, it did give Henry and me the kind of encouragement we so much needed.

Henry wasted no time but started selling the proposition to our New York members at once. He buttonholed them one by one, persuading, browbeating, hypnotizing. I trailed around in his wake, smoothing ruffled feelings and trying to dispel some of the suspicions that had been created about our motives. After a couple of weeks of this kind of violent promotion we got a lukewarm consent from our Eastern membership. Dr. Bob was dubious, but he also consented. He did think it would be unwise at this stage to lay the matter before the Akron membership. Some promotion might be justifiable in New York, but few Akronites would be able to see it, he thought. He felt, too, that we should try the idea out on the Board of Trustees. We surely could not ignore them.

Meanwhile Henry and I were perfecting our plan. It would take a persuasive prospectus to induce alcoholics to part with their money for stock in a company that had not yet produced even one book. But the more we investigated, the better the proposition looked. We went to Edward Blackwell, the president of Cornwall Press, one of the largest printers in the United States. Here we discovered that the printing cost of an average-size book is only about 10 per cent of its retail price. A 400-page volume could be printed for only a fraction of a dollar. If we were to price our new book at $3.50, as Henry and I figured it, this would be practically all net profit. There would be no bookstore commission, no paid advertising, and none of the usual losses that publishers had to take on books that did not sell. Our book of course *would* sell, and we could not fail to clean up. It looked too good to be true.

I laid this information before the next Trustees' meeting. I anticipated that the reaction would be bad, and it certainly was. To flatly disagree with these wonderful friends was the toughest possible assignment. Once more the Trustees' meeting adjourned without agreement. I knew we would have to go through with the deal despite all the objections. It was depressing.

But Henry was not depressed. He had been sitting up nights working on a prospectus. The main arguments were these: Harper had said the book was going to be a good one. And even if we paid our groups and outside bookstores a dollar a book for distribution there would still be a whopping profit margin. The book could be printed at very low cost and sold for $2.50 wholesale or $3.50 by mail order. And when the reviews and other publicity got rolling, we were certain there would be sales by the carload.

The prospectus suggested that a company be formed with stock of $25 par value. The New York alcoholics and their friends could buy one-third of these shares for cash. The other two-thirds would be distributed between Henry and me for our work. To mollify the Trustees it was decided that the author's royalty which would ordinarily be mine could go to the Alcoholic Foundation. To the prospectus Henry attached a chart which showed the estimated profits on sales of 100,000, 500,000, and even a million books! I have now forgotten just what his hopes were, but they were fantastic. I was not *quite* so optimistic, but I did feel sure that the proceeds of the book would enable several of us to become full-time workers and to set up a general headquarters for our society. Whether this worked out or not, I was nevertheless convinced that our fellowship ought to own and control its own literature.

Our enterprise still lacked two essentials. It was not incorporated and it did not have a name. Henry took care of these matters. Since the forthcoming volume would be only the first of many such "works," he thought our publishing company should be called, "Works Publishing, Inc." This was all right with me, but I protested that we had no incorporation on which to base shares and that incorporation would take money. Next day I found that Henry had bought a pad of blank stock certificates in a stationery store, and across the top of each certificate was typed this legend: "Works Publishing, Inc., par value $25.00." At the bottom there was a signature: "Henry P. ———, President." When I protested these irregularities, Henry said there was no time to waste; why be concerned with small details?

So the great enterprise was launched. It remained to be seen if it would float. Henry knew every stratagem of the super-salesman, and he got right down to work. He descended like a whirlwind on the New York alcoholics and some of their friends, suggesting that they take stock in the glittering new venture. I was no second-rater at this sort of thing myself, and I followed right along.

Well, we did not sell even one of our proposed 600 shares of Works Publishing, cheap as we claimed it was. The New York alcoholics said, "You fellows have certainly got nerve. What made you think that we would buy stock in a book not yet written?" But Henry was not discouraged. He still had ideas. "Bill," he said, "you and I know this book is going to sell. And Harper thinks it will sell. But these New York drunks just do not believe it. Some take it as a joke, and the rest talk high and holy about mixing a spiritual enterprise with money and promotion. But if they really *did* think that the book would sell, they would buy the stock all right, and fast. So why don't we go up and see *The Reader's Digest* people and find out if they will print a piece about our fellowship and this book? If the *Digest* runs an article about us, we will sell those books by the carloads. Anybody can see that, even these tightwad drunks. So what are we waiting for? Let's go!"

Two days later at Pleasantville, New York, we sat in the office of Mr. Kenneth Payne, then managing editor of the *Digest*. We drew a glowing picture of our fellowship and its book-to-be. We mentioned the high interest of Mr. Rockefeller and some of his friends. Mr. Payne was interested. After a while he said, "I am almost sure the *Digest* would like to handle this story, though of course I'll have to check it up with the other editors. Personally I think it is just the sort of thing we are looking for. When your book is ready next spring, let me know and I think we can put a feature writer to work. This should be a great story. But of course I must check it up with the staff first. That's understood, isn't it?"

Henry and I reached for our hats and sped for New York. Now we had *real* ammunition. That very night we started a fresh canvass, and the former doubters began to sign up. Nearly everybody was broke at the time, so we made things easy for them. They could buy their shares on the installment plan, five dollars a month for five months for each share. Many could afford only a single share. When the Trustees were brought up to date they loyally pitched in too. Some A.A.'s had friends who signed up for small amounts. Certain of my old Wall Street cronies tossed in a few chips. People like Dr. Silkworth and Dr. Tiebout lent a hand. Soon we had a subscription of 200 shares which amounted to $5,000, and a little actual money began to come in. However, the subscribers were not animated wholly by commercialism. After receiving just a little assurance that they might someday get their money back, they really got behind the deal.

At 17 William Street, Newark, New Jersey, Henry had an office which was the headquarters for a rapidly failing business. He also had a secretary named Ruth Hock, who was to become one of A.A.'s real pioneers. The other assets consisted of a huge desk and some plush furniture.

Each morning I traveled all the way from Brooklyn to Newark where, pacing up and down in Henry's office, I began to dictate rough drafts of the chapters of the coming book. As we seemed unable to come up with any genuine outline for the publication, I worked from a hastily drawn-up list of possible chapter headings. Week after week, Henry raced around among the stock subscribers, prodding them for their installments. In addition to this dribble of money, we were able to secure $2,500 from Mr. Charles B. Towns. Most of these funds had to be devoted to office expenses and groceries for Henry, Ruth, Lois, and myself, and we kept going on this basis until April, 1939, the publication date of the book *Alcoholics Anonymous*.

As the chapters were slowly roughed out I read them to the New York group at its weekly meeting in our parlor at Clinton Street, and copies were sent to Dr. Bob for checking and criticism in Akron, where we had nothing but the warmest support. But in the New York meeting the chapters got a real mauling. I redictated them and Ruth retyped them over and over. In spite of the heated arguments, the New York group's criticisms did help a lot, and to some extent their enthusiasm and confidence increased.

So the job went until we reached the famous Chapter 5. Up to that time I had done my own story and had drafted three more chapters with the titles "There Is a Solution," "More About Alcoholism," and "We Agnostics." It was now realized that we had enough background and window-dressing material, and that at this point we would have to tell how our program for recovery from alcoholism really worked. The backbone of the book would have to be fitted in right here.

This problem had secretly worried the life out of me. I had never written anything before and neither had any other member of the New York group. Progress on the book had been too slow for several of the stock subscribers and they had slacked off on their contributions. The hassling over the four chapters already finished had really been terrific. I was exhausted. On many a day I felt like throwing the book out the window.

I was in this anything-but-spiritual mood on the night when the Twelve Steps of Alcoholics Anonymous were written. I was sore and tired clear through. I lay in bed at 182 Clinton Street with pencil in hand and with a tablet of scratch paper on my knee. I could not get my mind on the job, much less put my heart in it. But here was one of those things that had to be done. Slowly my mind came into some kind of focus.

Since Ebby's visit to me in the fall of 1934 we had gradually evolved what we called "the word-of-mouth program." Most of the basic ideas had come from the Oxford Groups, William James, and Dr. Silkworth. Though subject to considerable variation, it all boiled down into a pretty consistent procedure which comprised six steps. These were approximately as follows:

1. We admitted that we were licked, that we were powerless over alcohol.
2. We made a moral inventory of our defects or sins.
3. We confessed or shared our shortcomings with another person in confidence.
4. We made restitution to all those we had harmed by our drinking.
5. We tried to help other alcoholics, with no thought of reward in money or prestige.
6. We prayed to whatever God we thought there was for power to practice these precepts.

This was the substance of what, by the fall of 1938, we were telling newcomers. Several of the Oxford Groups' other ideas and attitudes had been definitely rejected, including any which could involve us in theological controversy. In important matters there was still considerable disagreement between the Eastern and the Midwestern view-points. Our people out there were still active Oxford Group members, while we in New York had withdrawn a year before. In Akron and vicinity they still talked about the Oxford Groups' absolutes: absolute honesty, absolute purity, absolute unselfishness, and absolute love. This dose was found to be too rich for New Yorkers, and we had abandoned the expressions. But all of us, East and West, were placing increasing emphasis on Dr. Silkworth's expression describing the alcoholic's dilemma: the obsession plus the allergy. By now we knew from experience that the new prospect had to accept Step One or get no place.

This particular evening, as my mind ran over these developments, it seemed to me that the program was still not definite enough. It might be a long time before readers of the book in distant places and lands could be personally contacted. Therefore our literature would have to be as clear and comprehensive as possible. Our steps would have to be more explicit. There must not be a single loophole through which the rationalizing alcoholic could wiggle out. Maybe our six chunks of truth should be broken up into smaller pieces. Thus we could better get the distant reader over the barrel, and at the same time we might be able to broaden and deepen the spiritual implications of our whole presentation. So far as I can remember this was all I had in mind when the writing began.

Finally I started to write. I set out to draft more than six steps; how many more I did not know. I relaxed and asked for guidance. With a speed that was astonishing, considering my jangling emotions, I completed the first draft. It took perhaps half an hour. The words kept right on coming. When I reached a stopping point, I numbered the new steps. They added up to twelve. Somehow this number seemed significant. Without any special rhyme or reason I connected them with the twelve apostles. Feeling greatly relieved now, I commenced to reread the draft.

At this moment a couple of late callers arrived. One of them was my boon companion of those days, Howard A. With him was a newcomer, dry barely three months. I was greatly pleased with what I had written, and I read them the new version of the program, now the "Twelve Steps." [11] Howard and his friend reacted violently. "Why *twelve* steps?" they demanded. And then, "You've got too much God in these steps; you will scare people away." And, "What do you mean by getting those drunks down 'on their knees' when they ask to have all their shortcomings removed?" And, "Who wants all their short-comings removed, anyhow?" As he saw my uneasiness, Howard added, "Well, some of this stuff does sound pretty good after all. But, Bill, you've got to tone it down. It's too stiff. The average alcoholic just won't buy it the way it stands."

I sprang to the defense of the new creation, every single word of it. A terrific discussion developed which cooled only when Lois turned up a couple of hours later. "Why don't you forget about it for a while," she said, "and have a cup of coffee." This we did.

Akronites like Paul and Dick S. liked the new steps very much. As the remainder of the book text developed, based on the Twelve Steps, they continued to report their approval. But in New York the hot debate about the Twelve Steps and the book's contents was doubled and redoubled. There were conservative, liberal, and radical viewpoints. Fitz M., the Episcopal minister's son from Maryland and the second man to recover at Towns Hospital, made constant journeys to New York in order to reinforce the conservative position. Fitz thought that the book ought to be Christian in the doctrinal sense of the word and that it should say so. He was in favor of using Biblical terms and expressions to make this clear. Another early New York A.A., Paul K., was even more emphatic about this.

The liberals were the largest contingent and they had no objection to the use of the word "God" throughout the book, but they were dead set against any other theological proposition. They would have nothing to do with doctrinal issues. Spirituality, yes. But religion, no —*positively* no. Most of our members, they pointed out, believed in some sort of deity. But when it came to theology we could not possibly agree among ourselves, so how could we write a book that contained

[11] See The Twelve Steps, p. 50.

any such matter? There was no such thing as group opinion in these areas and there never could be. Alcoholics who had tried the missions were forever complaining about this very thing. The alcoholic's unreasoning rebellion against the specifically religious approach had severely handicapped the missions. The liberals said they did not intend to be critical; they only wanted us to remember the hard facts. These contentions could not be denied. It was true that we could not agree on a religious basis for our fellowship and that the straight religious approach had worked in relatively few cases.

Thus the spiritual pitch and tone of our book was greatly influenced by the liberals. But the atheists and agnostics, our radical left wing, were still to make a tremendously important contribution. Led by my friend Henry and obstinately backed by Jim B., a recently arrived salesman, this contingent proceeded to have its innings. At first they wanted the word "God" deleted from the book entirely. Henry had come to believe in some sort of "universal power," but Jimmy still flabbergasted us by denouncing God at our meetings. Some members had been so angered that they wanted to throw him out of the group. But most of us thought it better to let him talk on, believing that eventually he would change his mind, which he later did. What Henry, Jimmy, and company wanted was a *psychological* book which would lure the alcoholic in. Once in, the prospect could take God or leave Him alone as he wished. To the rest of us this was a shocking proposal, but happily we listened and eventually learned something of great value. Actually our group conscience was at work to construct the most acceptable and effective book possible. Every voice in it was playing its appointed part to create an outcome that was to be nothing less than providential.

As the one who had to do the writing, I was caught squarely in the middle of all this arguing. The liberals were the larger group, but they barely outnumbered the combined conservatives and radicals. For a while it looked as if we would bog down into permanent disagreement. Despairing of satisfying everyone, I finally asked that I might be the final judge of what the book said. Seeing that we would get nowhere without such a point of decision, most of the group agreed. We began to carry on again.

We had not gone much farther with the text of the book when it was evident that something more was needed. There would have to be a story or case history section. We would have to produce evidence in the form of living proof, written testimonials of our membership itself. It was felt also that the story section could identify us with the distant reader in a way that the text itself might not. At this point Dr. Bob and the Akronites played a vital role. The Akron group was the larger and had more case history material, and the means of putting it into story form now appeared. Two years earlier a former newspaperman, Jim S., had been lifted off skid row and nursed back to health and sobriety. Jim and Dr. Bob went after all the Akronites who had substantial sobriety records for testimonial material. In most cases Jim interviewed the prospects and wrote their stories for them. Dr. Bob wrote his own. By January the Akronites had produced eighteen fine stories. Two of them came from Clevelanders who had attended the Akron meeting, and one concerned Marie B., the wife of an Akron alcoholic, an early forerunner of today's Family Group development.

With somewhat more difficulty the New York group produced ten stories. At the time we were an oddly assorted crowd. Since New York had no one comparable to Akron's newsman Jim, it was thought that each New Yorker with a real record of sobriety could try to write his story himself. None of us had any writing experience, and when Henry and I tried to edit these amateur attempts there was plenty of trouble. Who were we, said the writers, to edit their stories? That was a good question, but still we did edit them. The cries of the anguished edited taletellers finally subsided and the story section of the book was complete in the latter part of January, 1939. So at last was the text. The end of our money supply was definitely in sight, and we were preparing to rush the book to press.

But someone, I do not remember who, sounded a note of caution. These points were raised: "How do we know for sure that this book will be widely acceptable to everybody? Maybe it still contains medical errors or material that might offend our friends of religion. Had we not better make a prepublication copy of the text and some of the stories and try the book out on our own membership and on every kind and class of person that has anything to do with drunks?" This method would consume still more time and money, and many objected, but at length we concluded that we had better be safe than sorry. Four hundred mimeograph copies of the book were made and sent to everyone we could think of who might be concerned with the problem of alcoholism. Each mimeograph was stamped "Loan Copy" in order to protect our coming copyright.

While we were waiting for the returns to come in, two hot controversies got under way. Though I had labeled the mimeograph issue "Alcoholics Anonymous," this title was still unacceptable to a great many people.

The Akron and New York groups had been voting for months on possible titles. This had become an after-the-meeting form of amusement and interest. The title "Alcoholics Anonymous" had appeared very early in the discussion, probably in October, 1938. We do not know who first used these words. After we New Yorkers had left the Oxford Groups in 1937 we often described ourselves as a "nameless bunch of alcoholics." From this phrase it was only a step to the idea of "Alcoholics Anonymous." This was its actual derivation.

At the beginning I had liked this title very much. But as the book-naming discussion went on, I began to have certain doubts and temptations. From the start the title "The Way Out" was popular. If we gave the book this name, then I could add my signature, "By Bill W."! After all why shouldn't an author sign his book? I began to forget that this was everybody's book and that I had been mostly the umpire of the discussions that had created it. In one dark moment I even considered calling the book "The B. W. Movement." I whispered these ideas to a few friends and promptly got slapped down. Then I saw the temptation for what it was, a shameless piece of egotism. So once more I began to vote for the title "Alcoholics Anonymous."

We considered more than a hundred titles all told. In New York "Alcoholics Anonymous" had slowly gained in favor. This trend had been helped by the appearance of our first literary light, Joe W., recently scraped out of the Bowery. Years before, he had been one of the founders of a popular and sophisticated magazine. He was all for "Alcoholics Anonymous." He made a burning issue out of it and the majority of the New York group rallied around him. But we had failed to reckon with our friends in Akron; out there a considerable majority favored calling our book "The Way Out," and the combined voting of the two groups still showed that "The Way Out" had a bare majority.

Here an advantage presented itself and we seized it. I sent a wire to good old Fitz, then on his farm in Maryland. I asked him to visit the Library of Congress in Washington and find out how many books were entitled "The Way Out" and how many were called "Alcoholics Anonymous." Two days later we got this reply: "The Library of Congress shows twelve books titled 'The Way Out.' No book there is called 'Alcoholics Anonymous.'" We said to ourselves, "We sure aren't going to make this book the thirteenth 'Way Out.'" We left the title "Alcoholics Anonymous" in the copy that went to the printer. That is how we got the title for our book, and that is how our society got its name.

Just before the manuscript was finished an event of great significance for our future took place. At the time it looked like just another battle over the book. The scene was Henry's office in Newark, where most of the writing had been done. Present were Fitz, Henry, our grand little secretary Ruth, and myself. We were still arguing about the Twelve Steps. All this time I had refused to budge on these steps. I would not change a word of the original draft, in which, you will remember, I had consistently used the word "God," and in one place the expression "on our knees" was used. Praying to God on one's knees was still a big affront to Henry. He argued, he begged, he threatened.

He quoted Jimmy to back him up. He was positive we would scare off alcoholics by the thousands when they read those Twelve Steps. Little by little both Fitz and Ruth came to see merit in his contentions. Though at first I would have none of it, we finally began to talk about the possibility of compromise. Who first suggested the actual compromise words I do not know, but they are words well known throughout the length and breadth of A.A. today: In Step Two we decided to describe God as a "Power greater than ourselves." In Steps Three and Eleven we inserted the words "God *as we understood Him.*" From Step Seven we deleted the expression "on our knees." And, as a lead-in sentence to all the steps we wrote these words: "Here are the steps we took which are suggested as a Program of Recovery." A.A.'s Twelve Steps were to be *suggestions* only.

Such were the final concessions to those of little or no faith; this was the great contribution of our atheists and agnostics. They had widened our gateway so that all who suffer might pass through, regardless of their belief or *lack of belief.*

God was certainly there in our Steps, but He was now expressed in terms that anybody—*anybody at all*—could accept and try. Countless A.A.'s have since testified that without this great evidence of liberality they never could have set foot on any path of spiritual progress or even approached us in the first place. It was another one of those providential ten-strikes.

By now great numbers of the 400 mimeographs which had been sent out had been returned. The total reaction was very good—indeed it was wonderful. Many helpful suggestions had been made, and two of these were critically important.

One of them came from Dr. Howard, a well-known psychiatrist of Montclair, New Jersey. He pointed out that the text of our book was too full of the words "you" and "must." He suggested that we substitute wherever possible such expressions as "we ought" or "we should." His idea was to remove all forms of coercion, to put our fellowship on a "we ought" basis instead of a "you must" basis. To make this shift throughout the text of the book would be a big job.

I argued weakly against it but soon gave in; it was perfectly apparent that the doctor was dead right. Dr. Silkworth and Dr. Tiebout gave us similar advice and much more besides. And we must never forget that it was Dr. Silkworth who wrote the Introduction to the first edition of *Alcoholics Anonymous,* giving the volume medical standing.

All this time much needed encouragement and advice had come from Dick Richardson, Frank Amos, and Dr. Leonard Strong of our Board of Trustees. They had followed our progress with eager interest and constantly rising hope.

It should here be emphasized that the creation of A.A.'s book brought forth much more than disputes about its contents. As the volume grew so did the conviction that we were on the right track. We saw tremendous vistas of what this book might become and might do. High expectation based on a confident faith was the steady and sustaining overtone of feeling that finally prevailed among us. Like the sound of a receding thunderstorm, the din of our earlier battles was now only a rumble. The air cleared and the sky was bright. We all felt good.

In the midst of this rejoicing still another wonderful thing happened. We had worried about how the world of religion would receive our book. We were not kept waiting long. Dr. Harry Emerson Fosdick expressed his deepest satisfaction with the volume and promised to review it when it was released. The New York group did not contain even one Catholic member at the time the book was in preparation. A Catholic member from Akron had written his story but had volunteered no further opinion. So we were entirely in the dark as to what Catholic clergymen would say about our book. A group of laymen whose combined religious training and experience had been small indeed had produced a volume which described release from alcoholism by spiritual means. What would our Catholic friends think? We had not the slightest inkling.

Then the good news came. By messenger we had sent the book *Alcoholics Anonymous* to the Catholic Committee on Publications in the New York Archdiocese. Our messenger was Morgan R., released only a few weeks before from Greystone asylum and himself the first Catholic to put in an appearance in New York. It turned out he knew a member of the Church Committee on Publications. So we sent Morgan. Not long after he returned with wonderful things to tell us.

The Committee, he said, had nothing but the best to say of our efforts. From their point of view the book was perfectly all right as far as it went. After reading the section on meditation and prayer, the Committee had made certain suggestions for improvement, though none for actual change. Morgan had brought these with him and they looked so good that we adopted them on the spot. In only one sentence of the entire book had they found it necessary to suggest a real change. At the conclusion of my own story, Chapter 1 of the original draft, I had made a rhetorical flourish to the effect that "we have found Heaven right here on this good old earth." Morgan's friend on the Committee pointed this out to him with a smile and said, "Don't you think that Bill W. could change that word 'Heaven' to 'Utopia'? After all, we Catholics are promising folks something much better later on!" The Committee took no official action; they just sent us word that we were all right. Indeed this has since been the verdict of practically all denominations, a fact for which we are devoutly grateful.

Nothing now remained except to prepare the printer's copy of the book. We selected one of the mimeographs, and in Henry's clear handwriting all the corrections were transferred to it. There were few large changes but the small ones were very numerous. The copy was hardly legible and we wondered if the printer would take it, heavily marked up as it was. Henry and I went to New York and soon found ourselves face to face with Edward Blackwell, president of the Cornwall Press. In high spirits, we told him we were ready to go.

Mr. Blackwell wanted to know how many copies we wished. With the promised *Reader's Digest* article in mind, we were still thinking of carloads. Though doubtless impressed, Mr. Blackwell suggested 5,000 copies for the first printing. Then he asked what financial terms we were able to make. We cautiously let it be known that our cash was temporarily low. Pointing out what the *Reader's Digest* article would do for us, Henry mentioned a figure of $500 for our first down payment on the 5,000 books. Mr. Blackwell was startled and looked it. "What about that Rockefeller connection?" he asked. We replied that we had better hold that in reserve; that we were trying to manage this thing on our own if we could. Mr. Blackwell, having already caught the A.A. spirit, said with a twinkle in his eye, "Well, I guess that will do. I'm glad to give you a hand." So the presses were set to roll and Alcoholics Anonymous had found another wonderful friend.

When making these arrangements with Mr. Blackwell we fixed the retail price of the book at $3.50. This figure was the result of long and heated arguments. Some members had insisted on a $1.00 book, others wanted a $2.50 printing. They had turned deaf ears to Henry's plea that we *must* make something on the deal or else we could never operate a headquarters office, much less pay off the shareholders. But Henry finally won through and, as a consolation to the contestants, we directed Mr. Blackwell to do the job on the thickest paper in his shop. The original volume proved to be so bulky that it became known as the "Big Book." Of course the idea was to convince the alcoholic purchaser that he was indeed getting his money's worth!

Very soon Henry, Ruth, Dorothy S. of Cleveland, and I wheeled up to Mr. Blackwell's big printing plant at Cornwall, New York, and checked in at the town's only hotel. We brought with us the mangled but precious printer's copy of *Alcoholics Anonymous*. When the Cornwall manager saw the mess our book was in he was so dismayed that he almost sent us home to make a fresh typing of the whole business. But salesman Henry prevailed upon him to try to make galleys, and day after day we corrected these as they issued from the shop.

By now our money supply was gone. The hotel bill was going to be twice as much as the cash we had. To Ruth and Dorothy and me this seemed pretty awkward, but Henry stated confidently that God would provide. Henry had lately adopted the comforting theory that if God wanted something done we only had to keep running up bills which eventually He would pay. This was a heartening example of faith, but it did leave the practical question of who would be God's agent in the matter of the money. Our stockholders were already loaded for every share they could take; they had had it. Maybe good old Charlie Towns would be the man. So it fell my lot to go to New York and put the touch on him. Mr. Towns was not too favorably impressed when he heard where we stood, but he came through with the hotel bill and about a hundred dollars to spare.

We took a cheerful view. Soon the book plates would be made, the presses would roll, and 5,000 books would be ready when the *Reader's Digest* piece broke. Henry and Ruth and I divided the last hundred dollars among us and we all returned to New York in high spirits. We could be patient now; prosperity was just around the corner.

I will never know why, in all the time during which the book was in preparation, none of us had thought of getting in touch with the *Reader's Digest*. Somehow the question of timing their article with the appearance of our book had not occurred to us. As Henry and I again rode up the parkway toward Pleasantville, we wondered about this. We estimated it might take them several months to produce the promised piece. But why worry; it was just a question of time, anyhow.

We were greeted by Managing Editor Payne at the door of his office. He did not remember exactly who we were. Henry gaily remarked, "Well, Mr. Managing Editor, we are all ready to shoot." And Mr. Payne, nonplused, weakly replied, "Shoot what?" Hastily we brought him up to date, and the memory of our visit during the previous fall came back with a rush. "Of course, of course," he said. "I remember you now. You are the representatives of that fellowship of alcoholics. You wanted a *Digest* piece about your society and the book you are preparing. You will remember that I told you I had to check this up with our editorial staff. Well, I did. To my surprise, they did not like the idea at all. They did not think there would be much interest in a society of alcoholics. And they thought besides that the whole business would be controversial, medically and religiously speaking. And worst of all, I forgot to let you people know. I am so sorry." [12]

This was shattering. Even the buoyant Henry was sunk. We protested, but it was no use. This was it. The book enterprise had collapsed.

Riding home in a daze, we wondered how we could face the groups, the stockholders, the printer, and Mr. Towns. The A.A. fellowship then had just about a hundred members. Twenty-eight books had been promised to those who wrote stories, and forty-nine had to be sent free to the alcoholic stockholders and their friends who had subscribed. Soon 5,000 books would land in Cornwall's warehouse with no market whatever. Maybe the printer would have to take them over to protect himself. We had not a cent left and certainly our $500 shoestring payment would not be much compensation to Mr. Blackwell. And what would the Trustees say? Maybe they had been right after all. What would we do? How could we face up to this catastrophe? We had no ideas at all.

Our homecoming, however, proved less distressing than we expected. A few of our people grumbled and said, "We told you so," but nearly everybody else took a sporting attitude and asked what had become of our faith. The Trustees were mighty nice about it, too; they suggested weekly meetings to consider ways and means of getting the book into circulation. Most cheering of all, Mr. Edward Blackwell said he had no intention of turning our book over to an outside publisher. He would see us through, he said. And so he did, for many an uncertain month and year to come.

It was obvious that we had to get some publicity in order to move those books. We tried magazine after magazine with no result. While

[12] As many are aware, no publication over the years has since been more generous to A.A. than the *Reader's Digest*. It has run many articles in which A.A. has been featured or prominently mentioned and it has given us invaluable help in translating our literature into foreign tongues. The late Fulton Oursler was both a Senior Editor of the *Digest* and a Trustee for Alcoholics Anonymous.

we were in the midst of these efforts, Cornwall Press told us the printing was ready. It was April, 1939. Henry, absolutely broke, was trying to get work. Ruth, living at home, was given meaningless stock certificates in the defunct Works Publishing as pay. She cheerfully accepted these and never slackened her efforts. All of us were going into debt just for living expenses.

Then, on May first, fresh calamity fell upon 182 Clinton Street. Lois and I had been living in a house which belonged to her parents before their death. The bank had taken it over and rented it to us for a nominal sum. The mortgage was so big the bank had found great difficulty in selling the place, so we had been able to stay there several years. But at this moment they found a purchaser and we had to get out. From its four floors the old brick house disgorged its furniture into a moving van. The warehouse had to pay the mover, since we could not. All our worldly goods were in hock with the warehouseman, and they were to stay that way for two years more. Where could we go?

Friends rallied around. A small fund, just about the first money our Foundation ever had, was set up as the "Lois W. Home Replacement Fund." To this, surrounding A.A. families began to make tiny contributions. Small, of course, because everybody was broke. Out of this, the Trustees began to pay Lois and me $50 a month. A newer member, Jack C. loaned us a battered Lincoln automobile. But where would we live? The question was settled by Howard and his mother, who owned a summer camp on a remote lake in western New Jersey. Here we stayed until snow flew in November. This interval gave us the needed opportunity to revive the bankrupt book project.

Shortly after the publication of *Alcoholics Anonymous* in April, Dr. Fosdick had beautifully reviewed the book, just as he promised. His review was reprinted, chiefly by religious periodicals, but it had no influence so far as book orders were concerned. We were delighted when the *New York Times* also gave us a review. But nothing happened. We still had no book orders. Right through the summer of

1939 all attempts to get national magazines to print pieces about Alcoholics Anonymous failed.

Then one day Morgan, our Irishman, came up with an idea. He said, "I used to be in the ad business and had a good deal to do with radio. I know Gabriel Heatter very well, and I'm sure he would give us a hand." So off he went to see Heatter and soon he was back, all smiles. "Sure thing," he said. "Gabriel is going to give us a lift." In those days Mr. Heatter was on a national network with a program called "We The People," consisting of three-minute interviews. Our story appealed to him at once. He planned to interview Morgan, quickly sketching his fall and rise, and then to elicit from him some facts about A.A. and to put in a plug for the book. This, we thought, was simply *great*. And on a national hookup, too.

Henry's promotional instincts were instantly revived. In connection with the broadcast he wanted to send a shower of postal cards to all physicians east of the Mississippi River. There were said to be some 20,000 of them. The card would exhort them to listen to the Heatter broadcast and buy the book *Alcoholics Anonymous,* "a sure cure for alcoholism." Here was another wonderful idea; all we needed was money. Among our new prospects a couple of the more prosperous variety had just turned up. Henry went after them, brandishing his pad of Works Publishing stock certificates. They did not want any stock, but they would take promissory notes signed by the defunct publishing company and personally endorsed by Henry and me. Quite unbelievably, Henry extracted $500 from them. A list of all physicians in the eastern United States was obtained from an agency which also designed the post card mailing. This made us feel sure of at least a few thousand book orders.

Gabriel Heatter meanwhile had set a date for Morgan's appearance before his microphone. It was only a week away, and we were very excited. With some of the past fiascos in mind, somebody sounded a note of caution: What if the lately released asylum inmate Morgan should be drunk the day of the broadcast! Hard experience told us this was a real possibility. How could such a calamity be averted?

Very gently we suggested to a resentful Morgan that he would have to be locked up somewhere until the night of the broadcast. It took all of salesman Henry's wiles to put this one over, but he did. How and where we would lock him up was the only remaining question. Henry, with full faith now restored, solemnly declared that "God would provide." He recalled that one of the prosperous newcomers had a membership in the Downtown Athletic Club. If we paid the charges, could a double room be arranged? Grumbling loudly, Morgan was conducted into captivity. For several days we took turns staying with him right around the clock, never letting him get out of our sight.

The postal card shower to the doctors was on its way and all was ready. Why had we not thought of radio before? This would be only a starter. Once more, talk was heard of book sales in carload lots. An hour before broadcast time, our whole membership and their families gathered about their radios to wait for the great moment. Sure enough, Gabriel spoke up right on the dot. Sighs of relief went up in every New York member's home when Morgan's voice was heard. He had hit the deadline without getting drunk. It was a heart-stirring three minutes. Gabriel Heatter saw to that, and he was well assisted by Morgan, who was no slouch as a radio man. We figured that the impact on America would be terrific, especially on the doctors who had already got our 20,000 postal cards. Within three days we figured that Post Office Box 658, Church Street Annex, New York City, would be flooded with pleas for help and book orders.

By a great effort of self-restraint we kept away for three whole days. Then we marched up the steps of the post office and headed straight for our box, each of us armed with a couple of suitcases to bring home some part of the first great influx. Peering through the glass, we were stunned to see less than a handful of postal cards. Henry, the optimist, rallied to exclaim, "Think nothing of it, folks. They just couldn't get them into the box. I'll bet they've got a whole mailbag full out back." The mail clerk handed us exactly twelve cards. Henry said to the clerk, "There must be a lot more.

Where are they?" And the clerk replied, "This is all there is, sir." Sick clear through, we looked through the twelve replies. Some ribbed us unmercifully. Others, evidently inscribed by medics in their cups, were totally illegible. The two remaining cards were orders for the book *Alcoholics Anonymous.* Radio as a medium lost considerable stature in our eyes and another $500 had gone down the drain.

A few days later our landlord in Newark got really tough. The sheriff appeared with an eviction notice. So in a near-by office building we found a tiny room barely big enough to contain Henry's large desk, his overstuffed chair, a couple of file cases, and Ruth and her typewriter. For callers there was standing room only. Somehow we made a small down payment on the rent, wondering how many months it would be before the sheriff showed up once more.

Howard's summer camp, facing the untroubled waters of the lake, was a wonderful place to relax and recoup. Besides, we had fifty dollars a month and a car to get around in. But what would happen when winter came? Lois began to wonder if she should not have kept her department store job. When prospects for the book had looked the brightest, I had persuaded her to quit. There was now nothing left but to press on. Somehow that book project must be revived. I confess we often reflected that after nearly four years of my sobriety we had no prospect of any income or the certainty of any place to live.

By July Henry had found himself a job, and so the revival of the book project was left pretty much up to Ruth and me. She was still on a theoretical salary of $25 a week, but that now consisted of a weekly ration of one Works Publishing stock certificate, par $25. Not a cent of cash could we give her. It wasn't until the following October that we could pay her anything.

One day in July I went into New York City, where I visited Mr. Charles Towns. As in the case of Mr. Blackwell of Cornwall Press, we owed Charlie plenty of money. But both men had cheerfully gone along. As I stepped off the elevator onto the hospital roof garden, Charlie greeted me with a broad smile. He had been raising heaven and earth to get publicity for us and had succeeded. He had known

Morris Markey, a well-known feature writer, for years. Intrigued with the story of A.A., Mr. Markey had approached Fulton Oursler, then editor of *Liberty* magazine. That great editor, writer, and friend-to-be had instantly seen the possibilities and had commissioned Morris Markey to do a piece. "So," inquired Charlie, "when can you go to York with Morris?"

To our great delight, Morris soon hammered out an article which he titled "Alcoholics and God." It was to appear in the September issue of *Liberty*. This time we really hoped and believed that we had turned the corner, and indeed we had.

But it would be October before we could get book orders as a result of the coming piece. What were we to do for money meanwhile? The rent would have to be paid and something ought to be done for Messrs. Blackwell, Towns, and certain other creditors. We simply had to find at least a thousand dollars.

One of our New York A.A.'s, Bert T., had a fashionable tailoring shop on Fifth Avenue which he had inherited from his father. But Bert's drinking had pretty nearly demolished the business and it was still going downhill. I phoned Bert and told him what we needed. When I said that *Liberty* would surely print a piece in September, he said, "Are you *really* sure this time? After all, you and Henry were awfully sure about the *Reader's Digest* piece. But come on down. Maybe I can do something."

Bert's clothing clients included many wealthy customers. Scanning the list, he chose one whom we shall call Mr. G.

Bert said, "Now here's a man who knows all about us. He is extremely interested in the alcohol problem, though I must admit he is on the bone-dry side of the argument." When I expressed doubt about accepting help from a dry crusader, Bert wryly remarked, "Listen, Bill, this is no time to quibble. We have got to get a thousand dollars from anybody who will give it to us." Bert went to the phone and asked for long distance. At first, he boldly asked Mr. G. for a contribution. Mr. G. was uncertain. Then Bert told his customer about Works Publishing, which at the moment had a large inventory of books but little cash. The *Liberty* piece, however, would bring in plenty of orders. Would Mr. G. care to buy some stock? Mr. G. was still more dubious. Then Bert proposed that Mr. G. make Works Publishing a loan. After all, the company had a large inventory of valuable books. Upon learning the true state of Works Publishing, Mr. G. emphatically declined. Bert tried once more. "Mr. G.," Bert said, "would you take the promissory note of Works Publishing for a thousand dollars if I endorsed it? As you know, I have a fine business right here on Fifth Avenue."

"Most certainly," said Mr. G., "I will take such a note if you endorse it. Send it right down and I'll be delighted to send you the money." This was a real godsend, which probably saved the book company, for it kept us going until the late fall of 1939. Bert had hocked his own business, virtually bankrupt by then, to save the book *Alcoholics Anonymous.* This was a friend indeed.

In September, 1939, the *Liberty* piece hit the newsstands. It was a bit lurid, and we thought the title, "Alcoholics and God," would scare off plenty of prospects. Maybe it did, but several hundred alcoholics and their families were not scared. *Liberty* magazine received 800 urgent pleas for help, which were promptly turned over to Ruth and me. She wrote fine personal letters to every one of them, enclosing a leaflet which described the A.A. book. The response was wonderful Several hundred books sold at once at full retail price of $3.50. Even more importantly, we struck up a correspondence with alcoholics, their friends, and their families all over the country. Ruth could at last draw a few dollars a week for herself. And all those moving appeals for assistance had made us forget our own troubles. Looking after all those new people by mail and relating them in some cases to each other and in others to the groups in Akron, New York, and Cleveland became our chief occupation until early 1940. Shortly after the *Liberty* article came out, Cleveland's *Plain Dealer* ran its great series of pieces, as already described. This brought in new book orders and new problems by scores. Alcoholics Anonymous was on the march, out of its infancy into adolescence.

As noted earlier, Lois and I moved to the home of Bob and Mag in Monsey, New York, to spend the winter of 1939 and the early spring of 1940. A little after this we moved to a friend's apartment in New York City, then briefly to a room in Greenwich Village, and finally to A.A.'s first clubhouse, "The Old Twenty-Fourth," where we remained until the spring of 1941. The contributors to the "Lois W. Home Replacement Fund" kept up their good work. Thus we were comfortable enough, and our happiness grew as we watched A.A. unfold.

One sad incident marred the early spring of 1940. Not knowing where any of us might live in the future, we had chosen Box 658 at one of New York's downtown post offices as the most central point of the whole metropolitan area, Long Island and New Jersey included. It now seemed right for us to establish a small office near this box. Backed by the book stockholders and by Ruth, I made this proposal. Henry, whose job took him into western New Jersey, objected violently. He wanted to take the book business and Ruth wherever he went. His job was not going too well, and he was on what we nowadays call a "dry bender." The more we insisted the more adamant and violent he became. He was heavily beset with other problems, too. At length he broke down completely and went on a terrific bender after four years of sobriety. He never again showed any real sign of recovery, and he went on drinking until his death recently. Considering what he had done for the book, and the further fact that he was one of our first New York members, this was hard to take. My own sponsor, Ebby, also continued his drinking and hadn't, as yet, shown any desire to stop. Our whole group shivered and we asked ourselves, "If stalwarts like these can relapse, what is going to become of the rest of us?" Actually, though, the effect was to make each one of us more vigilant. So no wave of slips followed in the wake of poor Henry's collapse.

Our expansion had been immensely accelerated by the *Liberty* piece and the frantic growth at Cleveland. Tiny beginnings had been made in many other towns and cities, which we denoted by placing pins in our office wall map. By early 1940 we could estimate that about 800 recoveries had been made. This number was a big jump from the figure of 100 at the time the book was published in April of the year before. The book had expressed the hope that someday A.A. travelers would find a group at every destination. That hope had begun to turn into reality.

All through the uncertain year of 1939 our nonalcoholic friends of the Board of Trustees had stayed with us. Another New York A.A. member, Bill R., had been made a Trustee, and Mr. A. LeRoy Chipman, who had been keeping an eye on us all along, now joined up himself and became the Foundation's treasurer. Nevertheless, the treasury itself was just as empty as before.

In 1940 we saw the establishment of the first clubhouse and the opening of the first rest farm.

The New York groupers had been complaining that weekly meetings in a rented parlor at Steinway Hall were not enough. We had to be together more. We needed something homelike, maybe a club. The idea caught on, and two of the elders, Howard and Bert, promptly spotted just the thing at 334½ West Twenty-fourth Street and personally guaranteed the rent. Tom B., another stalwart, did the same thing for the club's light, heat, and telephone.

Originally the club building had been a stable in the back yards of two brick houses. It opened onto the street by a narrow covered-over alley. Years earlier the horses had given way to artists, who had paneled the place and trimmed it up nicely. The quarters had become too small for the Illustrators Club, so they moved out and we A.A.'s moved in. The lower floor could hold a fair-sized meeting; the upper floor had a recreation room and two tiny bedrooms. One of these was soon to house old Tom, our famous first caretaker; and shortly thereafter Lois and I moved into the other one to stay for about a year. Our association there with others like Herb and Ila, Bobbie and Dick, Wilbur and Ruth, Henry and Lillian, and many another will always be unforgettable.

Of course the club promptly had its own peculiar troubles, just as hundreds of others have since had. But like most A.A. clubs this first one did us far more good than harm, especially after we learned that the club had to be on the side lines and could not be managed by the A.A. groups as such. The Old Twenty-Fourth Street Club witnessed much of A.A.'s early history. Still in busy operation, it is now a landmark visited by members from all over the world. Similar and far larger clubs were started in Philadelphia and Minneapolis later in 1940. Scores and scores of clubrooms and clubhouses now dot our landscape. Some of the more elegant ones, especially those in Texas, have to be seen to be believed.

Meanwhile up in the hills of Connecticut an interesting development had been taking place. A group of farms there belonged to a dear lady affectionately known to countless A.A.'s as Sister Francis. This wonderfully good soul out of her own pocket had operated these farms as a series of charities—one for the aged, one for children, and one for any wayfarer who passed by. In the summer of 1939 our New York member Marty had sponsored a prospect called Nona W. Nona, one of A.A.'s first women, had already enjoyed the farm's hospitality and eagerly conducted a party of us to Connecticut, where we met Sister Francis.

That good lady had fallen on hard times, and only one farm remained. She called it the Ministry of the High Watch. Sister Francis seemed to be as delighted with us as we were with her. She offered us full use of the place if some of us would create a board of trustees to look after it. Laughingly, she has since admitted that she was shocked as well as captivated by her early alcoholic visitors. Until then, she reflected, the greatest scandal in her family had been the time when in Rome her sister was seen in the company of an Italian Army officer without a chaperon! But Sister Francis made a ready adjustment to us. With each passing year we A.A.'s have loved her more, and she has returned our affection.

The rest farm which has come into being as a result of Sister Francis' gift is a charming place which, with its cabins, can accommodate more than twenty guests. It is a wonderful spot to send anyone who needs extra time to recuperate after hospitalization and many A.A.'s use it for vacations. Similar retreats can be found today throughout the length and breadth of our fellowship. Though they are not strictly A.A. enterprises, they do give many of us fine support and refreshment. On behalf of everyone I here set down our gratitude to Sister Francis and her much altered Ministry of the High Watch.

At the February, 1940, meeting, "Uncle Dick" Richardson turned up beaming and mysterious. Presently he broke the news that Mr. John D. Rockefeller, Jr., who had not been heard from since 1937, had been following our progress with intense interest.

Mr. Rockefeller had decided that he wanted to do something for Alcoholics Anonymous. He proposed a dinner meeting to which he would invite several hundred of his own friends and acquaintances, so that they might glimpse the beginnings of our remarkable fellowship. Uncle Dick produced the list of the people who were invited. It contained some 400 names, a veritable constellation of New York's prominent and wealthy. Anybody could see that their total financial worth might easily be a billion dollars. To us alcoholics it appeared that Mr. Rockefeller had at last changed his mind and that our money troubles would soon be a thing of the past. At this point we were comforted to learn that Dick Richardson's fund-raising friend, Mr. Carlton Sherwood, had been using his influence and good offices to bring about this promising prospect.

There is a reference to Mr. Rockefeller's dinner earlier in this book, but I think that a fuller description of that memorable event ought to go into our records. For this was the moment at which A.A.'s Tradition of declining outside contributions began to take definite shape and form.

On the evening of February 8, 1940, the dinner party foregathered at the Union Club in New York, a club even more conservative than the Union League itself. Some 75 of the 400 who were invited turned up. They looked like a fine lot of men. But as they gathered in the dining hall most of them did wear rather puzzled expressions. Obviously, they could not quite make out what Alcoholics Anonymous was all about. A few feared that A.A. was another scheme to dry up the whole world and said so. To take care of any questions, we had planted a New York A.A. member at each table. During dinner this thawed things out in a hurry. There were many queries, and some of our answers amazed the notables. At one table sat our hero, Morgan, as impeccably dressed as a collar-ad boy. One gray-haired banker inquired, "Mr. R., what institution are you with?" Morgan grinned and replied, "Well, sir, I am not with any institution at the moment. Nine months ago, however, I was a patient in Greystone asylum." The interest at that table took a sharp upturn.

Dr. Bob had arrived with an Akron old-timer, Paul, and had also brought Clarence, a founder of the flourishing Cleveland group. Dr. Russell Blaisdell, who during the previous fall had let us work with patients in his state asylum at Rockland, New York, was there, along with our good Dr. Silkworth.

Dr. Bob and I were scheduled to speak. Several other alcoholics were to handle a question-and-answer period, and the entire proceedings were to be backed up by Dr. Harry Emerson Fosdick, representing religion, and Dr. Foster Kennedy, the world-renowned neurologist, who would speak for medicine. We should here take special note of these two wonderful friends. Dr. Fosdick had been the very first clergyman to recognize us. Early in 1939 he had seen the prepublication copy of the book *Alcoholics Anonymous* and had at once volunteered to review it. This magnificent review, shown in the Appendix [13] of this volume, well illustrates his deep understanding and high approval of our fellowship. Likewise, Dr. Kennedy, our first friend in the field of neurology, never missed an opportunity to declare his great faith in A.A.[14]

Mr. Rockefeller himself had been taken ill suddenly and could not come. His son, Nelson, whom we all liked immensely, did the honors as chairman for the occasion. I was seated between Dr. Blaisdell and

[13] Dr. Fosdick's review appears in Appendix E:d.
[14] See Appendix E:c, Dr. Kennedy's remarks before the Medical Society of the State of New York.

Nelson Rockefeller. Directly in front of me was Wendell Willkie. The dinner was squab on toast. For a bunch of ex-drunks, we were doing remarkably well. We wondered how Mr. Rockefeller had dared to go so far out on a limb for an obscure and struggling fellowship of alcoholics.

After dinner Mr. Nelson Rockefeller rose to his feet. He expressed his father's regret for being unable to attend. He told how deeply Mr. John D., Jr., had been affected by his experience with this society of Alcoholics Anonymous. Promising a highly interesting evening, Nelson Rockefeller began to introduce the speakers. Dr. Fosdick gave us a most wonderful testimonial and expressed complete confidence in our future. Dr. Kennedy warmly endorsed us and read a letter of protest he had written to the *Journal of the American Medical Association* because in their review of the book *Alcoholics Anonymous* they had somewhat ridiculed us. Dr. Bob spoke briefly, and I gave a rapid account of my own experience as a drinker, my recovery, and the subsequent history of our fellowship. As we watched the faces of the guests, it was evident that we had captured their sympathetic interest. Great influence and great wealth were soon to be at our disposal. Weariness and worry were to be things of the past.

Finally the big moment came. Mr. Nelson Rockefeller, visibly moved, got to his feet once more. On behalf of his father he thanked us all for coming. He reiterated that few more affecting things than Alcoholics Anonymous had ever crossed his father's life. His father would be delighted, Nelson said, to know how many guests had availed themselves of the chance to see the beginnings of this most promising adventure of Alcoholics Anonymous.

Breathlessly we waited for the climax—the matter of money. Nelson Rockefeller obliged us. Continuing, he said, "Gentlemen, you can all see that this is a work of good will. Its power lies in the fact that one member carries the good message to the next, without any thought of financial income or reward. Therefore, it is our belief that Alcoholics Anonymous should be self-supporting so far as money is concerned. It needs only our good will." Whereupon the guests clapped lustily, and after cordial handshakes and good-bys all around, the whole billion dollars' worth of them walked out the door.

We were dazed. Why had Mr. Rockefeller gone to all that trouble—just for this? We simply could not figure it out. But a few days later we began to see, and as time passes Alcoholics Anonymous sees ever more clearly what he meant and what he did.

Dick Richardson had transcripts of all the talks that had been made at the dinner, and he asked me to condense and edit them. This really meant editing Dr. Bob and me, for who would edit Dr. Harry Emerson Fosdick and Dr. Foster Kennedy? Dick said that Mr. Rockefeller wanted to buy 400 books, and we let him have them at a whopping discount, too: one dollar each. He wanted to send one to every guest on the dinner list, along with a pamphlet containing the talks given at the dinner. And Mr. Rockefeller planned to write each dinner guest a personal letter, a copy of which would be presently shown us.

Mr. Rockefeller's letter, which was addressed to all who came to the dinner as well as to those who did not, reiterated his high confidence in Alcoholics Anonymous, the satisfaction he had in knowing that many of his friends had witnessed the start of a movement of such great promise, and his deep conviction that our society ought to be self-supporting. He followed this with a statement to the effect that a little temporary help might be needed; he, therefore, was giving Alcoholics Anonymous $1,000. In all probability this was a mild hint that the other diners might contribute modestly if they so wished.

Despite the curiosity of the press, no reporters had been allowed at the dinner. This was understandable, for Mr. Rockefeller was certainly taking chances. Had any of us alcoholics turned up stewed, the whole affair would have collapsed ignominiously. But as soon as it was seen that all had gone well, we were put in touch with the firm of Ivy Lee, Mr. Rockefeller's publicity consultants, and together we drafted a statement to the press.

The ensuing publicity was favorable and widespread. The news wires carried the news of Mr. Rockefeller's dinner all over the world.

A few of the stories that appeared were somewhat lurid and ran under startling headlines. One headline informed the public: "John D. Rockefeller dines toss-pots." But all the stories plugged A.A. just the same; even the tabloids gave us the glad hand. The total effect was to give Alcoholics Anonymous a public status of dignity and worth. Thus encouraged, considerable numbers of people went to their bookstores to buy the A.A. book. Orders poured in and our financial difficulties were much eased. Hundreds of requests for help came from alcoholics and their families all over the nation. These names were added to our growing list of correspondents that we hoped to reach later by personal contact as our fellowship grew. The awful letdown which had followed the departure of the dinner guests was now forgotten.

At about this time our trusteeship began to be enlarged. Mr. Robert Shaw, a lawyer and friend of Uncle Dick's, was elected to the Board. Two New Yorkers, my friends Howard and Bert, were also named. As time passed, these were joined by Tom B. and Dick S. Dick had been one of the original Akronites and was now living in New York. There was also Tom K., a hard-working and conservative Jerseyman. Somewhat later more nonalcoholics, notably Bernard Smith and Leonard Harrison, took up their long season of service with us.

The Board of Trustees conceived the idea of soliciting the dinner guests for contributions. Since Mr. Rockefeller had made a token gift of $1,000, it was supposed that the solicitation would not have any large money result. But it certainly might help. Mr. Rockefeller consented, and an appeal was directed to the dinner list. As we expected, no contribution was large, but the donations were fairly numerous. The smallest check was for $10 and the highest was for $300 (from a gentleman who had an alcoholic brother). The total of these gifts amounted to about $2,000 and this, plus Mr. Rockefeller's gift of $1,000, put our hitherto empty Foundation in funds for the first time.

Money-wise, Dr. Bob and I were still in a rather bad way. We were therefore allotted $30 a week, and enough was on hand to keep this up for a year. Thereafter the dinner guests were solicited annually and the proceeds were always divided in the same way. Four years later we were able to write Mr. Rockefeller and his friends of the Union Club dinner that we needed no more funds. By then royalties from the book were giving Dr. Bob and me the help we needed, and the A.A. groups had begun to pick up the load of supporting the Headquarters office. At that point the A.A. Tradition of "no outside contributions" went into full force and effect. Mr. Rockefeller and his friends had given us something more valuable than money. They had put A.A. on the map.

Now to flash back for a moment to the spring of 1940. Over Henry's strong objections, we had moved from the tiny cubicle of an office in Newark to one slightly larger at 30 Vesey Street, New York City, next door to our downtown post office box. Ruth and I set about answering the mass of inquiries that came in the wake of the Rockefeller dinner and the resulting publicity. Many new A.A. groups took shape as travelers from the older centers, armed with lists of prospects, visited new locations. The struggles at these distant outposts were quickly reflected in letters asking for advice on the growing pains and problems of the new groups. Almost every week we happily added a new pin to our wall map to mark another group in formation.

The sales of the A.A. book steadily increased, and we could now meet the cost of rent, postage, and supplies, and best of all we could pay Ruth a fair salary. Lois and I were living rent-free at the Old Twenty-Fourth Street Club, and we were able to get along nicely on the proceeds of the Rockefeller dinner and gifts still being made to the "Lois W. Home Replacement Fund" in the Foundation. Everybody began to breathe easier.

The affairs of Works Publishing, however, were still in pretty sketchy shape. It had never been incorporated, and the only evidence of its existence were the stock certificates that Henry and I had manufactured, the books in the warehouse, and the canceled checks that gave a rough idea of how the money had been spent. Four hundred shares of stock, to be equally divided between Henry and me, had never been issued and *could* not be issued, under our original agreement, until the cash subscribers had received all their money back.

When they heard that the book was making money, some of the cash subscribers, including even Charlie Towns, began to get restless. They wanted to know why all of the profits of the book were being spent to finance a Headquarters for A.A. We replied that there was not any other way; would they like to see all those pleas for help thrown in the wastebasket? But a few still insisted on getting their money back, and something had to be done.

Therefore Ruth and I set about making Works Publishing's first report to its stockholders. We outlined the history of the book project and painted a rosy picture for the future. From the mass of check stubs, old bills, and receipts we made an approximate accounting. As I remember, the publishing company had shown a profit of about $3,000, which had all been spent on A.A. work at the office.

Again we turned to our trusted pad of blank stock certificates. On a number of these we wrote: "Works Publishing, Inc., *Preferred Stock,* par value $100."

Equipped with these certificates, I went off to Washington. The new A.A. group there included some well-to-do members: Bill E., Hardin C., and Bill A. They cheerfully bought these strange and irregular stock certificates in the amount of about $3,000. Thus we satisfied a few of the grumbling stockholders and gratefully handed to Mr. Charles Towns all of the money which he had advanced to make the book project possible. He was delighted and so were we.

In this period, one of our nonalcoholic friends performed an outstanding service for us. This was accountant West, of West, Flint & Co., a lifelong associate of Dick Richardson. He saw that Works Publishing was properly incorporated and he personally audited its affairs and those of the Foundation from our beginnings in 1938. Ruth had had no time to keep books, and I did not know how. So a thorough CPA audit of the book company proved to be a real job. The tireless Mr. West spent days and days at it, without pay. When this difficult job of unscrambling our affairs was completed, we felt we could ask no more of Mr. West. From that point on, Wilbur S., a CPA as well as an early A.A., took over the job of keeping our records in shape. He did this for a long time gratis, and even today I doubt if we pay him enough.

By 1940 we had begun to see that the A.A. book should belong to our society itself. Its shares should not be forever scattered among forty-nine subscribers, Ruth Hock, Henry, and me. If the Foundation could acquire these outstanding shares, the book could be placed in trust for A.A. as a whole. The proceeds of the book would become tax-free if the cash shareholders were paid off, and they could no longer kick about the book's income being used to run the A.A. office.

Trustee A. LeRoy Chipman conceived the idea of borrowing enough money from Mr. Rockefeller, two of his sons, and the dinner guests to clear away certain debts and to buy all Works Publishing's shares (except Henry's and mine) from the cash subscribers at par. Every one of the cash subscribers gladly consented to this; they were happy to get out even. Mr. Chipman thereupon raised a total of $8,000 dollars, to be repaid to Mr. Rockefeller and the others out of book profits at a later date. The subscribers turned in their shares, received their money, and placed our Foundation in possession of a one-third interest in Works Publishing. A few of the subscribers, both alcoholic and nonalcoholic, were extra generous. Some sent all, and some half, of the money they had received back to the Foundation as gifts.

That left two-thirds interest in Works Publishing still coming to Henry and me. Seeing the necessity of the situation, I agreed to turn my 200 shares over to the Foundation. But poor Henry, still drinking, was not easily convinced. For a long time he resisted all our pleas. One day, completely broke and very shaky, he turned up at the Vesey Street office. He pointed out that most of our office furniture still belonged to him, particularly the huge desk and the overstuffed chair. This gave us an idea. Supposing, we said, that the Foundation would buy his furniture for, say, $200, would he then turn his Works Publishing stock over to the Trustees?

Henry finally consented and signed the necessary paper promising to do this. As a matter of fact we had once before allowed Henry money on his furniture in order to help him out. But the Trustees gravely produced still another $200; Henry turned in his stock; I turned in mine; and that is how the society of Alcoholics Anonymous, through its Trustees, came to own the Big Book.

There was a slow but steady growth of our society during 1940. As new groups were started, local newspapers began to print articles about this strange new fellowship. These pieces helped us greatly. Lois and Ruth each had started scrapbooks, and they happily pasted up the clippings as they came in. Groups were well under way in big towns like Boston, Philadelphia, Detroit, Chicago, San Francisco, and Los Angeles, and many smaller towns had equally promising beginnings. Cleveland continued its phenomenal boom which had begun the year before. The New York clubhouse could hardly seat its meetings. In Akron Dr. Bob had begun the historic partnership with Sister Ignatia in St. Thomas Hospital. Thus A.A. rolled along until the spring of 1941, when we could count 2,000 members, a gain of 1,200 in a single year. We thought this was good going, but actually we had not seen anything yet. We were on the threshold of the event that made Alcoholics Anonymous a national institution overnight.

Dr. A. Wiese Hammer, already champion of A.A. in Philadelphia, had drawn our fellowship to the attention of Curtis Bok, one of the owners of the *Saturday Evening Post*. At first the editorial board of the *Post* was dubious. But Mr. Bok had seen some of our Philadelphia members and had heard about their recovery at first hand; he knew whereof he spoke. And the next thing we knew Mr. Jack Alexander, a star feature writer for the *Post,* appeared at our Vesey Street office. Knowing the circulation and prestige of the *Saturday Evening Post,* we were thrown into great excitement.

Jack is an excellent reporter, and he by no means went overboard at once. The smell and taste of the Jersey rackets which he had just been investigating were still fresh to him. Seeing this, we gave him the most exhaustive briefing on Alcoholics Anonymous any writer has ever had. First he met our Trustees and New York people, and then we towed him all over the country.

Finally Jack said that he had enough; he was ready to write. But a serious difficulty arose. The *Saturday Evening Post* wanted pictures; indeed it said it *must* have them. It was all right, they said, for Dr. Bob, myself, and other alcoholics to be called by other than their real names. But pictures they *had* to have, and some of them had to be on the sensational side. We objected that this might keep people away. Finally the *Post* said, "No pictures, no article." The choice was ours, and it was a hard one. Over the protests of a good many conservative and fearful members, we told the *Post* to go ahead. It was a crucial decision which happily turned out to be the right one—that is, for the time being.

The article appeared in the March 1, 1941, issue. Jack's extensive investigation and his remarkable capacity for sympathy and rapport with us produced a piece which had immense impact. By mail and telegram a deluge of pleas for help and orders for the book *Alcoholics Anonymous*, first in hundreds and then in thousands, hit Box 658. Ruth and I laughed as we remembered the day less than two years before when the postal clerk had handed us those jeering post cards from the doctors. Pawing at random through the incoming mass of heartbreaking appeals, we found ourselves crying. What on earth could we do with them? We were really swamped.

We saw that we must have help. So we rounded up every A.A. woman and every A.A. wife who could use a typewriter. The upper floor of the Twenty-Fourth Street Club was converted into an emergency headquarters. For days Ruth and the volunteers tried to answer the ever increasing tide of mail. They were almost tempted into using form letters. But experience had shown that this would not do at all. A warm personal communication *must* be sent to every prospect and his family. The peak of the flood finally passed, but the regular correspondence traffic through Headquarters remained so great that we saw we would have to have permanent paid help. Volunteers could not handle the situation.

We also realized that these increased demands upon the office could not be met out of book income. So for the first time we asked the A.A. groups to help. Following the *Post* piece, Trustees Howard and Bert went on the road, one to Philadelphia and Washington, the other other to Akron and Cleveland. They asked that all A.A. groups contribute to a special fund in the Foundation which would be earmarked "for A.A. office expenses only." The contributions would be entirely voluntary. As a measuring stick, it was suggested that each group send in one dollar per member per year. Gradually group funds began to trickle in, and we were able to add two regular paid workers to the staff. The A.A. Tradition of self-support began to be a reality. The net book income could now go into the Foundation. Whenever the groups failed to meet office expenses this reserve fund could plug the deficit, as it frequently did for many years. The book *Alcoholics Anonymous* was not only helping to save alcoholics; it became the financial cornerstone of the Headquarters and the guarantor of our solvency.

At the end of 1941, when the group secretaries made their reports, we found that the membership had jumped to 8,000, an increase of 6,000 over 1940. We had begun to reach into Canada and into foreign lands. Everywhere we were growing rapidly. In many ways 1941 can be reckoned as the most exciting year in our history. We paid little attention to the low-lying clouds on the horizon which would soon involve us in storms. A.A. was just entering its fearful and wonderful time of adolescence, a phase which was to last almost fifteen years.

The pins on our office wall map showed scores of new groups springing up every week. Sometimes experienced A.A.'s moved away from established centers to make their homes in other cities. Such localities were the lucky ones. But in most cases the newly formed groups had no experienced guidance whatever, except for the A.A. book, an occasional traveler, and correspondence with Headquarters. Their worries and problems seemed endless. Committees quarreled, new clubs had unheard-of headaches, orators held forth, groups split wide open. Some members turned professional, selling A.A. therapy for money to new prospects. Sometimes whole groups got drunk, and local public relations went haywire. Such was the beginning of a truly frightening experience that lasted a long time.

Then in one of our larger centers the amazing story got around that the Foundation and the New York office and the book *Alcoholics Anonymous* were nothing but a huge racket for which Mr. John D. Rockefeller had foolishly fallen. At the height of this commotion a few A.A.'s set up a dinner in the city where these rumors had the largest currency. Dr. Bob and I were asked to speak. The dinner was not any too well attended and the usual good cheer seemed mysteriously lacking. When the festivities were over, the chairmen of all the groups in town conducted Dr. Bob and me to a hotel parlor. There they produced an attorney and a certified public accountant. They had been hearing awful stories about the Foundation. They had heard that the book *Alcoholics Anonymous* was making vast sums of money, that Dr. Bob and I shared profits of $64,000 the year before. They believed that I, the Wall Street promoter, had my truck backed right up to Mr. John D. Rockefeller's strongbox and had persuaded him to fill it with coin for me and my friends. The interrogating committee let us know that a member from their city had met one of our Trustees in New York who was said to have confirmed these appalling reports.

This incredible but more than half-believed fantasy hit Dr. Bob and me quite hard. Fortunately I happened to have with me a certified audit of all of our affairs from the beginning. This showed that Dr. Bob, though he had been assigned a royalty, had never received any because his money was needed for the A.A. office work. He was still on a $30-a-week stipend from the Rockefeller dinner. Like Dr. Bob I received $30 a week from the dinner guests, and since the *Post* article I had begun drawing $25 a week from the publishing company, which had seemed justified from the book sales. My total income was $55 a week. The Foundation itself still had practically no cash balance;

the group contributions coming into it were promptly spent on the office in order to carry on there.

The investigating committee's accountant read our modest financial statement aloud and testified to its correctness. The committee was crestfallen and we received an apology. The committee's chairman explained that the meeting had been called to set the record straight; that few of the committee members had actually believed the stories. He promised that he and his fellows would do all that they could to stop the spreading of these tales. But they never quite succeeded; the racket talk went on for years in that region.

It was a very good experience for Dr. Bob and me. It obliged us to carefully re-examine our status and seek the counsel of friends. This was one of the test cases out of which A.A.'s Tradition respecting professionalism and paid workers was evolved. It was certain that I could not continue full time nor Bob devote more than half his working hours to A.A. unless we both had some definite source of steady income. We could not expect the dinner guests to bolster us up indefinitely. That would be contrary to the then-forming Tradition of no contributions from the outside world. Neither could he and I receive group funds, which were already pledged to the support of the Headquarters office. Profits of the book were all going into the Foundation reserve fund and we had no business to touch them, either.

So royalties from the book, provided the sales ever got large enough, seemed to be the only answer to the problem. In this way we might be recompensed for authorship and for the labor of putting the publishing company together. But would this constitute professionalism within the meaning of our growing Tradition? Some members said that this *would* make us professionals; we would be making money out of A.A. But our experience elsewhere had begun to indicate that this was not necessarily so. Our clubs were paying for caretakers, most of them A.A. members. They were not paid anything for their Twelfth Step work, but they were recompensed as janitors and cooks. We simply had to have their full-time services. Our New York office had just engaged an alcoholic staff member, full time. Was she a "professional A.A."? Obviously not. She was being paid for special services, as a secretary.

Ever since the book project started, my own thinking had gone from one extreme to the other. Sometimes I had felt that I should hang onto my one-third stock interest and have my royalty too. I was entitled, I thought, to all the financial reward that my work on the book business justified. At other times I felt that I should not take a cent, no matter what difficulties that might cause Lois and me.

Shortly after the financial investigation episode, Father Ed Dowling, our Jesuit friend from St. Louis, turned up in New York. Still puzzled, I put the case up to him. He asked, "Do you think A.A. requires your full-time efforts?" I replied, "Yes, I think it does, perhaps indefinitely." Then he inquired, "Could you become a paid therapist, taking money for Twelfth Step work?" I told him that this issue had been settled long since. Most emphatically I could not, regardless of the consequences, nor could any other A.A. member. "Well, Bill," said Father Ed, "if you were the only one concerned, you could certainly start wearing a hair shirt and take nothing. But what about Lois? Once upon a time you made a marriage contract to support her. Suppose you put her on the charity of friends so that you can do a service organization job for A.A. free. Would that be the kind of support your marriage contract called for? I should think the royalties would be the best bet."

This meant that Dr. Bob and I must certainly never accept money for Twelfth Step work but that we could be recompensed for special services. We both accepted Father Ed's down-the-middle advice and have stuck by it ever since, and I am glad to say this status for Dr. Bob and me was later accepted as correct in principle by our entire fellowship.

In early 1942, nonalcoholic secretary Ruth Hock left us to be married, carrying the affectionate wishes of thousands of members. The work of that sturdy little pioneer of the book *Alcoholics Anonymous* and A.A.'s first Headquarters set us an example that will never be forgotten. She was replaced by Bobbie B., who became A.A.'s National Secretary number two. Bobbie's complete loyalty and devotion and her unbelievable energy and capacity for hard work were priceless helps during the confused and hazardous years which now lay ahead of us.

Just before Ruth left, a news clipping whose content was to become famous was called to our attention by a New York member, newsman Jack. It was an obituary notice from a New York paper. Underneath a routine account of the one who had died there appeared these words: "God grant us the serenity to accept the things we cannot change, courage to change the things we can, and wisdom to know the difference."

Never had we seen so much A.A. in so few words. While Ruth and I were admiring the prayer, and wondering how to use it, friend Howard walked into the office. Confirming our own ideas, he exclaimed, "We ought to print this on cards and drop one into every piece of mail that goes out of here. I'll pay for the first printing." For several years afterward we followed his suggestion, and with amazing speed the Serenity Prayer came into general use and took its place alongside our two other favorites, the Lord's Prayer and the Prayer of St. Francis.

No one can tell for sure who first wrote the Serenity Prayer. Some say it came from the early Greeks; others think it was from the pen of an anonymous English poet; still others claim it was written by an American naval officer; and Jack Alexander, who once researched the matter, attributes it to the Rev. Reinhold Niebuhr of the Union Theological Seminary. Anyhow, we have the prayer and it is said thousands of times daily. We count its writer among our great benefactors.

Our phenomenal expansion soon brought us face to face with the very important problem of public relations. The national spotlight was now on us; we had to begin dealing with the public on a large scale. Public ill will could stunt our growth or even bring it to a standstill. Public confidence could swell our ranks to numbers of which we had only dreamed before. The *Saturday Evening Post* piece had proved this. Public relations was not only a big problem but a very delicate one. Any blunders that could arouse general prejudice might prolong the suffering of many and cost the lives of some. A carefully thought-out public relations policy had to be formed and put into operation.

Prime consideration was given to our relations with medicine and religion. Under no circumstances must we get into competition with either. If we appeared to be a new religious sect, we would certainly be in trouble. And if we moved into the medical field as such, there would be more trouble. So we began to emphasize the fact that A.A. was a way of life that conflicted with no one's religious belief. We let the doctors know how much we needed hospitalization, and we suggested to psychiatrists and drying-out places the advantage of co-operating with us. At all times, religion would be the province of the individual and of the clergymen, and the practice of medicine would be for our friends the doctors. As alcoholic laymen, we were simply supplying the much-needed and long-lost missing link.

These public relations attitudes have been maintained over the years since, and they have brought heart-warming results. Today we have the unqualified support of nearly every religious denomination. Most medical practitioners who understand A.A. send their alcoholic patients to us. Our members speak frequently before religious gatherings and medical societies. And the men of medicine and religion are often seen at A.A.'s open meetings.

But medicine and religion, important as they are, proved to be only a fraction of our total public relations problem. We also had to determine how best to co-operate with the press, radio, motion pictures, and more recently television; how to deal with employers who wanted special help; what would be the right attitude toward the field of alcohol education, research, and rehabilitation, private and public. What would we say to prisons and hospitals who wanted A.A. groups within their walls? What were we to tell A.A.'s who went into some of these fields and who were then tempted to capitalize publicly upon the A.A. name for advertising or fund raising? What would we say or do if A.A. were ever widely exploited, defamed, or attacked by outsiders? Workable solutions to all these and many more such problems had to be found or A.A. might suffer serious consequences.

Finding answers to these public relations puzzlers has been a long process. After much trial and error, sometimes punctuated by painful mistakes, the attitudes and practices that would work best for us emerged. The basic ones can be seen today in the A.A. Traditions: 100 per cent anonymity at the public level; no use of the A.A. name for the benefit of other causes, however worthy; no endorsements or alliances; the carrying of the message as the single purpose for Alcoholics Anonymous; no professionalism; public relations by the principle of attraction rather than promotion—these were some of the hard-learned lessons.

It was natural that our Board of Trustees and the Headquarters office became the focal point around which the A.A. Traditions were formed. Problems of every description poured in upon us, but by 1945 a considerable degree of order had come out of what had been a chaotic situation. On all sides the membership of our society asked for the experience and guidance of the New York office in solving their problems. Things finally began to run so smoothly that the average A.A. member has taken our world service record for granted. Until recently these Headquarters services were largely invisible to him. Nevertheless, this unseen activity has surely been responsible for much of our growth and unity.

Over the years the functioning of the Foundation, the wide use of the A.A. book, the expansion of pamphlet literature, the answering of thousands of pleas for help, the response to requests for guidance on group problems, the working out of our relations with the public— all these constituted a growing service to the whole world of A.A. At long last our society really had begun to function as a whole.

The 1941-1945 period brought still other developments. Our downtown Vesey Street office was moved to 415 Lexington Avenue, just opposite Grand Central Station. We made this move because the need for serving the many A.A. travelers through New York had become urgent. Our new location near Grand Central brought us into contact with visitors who, for the first time, began to see Alcoholics Anonymous as a vision for the whole world. Thousands of A.A.'s, their families, their friends, their clergymen, their doctors, and their employers have since visited the New York Headquarters.

The growth of Alcoholics Anonymous continued at a pace which was to us sometimes staggering. By almost geometrical progression the multiplication went on year after year. We no longer counted by thousands; we began to reckon by tens of thousands.

But this was not the whole story. For the first time we had begun to sense that the character of A.A. was changing. We were beginning to have success with milder alcoholics and even some potential alcoholics. In the first years, those of us who sobered up in A.A. had been grim and utterly hopeless cases, almost without exception. But now younger folks began to appear. Lots of people turned up who still had jobs and homes and health and even good social standing. These in their turn were able to persuade others like themselves of the need for A.A. Of course it was necessary for these types of newcomers to hit bottom emotionally. But we found they did not have to hit every possible bottom there was in order to admit that they were licked. We began to develop a conscious technique of "raising the bottom" and hitting them with it. When one of these mild cases arrived at the conviction that he already had the principal symptoms of alcoholism, that was usually enough. He "hit bottom" then and there and so was spared years of anguish.

In something of the same fashion this idea began to work out with other kinds of prospects. In the beginning we could not sober up women. They were different, they said. But when they saw other women get well, they slowly followed suit. The derelict, the rich man, the socialite—all these once thought A.A. was not for them. So did certain people of other races and tongues and creeds. But when they clearly saw the alcoholic tragedy for which they were headed, they could forget their differences and join A.A.

As these new trends came into full view, we were overjoyed. Today more than half of A.A.'s membership consists of mild cases and those who once thought they were "different."

Then the spread to foreign lands began. This development brought us a whole new set of problems to solve. Each new distant beachhead had to go through its flying-blind and pioneering period just as we had in the United States. Soon we were running into language barriers, and more and more of our pamphlet literature had to be translated into other tongues.

In addition, our foreign friends raised new and special doubts. Maybe A.A. was just a Yankee gadget that would be no good for Ireland, England, Holland, Scandinavia, Australia, and the Pacific. Since their countries were so different, maybe their alcoholics were different too. "Will A.A. work in our cultures?" they asked. We became heavily involved in correspondence, much helped by our American members in New York who could translate for us. We searched out and briefed A.A. travelers going abroad. Gradually headway was made. It was a long time, however, before we knew for sure that A.A. could cross the barriers of distance, race, creed, and language. But today, the A.A. map shows our society in more than seventy countries and U.S. possessions. We now feel sure that it is only a question of time until every alcoholic in the world may well have as good a chance to recover as we have had here in America. Serving the foreign groups has become a major Headquarters activity, although we have scarcely scratched the total possibilities so far.

Good translations of A.A. literature are ever more urgently needed. But able helpers have always turned up to meet that need. Some ten years ago, Frank M. translated the A.A. book into Spanish. He worked daytimes as interpreter for a New York importer and at night he labored over his love, the book, *Alcoholics Anonymous*. Today his translation is the foundation cornerstone for A.A. in Spanish-speaking countries. Somewhat later certain Quebec members did an equally fine piece of work, this time in French. At Oslo, we hope our Big Book will soon be published in Norwegian. Because of the language similarity, the Danes and the Swedes will also be able to read our basic text when it appears in Norwegian.

Many of our pamphlets have already been published in still other tongues—notably, German, Dutch, and Finnish. We strive constantly to cross more language barriers, thus throwing new lifelines to those who don't yet know that there is a way out.

Since A.A. was growing so fast, Headquarters had to grow, too. Thousands of group contributions and our increasing literature sales soon demanded a full-time bookeeper. Getting out our Directory of A.A. groups began to be a job rather like publishing a suburban telephone book. Letter and Kardex files began to appear in rows. More alcoholic staff members had to be engaged. As the work was divided among them, departments began to be created. Today's office is departmentalized to cover the following activities: group relations, domestic and foreign, public relations, General Service Conference, office management, mailing, packing, accounting, stenographic, and special service to prison and hospital groups.

Fortunately the office did not have to grow as fast as A.A. did. The bill would never have been paid if it had. A.A. was getting so big that we could not possibly educate all members on what Headquarters was doing. Many groups, preoccupied with their own affairs, failed to help us at all. Less than half of them contributed anything. We were plagued by constant deficits in contributions which luckily could be plugged up with money from the sale of the Big Book and our growing pamphlet literature. Without this book income we would have folded up entirely.

The year 1944 brought a vital development. In New York City a few literary and newsminded A.A.'s began to issue a monthly publication. This original group consisted of Marty, Priscilla, Lois K., Abbott, Maeve, and Kay. Besides these, Grace O. and her husband turned up among its moving spirits. They called their magazine the *Grapevine*. It was by no means the first local A.A. bulletin or magazine. The *Cleveland Central Bulletin,* the Los Angeles *Eye-Opener,* and several others had preceded it. But the *Grapevine* caught on nationally.

After the first few months it encountered a strange kind of difficulty. It turned out that the FBI for a long time had published a sheet called the *Grapevine*. It was largely devoted to keeping FBI men up to date on the doings of their great service. Things were finally ironed out when we began to call our monthly magazine the *A.A. Grapevine*. With this minor difficulty overcome, our *Grapevine* grew and grew. The circulation has since risen to more than 40,000 [15] copies a month.

The *Grapevine* is the mirror of A.A. thought and action, worldwide. It is a sort of magic carpet on which all of us can travel from one distant A.A. outpost to another, and thus it has become a wonderful exchange medium of our current thought and experience.

After a while the Grapeviners discovered that they had a bear by the tail. It was always fun to get in the material and edit the pieces, but licking all those postage stamps and mailing thousands of copies finally became an impossible job. So they asked that the Foundation take over. When the Trustees inquired of the A.A. groups if they would like to make the *Grapevine* their international magazine, their answer was yes. The journal was incorporated, and two Foundation Trustees were seated on its Board of Directors, along with the editors.

The *Grapevine* had to have full-time help; this created a mounting deficit and again funds from the Big Book had to come to the rescue. Without this aid the magazine would have suspended publication.

Even more than the Headquarters office, the *A.A. Grapevine* can always use a large staff of volunteers. Only the managing editor, her assistants, the head of the subscription department, and a few routine workers are on the pay roll. The editor, the editorial board, the artists, and many writers always do a vast amount of volunteer work on every issue. Without such expert volunteers we could have no magazine at all. Were we to pay them for their services, the bill would be prohibitive. How these busy professional men and women are able

[15] As of 1957. Office procedures described here also have changed.

to meet the *Grapevine* deadline every month will always be a mystery to the rest of us. It is one of the most consistent and brilliant volunteer efforts that A.A. has seen.

Even as early as 1945, the solution of group problems by correspondence had put a large volume of work on Headquarters. Letters to metropolitan A.A. centers filled our bulging files. It seemed as if every contestant in every group argument wrote us during this confused and exciting period.

The basic ideas for the Twelve Traditions of Alcoholics Anonymous came directly out of this vast correspondence. In late 1945 a good A.A. friend suggested that all this mass of experience might be codified into a set of principles which could offer tested solutions to all our problems of living and working together and of relating our society to the world outside. If we had become sure enough of where we really stood on such matters as membership, group autonomy, singleness of purpose, nonendorsement of other enterprises, professionalism, public controversy, and anonymity in its several aspects, then such a set of principles could be written. A code of traditions could not, of course, ever become rule or law. But it might act as a guide for our Trustees, Headquarters people, and especially for A.A. groups with growing pains.

Being at the center of things, we of Headquarters would have to do the job. Aided by my helpers there, I set to work. The Traditions of Alcoholics Anonymous were first published in the so-called "long form" in the *Grapevine* of May, 1946. Additional *Grapevine* pieces then explained the Traditions in detail. These continued to appear for several months. Later on these articles were incorporated in a pamphlet called *A.A. Tradition*. All of our Headquarters staff members and many group secretaries still rely on well-thumbed and battered copies of this first Tradition pamphlet for their guidance in times of trouble.

At the Foundation, meanwhile, we had taken a significant action that was incorporated in these Traditions. In 1945 we wrote Mr. John D. Rockefeller, Jr., and the 1940 dinner guests that we would no longer need their financial help. The book royalties could now look after Dr. Bob and me; group contributions could pay the general office expenses. If these were insufficient, the reserve accumulated out of literature sales could meet the deficit. This meant that we had finally declared for full self-support. Since that time A.A.'s Board of Trustees has steadfastly refused outside contributions.

When first published the Traditions got a mixed reception. Only groups in dire trouble took them seriously. But in some quarters there was a violent reaction against them, especially in groups that had long lists of "protective" rules and regulations. At the other extreme, there was much apathetic indifference. Still others said, "Let's keep A.A. simple." To them, the Twelve Traditions seemed only a needless expression of the hopes and fears of General Headquarters for A.A.'s future.

At this point I began to travel and talk a lot about the new principles. The members listened, but were obviously bored. After a while I received letters like this: "Bill, we would love to have you come and speak. Tell us where you used to hide your bottles and tell us about that hot-flash spiritual experience of yours. But please don't talk any more about those damned Traditions."

Time has changed all that. Several years later it was recognized that the Twelve Traditions were going to be just as necessary to the life of our society as the Twelve Steps were to the life of each member. We saw that the A.A. Traditions were the key to the unity, the functioning, and even the survival of Alcoholics Anonymous.

In reality I had not been the author of the Traditions at all. I had merely put them on paper in such a way as to mirror principles which had already been developed in A.A. group experience. A.A.'s General Headquarters, its Trustees, and its staff had actually made the formulation of these vital principles possible. Had there been no Headquarters to bring our group problems into focus, the Twelve Traditions of Alcoholics Anonymous could never have been written.

By this time A.A. had begun to find favor in the world of medicine. Two of America's great medical associations took unprecedented steps in recognizing us. In 1944 the Medical Society of the State of New York had invited me to read a paper at its annual meeting. After the reading, three of the physicians present—Dr. Harry Tiebout, Dr. Kirby Collier, and Dr. Foster Kennedy—stood up and gave A.A. the firmest kind of endorsement. The Society itself went still farther. It published the paper in its journal and permitted A.A. to make reprints. Large numbers of this pamphlet have since been distributed all over the world, carrying the assurance to doctors everywhere that A.A. is medically sound.

In 1949 the American Psychiatric Association did exactly the same thing. I read a paper at its annual meeting in Montreal. This was a still more exacting assignment, and I frankly wondered what I should say. I wound up by describing the spiritual experience as we understand it in A.A. As I read, I doubted if even a handful of the audience could possibly agree with the views expressed in my paper. To my astonishment there was a sustained round of applause. But this was not at all a tribute to me or to the contents of my paper; it was instead a tribute to Alcoholics Anonymous, a tribute to a way of life which had worked for alcoholics when other approaches had failed. This generous response was evidence that our friends the psychiatrists were being much more tolerant of us than we had been of them. If we ourselves became more open-minded, then far greater co-operation with this profession would be assured.

The Association promptly confirmed the view of its members in Montreal. My paper was carried in the *American Journal of Psychiatry* and we were permitted to reprint it in a pamphlet, now entitled *Alcoholism the Illness*.[16] Our standing with the psychiatric profession has increased greatly since that time. State and county medical associations began to ask A.A. members to make appearances before them. All these medical papers have served our foreign groups especially well, saving them the years that were once required here in America to demonstrate A.A.'s worth to physicians.

[16] Later retitled *Three Talks to Medical Societies by Bill W.*, this pamphlet also includes Bill's paper before the Medical Society of the State of New York.

The medical aspect of alcoholism includes the problem of hospitalization, and here also great progress has been made. Many hospitals have been reluctant to take alcoholics at all. State and Provincial institutions usually have required alcoholics to stay for long periods of commitment. Therefore it has been difficult—and it still is—to persuade the average general hospital to take in A.A. prospects for short periods of treatment and to grant sponsors the necessary visiting privileges in co-operation with our local Intergroup Associations.

It is good to report that this condition is rapidly changing for the better. Our pioneering activity in this field, together with the use which A.A. Headquarters has been able to make of that experience, has a special interest for us all. Two American hospitals have afforded fine examples of how medicine and A.A. can best co-operate. At St. Thomas Hospital in Akron Dr. Bob, the wonderful Sister Ignatia, and the hospital staff presided over an alcoholic ward which had treated several thousand alcoholics by the time of Dr. Bob's death in 1950. And beginning in 1945, Knickerbocker Hospital in New York provided an A.A. ward under the care of our first friend in medicine, Dr. William D. Silkworth, who was assisted with rare devotion and skill by nurse Teddy. By 1954, 10,000 alcoholics had been referred to Knickerbocker by the New York Intergroup Association and had passed through this ward, the majority on their way to freedom. Since proper hospitalization is one of A.A.'s greatest problems, the New York Headquarters continues to pass on the knowledge gained from this early experience, along with its many subsequent developments and ramifications, to A.A. groups all over the world.

Meanwhile a great tide of public approval, stimulated by A.A.'s friends of press, radio, and in recent times television, began to sweep in upon us and it has never ceased. Each month a clipping service feeds our Headquarters scrapbooks with a very large amount of material. Writers constantly ask Headquarters to check their manuscripts. A.A. members are helped to appear anonymously on radio and TV programs. The making of arrangements for publicity has become a constantly increasing activity of our A.A. office. How many lives have been saved, how many years of misery have thus been averted for thousands of alcoholics and their families, only God knows.

To maintain these ever lengthening life lines of service, our office had to go on expanding. In 1950 we moved to 141 East Forty-fourth Street, still closer to Grand Central. Today this office is presided over by Chairman Hank, on part time, and six fine staff secretaries. These paid staff members are greatly helped by volunteer committeemen who are experts in law, finance, and public relations. On the routine service staff about twelve nonalcoholics look after bookkeeping, filing, and stenography, and two receptionists preside over the outer office. There visitors see the walls covered with sectional maps showing the world-wide reach of our fellowship. On a table stands a Winged Victory, symbol of the Lasker Award given to A.A. by the American Public Health Association in 1951.

The editorial offices of the *Grapevine* are on the floor below. Here editor Don and his volunteer assistants confer with the managing editor and her assistant to meet the monthly deadline. Farther downtown, where rents are cheaper, there is a large floor space where the circulation department looks after the *Grapevine's* 40,000 readers and their needs.

Three blocks away from the main office we have a good-sized loft space where all shipping and mailing is done. This activity now runs into tons of material a month. Six busy lads spend full time at it. Last year they shipped about 40,000 books and hundreds of thousands of pamphlets, many of them newly designed and edited largely through the work of Ralph, our consultant on pamphlet literature. They mailed about 30,000 letters and bulletins and did huge quantities of mimeographing.

Down one side of the long packing room, on shelves reaching to the ceiling, are scores of boxed-up files. These are the old records of our Headquarters, going clear back to the days at Vesey Street. The world story of A.A. is hidden in these boxes, waiting only to be searched out, and we have just begun the job. In a partitioned-off corner office near the files our research librarian is digging into the history of Alcoholics Anonymous. In addition to the present brief sketch, I hope that some day the full-length history of Alcoholics Anonymous will be written. Because of this research activity, it is now certain that the basic facts of A.A.'s growth and development never can become distorted. Such is one of our newest undertakings.

No description of A.A.'s world services would be complete without acknowledgment of all that has been contributed by our nonalcoholic Trustees. Over the years they have given a great amount of time and effort. Theirs has been the wisdom that has caused our affairs to make financial sense; and frequently in times of heated debate they have headed off the rash decisions that we volatile alcoholics would surely have made. Some of them—like Mr. Jack Alexander, Mr. Fulton Oursler, Mr. Leonard V. Harrison, and Mr. Bernard B. Smith—have given much to us out of their special fields of literature, social service, finance, and law. Their example is being followed by more recent Trustees such as Mr. Frank Gulden, Dr. John Norris, Mr. Archibald Roosevelt, and Mr. Ivan Underwood. The very special contributions of my brother-in-law, Dr. Leonard V. Strong, Jr., Mr. Willard Richardson, Mr. A. LeRoy Chipman, and Mr. Frank B. Amos have already been described. And a little farther on we shall consider at some length the vital role that Mr. Leonard Harrison played as long-time Chairman of the Foundation during the uncertain period of our adolescence.

That period, 1945 to 1950, was one of immense strain and test. We were confronted by three grave issues. The first had to do with money, the second with anonymity; and, most dangerous of all, there was the question of what was to become of Alcoholics Anonymous when its old-timers and founders had gone.

In 1945 we had begun to decline "outside contributions," but another similar hazard soon presented itself. Wealthy people, some of them A.A. members, began to insert large bequests in their wills with a direction that these funds be given to the Alcoholic Foundation in trust for Alcoholics Anonymous. One of these bequests became available during a period when A.A.'s Headquarters was in severe financial straits. At one point group contributions to the office failed to meet the bill by $2,000 a month and the *Grapevine* deficits were almost half that amount. The question was then asked: "Even if we cannot take money from living contributors, what reason is there for not accepting it from deceased ones?" But after long debate and soul-searching, the trustees finally turned all these bequests away, thereby consolidating and cementing the A.A. Tradition of self-support for all time to come. To thoughtful A.A.'s everywhere this action of the Trustees brought a deep new feeling of relief and security. A real peril had been averted.

The intense drive that most of us alcoholics have for money, prestige, and power then crashed into the open by way of broken anonymity at the public level. This development of the 1945–1950 period was made even more dangerous by the fact that most of the anonymity breakers meant well. Having done some anonymity breaking at an earlier period myself, I could well appreciate their good intentions. Sometimes these folks wanted to use the A.A. name publicly in order to help other good causes. Sometimes they just wanted their names and pictures in the papers—always, of course, to help A.A. They actually believed that being photographed with the Governor would really help. Finally we saw that the risk to A.A. would be appalling if all our power-drivers finally got loose at the public level. Scores of them were already doing it.

So A.A. Headquarters got to work. We wrote remonstrances, kind ones, of course, to every breaker. We sent letters to nearly all press, radio, and publishing outlets, explaining why A.A.'s should not break their anonymity before the general public. Group feeling, combined with the Headquarters efforts, finally squeezed the anonymity breakers down to a mere handful within a few years. Had this tendency not been checked, the whole character of our society could have changed, and its future could have been fearfully compromised.

In 1947 Dr. Bob had been stricken by an ailment that we all knew might prove fatal. At Headquarters this gave us plenty to think about. The main link between our world services and A.A. itself had been Dr. Bob, our secretarial staff, and me. To our world-wide fellowship its devoted Board of Trustees was scarcely known at all. Not one A.A. in a thousand could name even half of them. When death or disability finally took us few old-timers out of the picture, where would that leave the Trustees and the Headquarters? A single blunder on their part might cause a failure of confidence that could not be repaired. Lacking the moral and financial support of the groups, the whole Headquarters effort might collapse completely. Our services might never be reinstated because nobody could be authorized to do the job.

It was evident that here was a world-wide movement that had no direct access to its own principal service affairs. The Trustees had authority over our services; A.A. itself had no authority. The simple trusteeship had been the ideal guardian for our infancy and adolescence, but how in future years could it possibly go on functioning as it had?

This situation had been a matter of great concern to me ever since the publication of the Traditions in 1946. I had sent the Trustees many memorandums on the subject. There had been considerable discussion. At first we had talked vaguely about a hand-picked advisory council or an elected conference of some sort. But since there was no imminent danger, no action was taken. When Dr. Bob became ill, I began to feel the serious urgency of the problem. So did Mr. Bernard Smith and one or two of the others.

But the majority of the Board did not share our apprehension. They felt that creating a conference or even an advisory council would entail unnecessary politics and expense. The Foundation had done well for ten years, so why could it not go on in just the same way?

Typically alcoholic, I became very excited, and this turned the passive resistance of my fellow workers into solid opposition. A serious rift developed between me and the alcoholic members of the Board, and as the months went by the situation became worse and worse. With much reason, they resented my sledge-hammer tactics and my continued violence. As the tempest increased, so did my blistering memorandums to the Board. One of them was an amazing composition. Following a long plea for an elected A.A. conference and other reforms, and after having pointed out that the Trustees had all the authority there was, with no responsibility to anyone, even to Dr. Bob and me, I finished the memo with this astonishing sentence: "When I was in law school, the largest book I studied was the one on Trusts. I must say, gentlemen, that it was mostly a long and melancholy account of the malfeasances and misfeasances of boards of trustees." I had written this to a group of the best friends I had in the world, people who had devoted themselves to A.A. and to me without stint. Obviously I was on a dry bender of the worst possible sort.

This sizzling memorandum nearly blew the Foundation apart. Our nonalcoholic friends were dumbfounded. My alcoholic colleagues among the opposition Trustees darkly murmured that I must have gone crazy. They felt sure of it when I set out on the road in 1948 to sound out among the groups the possibility of an elected conference to which the Board of Trustees could eventually become accountable.

Soon after I left on my travels, the alcoholic Trustees got hold of old-timers in Akron, New York, and Cleveland to decide in conclave what could be done about the situation, and especially about me. They supposed that out on the road I was widely airing the dispute and looking for backing. Happily I refrained from doing this. And the conclave of old-timers exercised some restraint too. They merely advised the Board that things were all right as they were, that no elected conference or advisory council was necessary, and that there was no need for any of the internal changes that I had suggested.

But although I had not generally raised the issue among the groups, I did come back with the conviction that they would like to have full access to their own affairs through an elected conference. Of this much I was now certain.

By 1949 Dr. Bob was definitely failing. At the office Bobbie, caught squarely in the middle of this fracas about the Conference, was already exhausted to the cracking point.

This was low ebb. Then, slowly the tide began to turn. Had it not been for our nonalcoholic friends on the Board, I doubt if the impasse could ever have been resolved. As we entered 1950 this conflict had been going on almost five years. The two men who ultimately saved the situation were Mr. Leonard Harrison and Mr. Bernard Smith. Though Mr. Harrison did not then see the necessity for the elected conference, his unfailing tact and good sense, together with the respect and affection he had engendered among us all, were the qualities that kept our shaky Foundation on its course.

Most of the nonalcoholics on the Board at the time had been institutional men. Bernard Smith on the other hand was a businessman and lawyer. From the time he had joined the Board, three years earlier, he had always favored corporate management for the A.A. office and an elected conference to sit with the Trustees as the final plan of service structure for Alcoholics Anonymous.

At this critical juncture, Mr. Harrison appointed Bernard Smith as Chairman of the Trustees' committee on the proposed Conference. Considering their differences of opinion, this was a most magnanimous and generous act on Leonard's part. The recollection of it never fails to inspire me.

Bernard Smith has a remarkable faculty for persuasion and negotiation. Moreover, his ideas about a conference had already taken a deeper hold than any of us realized. After the air had cleared somewhat, he took up the task of convincing the Trustees' committee on the Conference. Following only two meetings he put this question to the committee: Shall we set up this Conference of delegates, or shall we forget about it? To my astonishment the committee unanimously said, "Let's give the Conference a try." It seemed like a miracle.

Just before this crucial decision Alcoholics Anonymous had taken another step toward world-wide unity and function.

In the summer of 1950 we held our first international convention in Cleveland, Ohio. About 3,000 were in attendance. The highlights of this occasion were Dr. Bob's last appearance and the confirmation of our Twelve Traditions by the Convention as the permanent platform of unity and function on which our fellowship would henceforth stand.

The Twelve Traditions had already been reduced from the old "long form" of 1946 to capsule statements which in length matched our familiar Twelve Steps of Recovery.

This had been done at the wise suggestion of Earl T., founder of our Chicago group. One day in 1947, or thereabouts, he turned up at my home with this excellent idea. After a week of wrestling with the problem of cutting down the "long form" we came up with a first draft which much resembled the Twelve Traditions as they are today. After several months more of consultation and refining, the final draft was ready. The *Grapevine* commenced to carry the newly stated Traditions in every issue and thus the average A.A. member was made Tradition-conscious. By the time the Cleveland Convention met, the understanding and approval of the Traditions had become general throughout our society.

At the Cleveland Convention we sensed that Dr. Bob was soon going to leave us and that many another early A.A. would soon follow him. The old order was changing. In the future we could no longer depend upon the authority and influence of our pioneering people for A.A. unity. Henceforth we would have to rely upon spiritual principles, as set forth in the Twelve Traditions.

Several speakers presented the Twelve Traditions to the Convention. I then summed them up and asked the Convention for final approval. Today one can still listen, by means of a recording, to the Convention's unanimous voice of consent. It was a fine hour in that month of July, 1950. Alcoholics Anonymous had passed its fifteenth milestone; its Second Legacy of Tradition was secure.

Only a few weeks later, I saw Dr. Bob at Akron and was able to bring the good news that the Trustees would, in all probability, consent at last to the formation of a world service Conference. This development could do for A.A.'s services what the Traditions were doing for A.A. unity.

Dr. Bob was visibly relieved by my message, but he made no immediate comment. Though still up and around, he was desperately ill. Hard as it was going to be, I realized that I must press for his consent to the Conference.

I remember suggesting that if he and I did not act on this matter but continued our silence we would *still* be taking action. If we both passed off the scene without making any move, everybody would suppose that the present state of affairs met with our full approval. If thereafter the Headquarters should collapse for lack of Conference linkage, the A.A.'s could rightfully say, "Why didn't Dr. Bob and Bill tell us? Why didn't they give us a chance to look after our own business and policy?" I ventured the idea that we ought to call the Conference anyhow, even if it was a failure at first. The movement's delegates could come down to New York and see what A.A.'s world affairs were really like. They could then decide whether they would take responsibility or whether they would not. That would make it a movement decision, rather than one taken in silence by Dr. Bob and me.

He continued to reflect, and I waited. Finally he looked up and said, "Bill, it *has* to be A.A.'s decision, not ours. Let's call that Conference. It's fine with me."

A few hours later I took my leave of Dr. Bob, knowing that the following week he was to undergo a very serious operation. Neither of us dared say what was in our hearts. We both knew that this might well be the last decision that we would ever make together. I went down the steps and then turned to look back. Bob stood in the doorway, tall and upright as ever. Some color had come back to his cheeks, and he was carefully dressed in a light gray suit. This was my partner, the man with whom I never had a hard word. The wonderful, old, broad smile was on his face as he said almost jokingly, "Remember, Bill, let's not louse this thing up. Let's keep it simple!" I turned away, unable to say a word. That was the last time I ever saw him.

Soon after I arrived home, the Trustees approved the Conference plan and gave me authority to proceed.

The money cost of holding such a yearly affair was not an obstacle. Even if the outlay might be $20,000 annually, this would be only a few cents extra for each A.A. member, and well worth it.

But how, in electing delegates, could we cut down destructive politics with all the usual struggles for prestige and vainglory? How many delegates would be needed and from where should they come? When they arrived in New York, how could they be related to the Board of Trustees? What would be their actual powers and duties? Whatever the plan, it had to be sound enough to work fairly well from the start. No blunders big enough to create a fiasco could be allowed.

Consequently it was with many misgivings that I began work on the draft of a detailed plan. Headquarters people and Trustees alike made many fine suggestions. Helen B. of the office staff had a real flair for statesmanship in the best sense of the word, and she understood practical politicking too. Her assistance throughout proved invaluable.

Though the Conference might someday be enlarged to include the whole world, we felt that the first delegates should come from the U.S. and Canada only. Each state and province might have one delegate each with the provision that those containing heavy A.A. population could have additional representation. To give the Conference continuity the delegates would be divided into two panels: Panel One to be elected in 1951 and Panel Two the following year. Hence only half the delegates would drop out at one time and the conference membership would rotate. Elections could take place at the largest centers of population in each state or province. Yet how could these assemblies of group representatives choose their committeemen and delegates without terrific political friction?

As veterans of many a group hassle and Intergroup brawl, we worried seriously about this. Then came a happy thought. We knew that many of our election troubles were caused by personal nominations, whether from the floor of a meeting or by a self-appointed committee from a back room. Another prime cause of grief was the hotly contested close election, which nearly always left behind a large and discontented minority.

We therefore devised a scheme of choosing committeemen out of Group Assemblies by written ballot with no personal nominations at all. But the chief friction would most certainly center around the election of the delegate. How could that pressure be kept down? It was stipulated that each delegate must receive a two-thirds vote of his Assembly for election. With a majority of this size the minority could not kick very much. But suppose the contest was a neck-and-neck affair, with nobody able to get the two-thirds vote? Here we would have to invent something. Maybe the lead man and one or two of his runners-up might place their names in a hat and take their chances on a drawing. The winner of such a painless lottery would become the delegate. Since the high men in the running would almost always be good ones, we could not miss getting a fine panel of delegates by such a method. Of course these ideas were quite speculative. We dearly hoped they were going to work. But *would* they?

It was felt that the elected delegates, meeting in New York in conference, should have very real authority. Therefore the tentative Charter [17] drawn for the Conference provided that the delegates, on a two-thirds vote, could issue flat directives to the Trustees. Even a simple majority could issue a strong suggestion to the Trustees. Nevertheless this type of suggestion would be a powerful one, because if it were not carried out the discontented majority could return home and see that contributions to Headquarters were cut. Under the proposed plan, it would also become traditional for the Trustees to submit the names of all proposed Board members to the Conference for confirmation. This would give the Conference an effective voice in the selection of Trustees.

Along with a temporary scheme for financing the new operation, we put these ideas and their detailed application into a pamphlet

[17] See Appendix C, the final draft of A.A.'s Service Charter.

called *The Third Legacy*. We shipped 50,000 of these documents to the groups and asked them to form their Assemblies for the election of committeemen and delegates.

Fortified with the approval of the Trustees and of Dr. Bob, I stumped the country for the Third Legacy plan, talking to large A.A. audiences and watching Assemblies select their delegates in more than two dozen states and provinces.

I remember particularly the first tryout of the new plan in Boston. Before the meeting some of the elder politicos made a microscopic examination of the whole scheme and came up with the verdict that it was going to work. This was comforting, since those folks in Boston knew politics as few of the rest of us did. Their interest was everywhere intense, and members turned out in force for the mass meeting where I highlighted the Third Legacy plan. When the area's group representatives finally met to elect their committeemen and the delegate, the proceedings were as unruffled as a mill pond. The committeemen were duly elected and seated in front of the Assembly meeting. Then the Assemblymen voted and voted, but nobody could get a two-thirds majority. At last it was decided that the names of the whole committee be dumped into the hat. And out of that traditional receptacle there was drawn a fine delegate. Everybody was elated; we knew the heat was off. Right there we had our first glimmer that A.A. had begun to move from partisan politics into true statesmanship.

When the first General Service Conference met in April, 1951, we found that about a third of its delegates were real old-timers. The rest were active A.A.'s sober four to eight years. Best of all, the majority of them had been chosen by a two-thirds vote, only a few of the elections going to lot. It was tremendously encouraging.

On their first day, the delegates inspected our Headquarters, got acquainted with the service staff, and shook hands with the Trustees. In the evening there was a briefing session under the name of "What's on your mind?" We answered questions of every description. The delegates began to feel at home. Seeing their quick understanding and confidence, our spirits rose. We all sensed that something momentous was happening; that this was a historic moment.

One strenuous session followed another, morning, afternoon, and evening. The delegates inspected A.A.'s finances and listened to reports from the Board of Trustees and from all of the services. There was warm but cordial debate on many questions of A.A. policy. The Trustees submitted several of their own serious problems for the opinion of the Conference. With real dispatch the delegates handled several tough puzzlers about which we at Headquarters were in doubt. Though their advice was sometimes contrary to our own views, we saw they were frequently right. They were proving as never before that A.A.'s Tradition Two was correct. Our group conscience could safely act as the sole authority and sure guide for Alcoholics Anonymous. As the delegates returned home, they carried this deep conviction with them.

For example, at its very first session the Conference had suggested that the Alcoholic Foundation ought to be renamed the General Service Board of Alcoholics Anonymous. But they would not hurry this matter. It was after two more years of careful consideration that this suggestion became a decision and was carried out. To their minds the word "Foundation" had stood for charity, paternalism, and maybe big money. What had been good for our infancy would be no good for our future.

Now that the General Service Conference was successfully launched upon its five-year trial period, A.A.'s fellowship and its Headquarters entered a time of quiet progress and consolidation. The growing pains of our youth here in America had abated and we no longer felt fearful when they began to recur in lands overseas.

This heartening state of affairs was reflected in our Trustees' meetings and in our daily work at Headquarters. The final outlines of A.A.'s structure of service could now be seen. Wonderful co-operation and effective work replaced the fear, indecision, and violent debate of earlier times. The Board was again enlarged and new members, alcoholic and nonalcoholic, joined the ranks of trustee service. In the new

Conference we could begin to hear the voice of A.A.'s conscience, world-wide. And we already knew that this voice could be relied upon. For the first time we seemed to fully understand what we were doing and where we were going.

In this era of smooth sailing death claimed two more of our old friends, Uncle Dick Richardson and Silky. Like Anne and Dr. Bob, these two died happily confident that A.A. was at last secure and on its way. What Willard W. Richardson and William D. Silkworth had left us in pioneering service and in love was a never-to-be-forgotten heritage.

One more noteworthy event marked this period of quiet: the publication of A.A.'s *Twelve Steps and Twelve Traditions* in 1953. This small volume is strictly a textbook which explains A.A.'s twenty-four basic principles and their application, in detail and with great care.

Helped by my editorial team, Betty L. and Tom P., I had begun work on this project in early 1952. The final draft was widely circulated among our friends of medicine and religion and also among many old-time A.A.'s. This rigorous checkup was topped off by none other than Jack Alexander, who added the final editorial touch. For group distribution we published the volume ourselves, and our old friend Gene Exman of Harper offered favorable terms for distribution through his firm to bookstores.

The response was far greater than expected; about 50,000 volumes are in circulation as of 1957. It is the general feeling that the book has deepened the meaning of our Twelve Steps as they can be applied to the individual's problem of daily living, and that our Twelve Traditions can now be better understood and used in guiding the life of our whole society.

This new book was doubtless another sign and portent that A.A. was soon to come of full age. For us who staffed A.A.'s services, these years of consolidation and promise will be remembered as among the best that we can ever know.

As 1955 came into view we became very confident that Alcoholics Anonymous was at last safe; that its future was assured.

Everyone here at St. Louis knows that we have just published the second edition of the book *Alcoholics Anonymous.* Many of you have it in your hands already. Today as we pass A.A.'s twentieth milestone, it is quite fitting that this long-pondered edition is now in readiness for the future. The scope and power of its case history section has been increased, but of course the old familiar text of the book stands unchanged. This edition contains an interesting review of what actually happened to the twenty-eight pioneer authors who in 1939 wrote the first-edition stories. We find that twenty-three of them made a recovery from alcoholism. Of these, fifteen have never had even a single relapse. The sobriety records of those veterans range from fifteen to nineteen years. This demonstration is a marvelous inspiration for us all. It clinches A.A.'s claim that almost any alcoholic who can continuously work the A.A. program has better than a three-to-one chance of staying sober for his lifetime.

Now a final word. Nearly all of the last fifteen years of my life have been invested in the construction of A.A.'s General Service Headquarters. My heart is still there, and it will continue to be. To me, A.A.'s world services are that important.

No words can express the gratitude I feel toward my associates, the people who have really done this job. Our thanks go out to all of you who have given this work of world service your unstinted attention and support. Lois and I also want to set on the record our special gratitude to nearly 300,000 purchasers of the book *Alcoholics Anonymous.* As you have seen, the income from the Big Book has made our Headquarters possible. But it has done even more than this; the royalties from it have provided Lois and me with a home, where we have seen more than 3,000 of you over the years.

For Lois and me the autumn of life has now rolled around. For your sake and for ours, we think that we should no longer pursue the strenuous activities of other days. We feel that we are facing a season of reflection upon all that has happened. Perhaps we can commit to writing more of the great experiences of A.A.'s past so they may be put in permanent store for the future. We think, too, we ought to grow up a great deal more ourselves. As one-time teachers in A.A.'s school of the spirit, we find that thousands of our pupils have made far better personal demonstrations than we. So it is high time that we now try to catch up with you.

Of course I feel not a little sad that I can no longer be your Headquarters handyman. But I do rejoice that Alcoholics Anonymous has come of age and, through its great Service Conference and by God's grace, can take its own destiny by the hand.

FROM THE CONFERENCE CHARTER . . .

In all its proceedings, the General Service Conference shall observe the spirit of the A.A. Tradition, taking great care that the Conference never becomes the seat of perilous wealth or power; that sufficient operating funds, plus an ample reserve, be its prudent financial principle; that none of the Conference members shall ever be placed in a position of unqualified authority over any of the others; that all important decisions be reached by discussion vote and, whenever possible, by substantial unanimity; that no Conference action ever be personally punitive or an incitement to public controversy; that though the Conference may act for the service of Alcoholics Anonymous, it shall never perform any acts of government; and that, like the Society of Alcoholics Anonymous which it serves, the Conference itself will always remain democratic in thought and action.

III

Four o'Clock Sunday Afternoon

THE following section portrays the high points of the St. Louis
Convention and the culmination of twenty years of Alcoholics
Anonymous.

The General Service Conference of A.A. is seated on the auditorium
stage. Bernard Smith, Chairman of A.A.'s Board of Trustees, introduces Bill, who reads the resolution by which he and A.A.'s old-
timers deliver their twenty-year stewardship of our society into the
hands of its elected representatives.

This ceremony is followed by the concluding talks of Lois and
Bill, marking the end of an era and the beginning of the time when
A.A. assumes full responsibility for its own affairs.

BERNARD SMITH: I now declare the Fifth Annual Conference of
the General Service Conference in session. We have completed in four
days all of the tasks that have been allotted to us, save only one; that
is the adoption of the resolution authorizing the General Service Conference to act for Alcoholics Anonymous and to become the successor
to its co-founders. Only this Conference, in all humility, has the
power, within the concepts of A.A., to adopt this resolution, and
only after it has evidence of the acceptance by all of A.A., in this Convention here assembled. I propose, therefore, to call upon Bill to read
this resolution, and then to ask this Conference to observe the action
of the Convention thereon, and when the Convention has acted I will
then call upon the Conference to carry into effect, within the body of
its principles and traditions, the action of this Convention. The Con-

ference will remain convened and will adjourn simultaneously with the adjournment of the Convention. And now, Bill, will you be good enough to read the resolution, and then, if you will, sense the feeling of the Convention, so that the Conference will be in a position to act.

BILL: We stand on the brink of a momentous decision. It is one of the most solemn hours in which this society will ever live, for we are about to confirm its permanent structure.

We of A.A. are apt sometimes to brag of the virtues of our fellowship. Let us remember that none of these are *earned* virtues. We have been forced into them, to begin with, by the cruel lash of John Barleycorn. We have adopted these attitudes, these practices, this structure, not at first because we wished to but because we *had* to. And then, as time confirmed the seeming rightness of our basic principles, we began to conform because it was right to do so. Some of us, notably myself, conformed even then with reluctance. But at last I think we have come to a summit here today where we stand willing to conform permanently and gladly to the principles which experience, under the grace of God, has taught us.

Some of us may think that, structurally speaking, we are quite unique. But this is not entirely so. Our principles of recovery are borrowed, and so are most of our structural ideas. In A.A. we can see many of the means by which men and women over the centuries have tried to unite themselves, and each of these techniques of association has its assets and its liabilities.

When we first come into A.A. we find here, as we have observed before, a greater personal freedom than any other society knows. We cannot be *compelled* to do anything. In that sense this society is a benign anarchy. The word "anarchy" has a bad meaning to most of us, probably because one of its excitable adherents long ago threw bombs around in Chicago. But I think that the gentle Russian prince who so strongly advocated the idea felt that if men were granted absolute liberty and were compelled to obey no one in person, they would then voluntarily associate themselves in a common interest. Alcoholics

Anonymous is an association of the benign sort the prince envisioned.

This kind of association among us is wonderful and free and simple and joyous. So far so good. But we have found that this is not enough. When we had to go into action—to function as groups—we found that we had to become a democracy. As the old-timers retired, we began to elect our servants by majority vote. Each group in this sense became a town-meeting democracy.

When we first put our world services into effect, Dr. Bob and I and our old-time friends were self-appointed guardians and custodians of this society. We took it upon ourselves to provide services. I do not mean it in any irreverent or exaggerated sense when I say that our setup of those days was a sort of a double-headed papacy and a college of cardinals. Structurally we had created a hierarchy of service.

But we have learned that such a hierarchy cannot forever float alone; it must somehow be connected with the great sea of democracy all about it. The General Service Conference of Alcoholics Anonymous is now about to provide that permanent connection so much needed between our society and its Trustees. But our Conference will be more than a connection; it will represent the conscience of A.A. world-wide, to which our Trustees will in this very hour become directly accountable.

In A.A. there is active still another form of association, a form of which the world is today in great doubt. It has its virtues, nevertheless, especially for us of Alcoholics Anonymous: I am speaking of dictatorship. In A.A. we have two dictators, and we profit and grow through both. One is John Barleycorn, who is never very far from the elbow of each of us. The other is the Father of Lights, who presides over all men. God is saying to us, "Learn my will and do it." And John Barleycorn is saying to each of us, "You had better do God's will or I will kill you!"

Perhaps it is something new for a society to borrow from so many forms of human association. But clearly enough, we have borrowed from anarchy, democracy, the republic, the hierarchy, and dictatorship.

We hope that we have avoided the liabilities of each. And we especially hope that we have inherited most of the assets of each.

I pray with you that the resolution which we are about to propose is God's will for us. I shall now offer it to you and ask for a voice vote. If you agree, if your conscience says, "This is right to the best of my knowledge and belief," then your General Service Conference and its hierarchy of service at the center will confirm your will for all the long future of Alcoholics Anonymous. This is the resolution:

We, the members of the Twentieth Anniversary Convention of Alcoholics Anonymous, here assembled at St. Louis in July of the year 1955, declare our belief that our Fellowship has now come of age and is entirely ready to assume full and permanent possession of the Three Legacies of our A.A. inheritance—the Legacies of Recovery, Unity, and Service.

We believe that the General Service Conference of Alcoholics Anonymous, as created in 1951 by our co-founders, Dr. Bob S. and Bill W. and authorized by Trustees of the Alcoholic Foundation, has now become entirely capable of assuming the guardianship of A.A.'s Twelve Traditions and of taking over full guidance and control of the World Service of our Society, as provided in the Third Legacy Manual of World Service recently revised by our surviving co-founder, Bill W. and the General Service Board of Alcoholics Anonymous.

We have also heard with approval Bill W.'s proposal that A.A.'s General Service Conference should now become the permanent successor to the founders of Alcoholics Anonymous, inheriting from them all their former duties and special responsibilities, thus avoiding in future time all possible strivings for individual prestige or personal power, and also providing our Society with the means of functioning on a permanent basis.

BE IT THEREFORE RESOLVED: That the General Service Conference of Alcoholics Anonymous should become, as of this date, July 3rd, 1955, the guardian of the Traditions of Alcoholics Anonymous, the perpetuator of the World Services of our Society, the voice of the group conscience of our entire Fellowship, and the sole successors to its co-founders, Dr. Bob and Bill.

AND IT IS UNDERSTOOD: That neither the Twelve Traditions of

Alcoholics Anonymous nor the warranties of Article XII of the Conference Charter shall ever be changed or amended by the General Service Conference except by first asking the consent of the registered A.A. groups of the world. These groups shall be suitably notified of any proposal for change, and shall be allowed no less than six months for consideration thereof. And before any such Conference action can be taken, there must first be received in writing, within the time allotted, the consent of at least three-quarters of all those registered groups who respond to such a proposal.

AND WE FURTHER UNDERSTAND: That, as provided in Article XII of the Conference Charter, the Conference binds itself to the society of Alcoholics Anonymous by the following means:

That in all its proceedings, the General Service Conference shall observe the spirit of the A.A. Tradition, taking great care that the Conference never becomes the seat of perilous wealth or power; that sufficient operating funds, plus an ample reserve, be its prudent financial principle; that none of the Conference members shall ever be placed in a position of unqualified authority over any of the others; that all important decisions be reached by discussion, vote, and, whenever possible, by substantial unanimity; that no Conference action ever be personally punitive or an incitement to public controversy; that though the Conference may act in the service of Alcoholics Anonymous and may traditionally direct its World Services, it shall never enact laws or regulations binding on A.A. as a whole or upon any A.A. group or upon any member thereof, nor shall it perform any other such acts of government; and that, like the Society of Alcoholics Anonymous which it serves, the Conference itself will always remain democratic in thought and action.

BERNARD SMITH: Members of the Conference, you have now heard the resolution authorizing the General Service Conference to act for Alcoholics Anonymous and to become the successor to its co-founders approved by the society of Alcoholics Anonymous in Convention assembled this third day of July. I will now ask for a motion that the resolution, as read by Bill and as approved by this Convention, be adopted by this Conference and be spread upon the minutes of this meeting. Will someone so move? (The motion was made.) Will someone second it? (The motion was seconded.) Will all those in favor say "Aye"? (The motion was carried unanimously.)

BERNARD SMITH: In the lives of men who have made a powerful impact on human society there is not infrequently a great woman, the wife and partner who has provided inspiration and unfailing devotion in times of triumph and of trial, without which support the man's impact might never have been made. To us, Lois is not only such a woman as the wife of Bill but is, indeed, a symbol to all of us of the A.A. wife.

LOIS: Good afternoon, everybody. I want to express here before you all my gratitude for this great occasion, and my thanks for being allowed to share in it. It is this sharing that makes A.A. the power for good that it is. Through these twenty years, and climaxed today by this thrilling Convention, you have not only been an inspiration to me and to many others like me, but you have given us proof of the power of good over evil. You have given us a demonstration that lives, no matter how low and sordid they may become, can be changed, and that men and women, through God's grace, can be remotivated to become constructive, useful forces. I believe all these miracles have come about because the principles of A.A. coincide with the highest precepts that we know, with the fundamental laws of the universe. These principles teach us how to step aside so that God can act through us.

I am particularly grateful to A.A. for showing me personally, and all the other wives and husbands of A.A., the way to a better and a more useful life. From the very beginning, A.A.'s example has made many of us want to live by the Twelve Steps ourselves and to help others like us, who still are frustrated and alone, to do likewise.

In the last ten years the numbers of partners of alcoholics who share this same feeling of need have increased so greatly that it has become possible to band together in groups in order to better solve our problems of fear and insecurity, and to pass our experience on to others who seek our help. The Al-Anon Family Groups are a spontaneous response to a vital need. In the Family Groups we follow the lead of you in A.A. We admit that we too are powerless over alcohol. We try to take our hands off your problems. We try to stop bossing and nagging, acknowledging the integrity of your lives as well as our own. We try to take our own inventories, to admit to God and to another human being the exact nature of our own wrongs. We make amends to those we have harmed. We seek through prayer and meditation to improve our conscious contact with God as we understand Him, and we try to carry this message to others. In the Family Groups we are trying to the best of our ability to live by the very same principles that have done so much for you. This effort on our part seems to have favorable results for you, the alcoholics, as well as for us. And as a consequence many upset homes have become serene, united, and joyous places.

As Bill told you last night, at the time of the A.A. International Convention in Cleveland in 1950 there were probably less than 100 Family Groups in existence. Now there are nearly 700 on the American continent, and there are groups in ten countries abroad. We have not only grown in quantity but, we hope, in quality too. We are proud to have a part in this great Convention, and we feel sure that the benefit to the A.A., as well as to his family, will be great.

We thank you, A.A.'s, for this tremendous opportunity to spread your message, which we have adopted as our own.

BERNARD SMITH: And now as this great afternoon in our lives draws to a close, there is only one human being who can properly close the meeting. To this man and to Dr. Bob, who together founded Alcoholics Anonymous, this age and the ages that follow will one day recognize that they have as great a debt as that of you who sit here this Sunday afternoon. I cannot help thinking of those countless human beings, living in the centuries that preceded ours, who went down to destruction in dissolution and death through the ravages of alcohol because in those times there did not come upon the scene a man called Bill. Let us who are here today give thanks that Providence has selected for this age of ours the privilege of having him among us. Here he is.

BILL: I expect some of you are asking, "Does this great event change the status of Lois and me with respect to you?" The answer we think is both yes and no. Let us look at this question.

Is it not true that most of us have been victimized by faulty parental relations? I don't say this in any sense of blame; but is it not true of most of us alcoholics that our parents either quit too soon and turned us loose before we were ready or else overstayed their time and never let us come of age at all? And when we alcoholics married, did not we, by our incapacity, force our wives or our husbands to become our mothers or our fathers? These were faulty parental relationships, always defeating growth, always defeating partnership. It is therefore the duty of every parent at some time to say, "Here is our experience together in this family. This is your inheritance. This is for you to multiply or to squander. Take it. Go out and meet life. We'll stand by. We'll help when the going is tough. But now you are on your own. We can no longer decide for you, act for you, protect you. We can only love you with all our hearts. The rest is up to God and yourself." When parents fail to do this, the seeds of misery are almost inevitably sown.

So Lois and I, along with many another old-timer in this outfit, are trying not to overstay our time. Back in 1948, we were thinking of this. Dr. Bob and I once wrote a joint piece in the *Grapevine* asking, "Why can't we join A.A., too?" Well, this is the day when we *do* join A.A.

I suppose that when children are weaned and declared to be of age —not grown up, mind you, just come to the age of responsibility—it is suitable for their parents to give them a word or two of admonition along with the final pat on the back.

Our three great days here together have reached their climax and are drawing to a close. We shall soon bid each other godspeed as we return to the tasks appointed for each of us. From this hour, we know that the beloved fellowship of Alcoholics Anonymous can gladly and confidently accept whatever destiny God may have in store for us all. I do not think that any of us would presume to believe that Alcoholics Anonymous in its present form will necessarily last forever. We can only hope that it will lead to better things for those who suffer from alcoholism; that the lessons and examples of our experience may in some measure bring comfort and assurance to the suffering and confused world about us, the world in which it is our privilege to be alive in this exciting and perilous time, this century in which spiritual rebirth may be the only alternative to extinction.

In the years ahead we shall, of course, make mistakes. Experience has taught us that we need have no fear of doing this, providing that we always remain willing to confess our faults and to correct them promptly. Our growth as individuals has depended upon this healthy process of trial and error. So will our growth as a fellowship. Let us always remember that any society of men and women that cannot freely correct its own faults must surely fall into decay if not into collapse. Such is the universal penalty for the failure to go on growing. Just as each A.A. must continue to take his moral inventory and act upon it, so must our whole society do if we are to survive and if we are to serve usefully and well.

I have great faith that we shall never embrace and persist in a fatal error; and yet we still *might* do so, fallible human beings that we are. This is the area in the future life of A.A. where we can never be too prudent or too vigilant. Let us not suppose, just because A.A. as a whole has never had a grievous problem, that it never can have one. If such a difficulty ever comes, I feel sure that it will center about false pride and anger, the two most destructive defects that we alcoholics have.

As a society we must never become so vain as to suppose that we have been the authors and inventors of a new religion. We will humbly reflect that each of A.A.'s principles, *every one of them,* has been borrowed from ancient sources. We shall remember that we are laymen, holding ourselves in readiness to co-operate with all men of good will, whatever their creed or nationality.[1]

Then, too, it would be a product of false pride to believe that Alcoholics Anonymous is a cure-all, even for alcoholism. Here we must remember our debt to the men of medicine. Here we must be friendly and, above all, open-minded toward every new development in the medical or psychiatric art that promises to be helpful to sick people. We should always be friendly to those in the fields of alcoholic research, rehabilitation, and education. We should endorse none especially but hold ourselves in readiness to co-operate so far as we can with them all. Let us constantly remind ourselves that the experts in religion are the clergymen; that the practice of medicine is for physicians; and that we, the recovered alcoholics, are their assistants.

There are those who predict that Alcoholics Anonymous may well become a new spearhead for a spiritual awakening throughout the world. When our friends say these things they are both generous and sincere. But we of A.A. must reflect that such a tribute and such a prophecy could well prove to be a heady drink for most of us—that is, if we really came to believe this to be the real purpose of A.A., and if we commenced to behave accordingly. Our society, therefore, will prudently cleave to its single purpose: the carrying of the message to the alcoholic who still suffers. Let us resist the proud assumption that since God has enabled us to do well in one area we are destined to be a channel of saving grace for everybody.

On the other hand, let us never be a closed corporation; let us never deny our experience for whatever it may be worth to the world around us. Let our individual members heed the call to every field of human endeavor. Let them carry the experience and spirit of A.A.

---

[1] Speaking for Dr. Bob and myself I would like to say that there has never been the slightest intent, on his part or mine, of trying to found a new religious denomination. Dr. Bob held certain religious convictions, and so do I. This is, of course, the personal privilege of every A.A. member.

Nothing, however, could be so unfortunate for A.A.'s future as an attempt to incorporate any of our personal theological views into A.A. teaching, practice, or tradition. Were Dr. Bob still with us, I am positive he would agree that we could never be too emphatic about this matter.

into all these affairs, for whatever good they may accomplish. For not only has God saved us from alcoholism; the world has received us back into its citizenship. Yet believing in paradoxes as we do, we must still realize that the more the society of Alcoholics Anonymous as such tends to its own affairs and minds its own business, the greater will be our general influence, the less will be any opposition to us, and the wider will be the circle in which our fellowship will be likely to enjoy the confidence and respect of men.

Having examined the perils of pride, let's look briefly now at how anger, even so-called righteous indignation, could harm us. Within A.A., I suppose, we shall always quarrel a good bit. Mostly, I think, about how to do the greatest good for the greatest number of drunks. We shall have our childish spats and snits over small questions of money management and who is going to run our groups for the next six months. Any bunch of growing children (and that is what we are) would hardly be in character if they did less. These are the growing pains of infancy, and we actually thrive on them. Surmounting such problems, in A.A.'s rather rugged school of life, is a healthy exercise.

But there are nevertheless certain areas where anger and contention could prove to be our undoing. We know this because stronger societies than our own have been undone. The whole modern world is in fact coming apart as never before because of political and religious strife; because men blindly pursue wealth, fame, and personal power regardless of the consequences to anyone, even to themselves. These are the destructive drives that are inevitably spurred by self-justification, and in all their disastrous collisions they are powered by righteous indignation, then by unreasoning anger, and finally by blind fury.

With the most heartfelt gratitude I can report that we have never yet had to endure any such trials by fire in A.A. In all these twenty marvelous years no such thing as religious or political dissension has touched us. Very few have tried to exploit A.A. for wealth or fame or personal power. We have had great problems, but they have always been resolved. Never has a grave issue cut across and scarred the face of this far-flung fellowship. But, again, this is no earned virtue of ours. Too many of us in our drinking days have suffered the terrible penalties of proud and angry pursuits to forget them now. These very pains have been the beginning of whatever wisdom we have since incorporated in A.A.'s Twelve Traditions. Hence, I feel confident that these forces of destruction will never rule among us. We are prepared to pay the price of peace. We will make every personal sacrifice necessary to insure the unity of Alcoholics Anonymous. We will do this because we have learned to love God and one another.

As these meetings began on a theme of gratitude, so should they end. We give thanks to our Heavenly Father who, through so many friends and through so many means and channels, has allowed us to construct this wonderful edifice of the Spirit in which we are now dwelling. It seems as though He had directed us to construct this cathedral whose foundations already rest upon the corners of the earth. On its great floor 200,000 of us are now sustained in peace, and long since we have inscribed thereon our Twelve Steps of Recovery. The older ones among us have seen the side walls of this cathedral going up, and one by one they have seen the buttresses of the A.A. Tradition set in place to contain us in unity for so long as God may will it so. And now eager hearts and hands have lifted the spire of our cathedral into its place. That spire bears the name of Service. May it ever point straight upward toward God.

IV

Medicine Looks At
Alcoholics Anonymous

WITHOUT its friends of medicine, Alcoholics Anonymous might never have been born. It was from the medical profession that we of A.A. learned the physical and emotional nature of our malady. Today thousands of physicians throughout the world are working in closest co-operation with us.

In the following section we introduce two of these medical friends, both of whom freely gave us their warmest endorsements at A.A.'s twentieth anniversary celebration in St. Louis in July, 1955.

Here we reproduce the proceedings of the Twentieth Anniversary Convention's Medical Panel. The first address was given by Dr. W. W. Bauer of the American Medical Association. This was followed by a paper read by Dr. Harry M. Tiebout, A.A.'s first friend in the profession of psychiatry. Both physicians gave their view of Alcoholics Anonymous and told how they co-operate with us and how A.A. has influenced their own thinking and practice. This session opened with an A.A. member, Dr. Clarence P., in the chair.

A.A. CHAIRMAN DR. CLARENCE P.: To be transplanted from a small town of 9,000 people into an auditorium like this is a little bit overwhelming. And to be presented with the array of talent that we have here this morning is also a little overwhelming.

You have done me a great honor in permitting me to act as your chairman. We will run this pretty much as a medical meeting. We will dispense with all formalities and get down to the business of medicine and A.A.

This morning, first, we have with us the greatest of living A.A.'s, who in his humility has refused a doctor of laws degree. It seems to me that this was a great decision. I will only say, thank God he passed this way and that we have known him. There are no words to describe our feelings toward Bill.

BILL: I know you all sense that this is a very significant meeting on a very significant occasion, because it has to do with our relations to the men of medicine. A.A. can be likened to a temple supported by three pillars: one is religion, another is medicine, and the third is our own experience as people who have suffered from alcoholism. Medicine in its broad aspects includes the science of the mind and its effect upon the body, as well as the effect of a physical malady upon the mind. In our two distinguished guests, Dr. Bauer and Dr. Tiebout, we have here people truly expert in each of these departments.

It would be a sorry day for A.A. if we ever came to think that we had a monopoly on fixing drunks. I think we ought to encourage every research in this area, whether it concerns the mind or the body. As individuals we often ought to associate ourselves with such enterprises.

As excuse-makers and rationalizers, we drunks are champions. It is the business of the psychiatrist to get behind our excuses and to find the deeper causes for our conduct. Though uninstructed in psychiatry, we can, after a little time in A.A., see that our motives have not been what we thought they were and that we have been motivated by forces unknown to us. Therefore we ought to look, with the deepest respect, interest, and profit upon the findings of psychiatry, remembering that up to now the psychiatrists have been far more tolerant of us than we have been of them. So we thank them for the steadfast friendship and support which they have given us in nearly every quarter of the profession. When it comes to the general practitioner or specialist in the chemistry of the body, his findings too ought to be made use of by us as individuals. Of course as a movement we should never presume to intrude on the province of medicine. The practice of medicine is for doctors; the teaching of formal religion is for clergymen. So let us modestly fill our role; let us make our link, the once-missing one, strong. And let's thank God for folks like Dr. Bauer and Dr. Tiebout.

CHAIRMAN: On this morning's program I have shifted my own responsibilities. I have had the pleasure of meeting Dr. Earle M. from San Francisco. Without ever having met this gentleman before, but having had some previous correspondence with him, I feel as though I had known him for years. I am going to ask him to act as a co-chairman to introduce our next speaker. Let me present Dr. Earle M.

DR. EARLE M.: Fellow members of Alcoholics Anonymous, and distinguished guests: My remarks will be brief. We are indeed fortunate to have with us a man of the caliber that you are about to hear. He is one of the men in an exceedingly high position in the American Medical Association; one who carries you and me very close to his heart. We could ask for no better ally than the next speaker to confirm and strengthen the already growing friendship between A.A. and the medical profession. It is a deep pleasure and a great honor to introduce you to my boss—and your and my friend, Dr. W. W. Bauer.

DR. W. W. BAUER: Thank you, doctor, for that gracious introduction. I want to assure you that I am nobody's boss; I'm just one of the hired hands of the American Medical Association, or perhaps I should say, a perambulating loud-speaker. I think my status in the Association was expressed one day at an annual meeting in Atlantic City, when someone asked me at what hotel I was staying. I mentioned the hotel, and he said, "Oh you're not staying at such and such a hotel where the heads are; you're staying with the shoulders."

As a perambulating loud-speaker, I have faced innumerable audiences. One of my staff told me not so long ago that I had made over a thousand speeches, which is a magnificent tribute to the long-suffering of the American people. Ordinarily I take an audience in my stride, but I had an invitation about a year ago, when the A.M.A. met in San Francisco, to address an open meeting of A.A. in the downtown area of that city, and I admit that I never suffered more trepidation in all my life than I did in anticipation of meeting that audience, because I didn't see any good reason why I should be standing up there talking to you A.A.'s.

I reminded myself of the young rector in the Episcopal Church to which I belonged. He was consecrated Bishop, which was, of course, a great event in the life of a young Episcopal clergyman. After the solemn service of consecration there was a banquet, and the speakers' table was raised high on a platform so we could all see the new Bishop. He was given some very fine tributes, and when it came to his turn to respond, he said, "I feel like the slightly inebriated gentleman on a bright moonlight night, who walked out onto the middle of a bridge, looked down at the water, saw the moon reflected there, shook his head, and remarked to himself, "How in hell did I get way up here?"

I don't feel quite so apprehensive this time because that audience of A.A.'s proved to be just like any other audience; they were very kind and considerate to the speaker; they listened to him with courtesy, and they were even good enough to tell him afterward that they liked him. But the reason why I am much more at home this time is because of what happened to my wife, who accompanied me on that day. After the meeting, we were standing in a group with the people in charge, and with other A.A.'s and, I suppose, guests, and as we were chatting a gentleman joined the group and was introduced around, and when he saw my wife he looked at her and said, "Where have you been? It's been two years since you attended a meeting." This was particularly good because my wife is practically a teetotaler.

My experience with A.A. goes back to the days when I used to put radio shows on the NBC network every week, and I had the privilege of putting on a show under the guidance and direction of one of your members in the Chicago area. From that time on, I began to understand a little of what A.A. was all about. Of course, a person like me can never understand it fully. I am not a psychiatrist like Dr. Tiebout, so my practical knowledge is only that of a practitioner. I am not a member of A.A., so I do not have the background of experience that you have, and I am quite serious when I say I feel most humble in this position before a group of people like you.

All I can do is to try to express to you the feeling of the medical profession, a feeling which has been growing steadily throughout the life of your organization and which now, I believe, may be said to be fully crystallized—a feeling that A.A. has a very large and important part of such answers as we possess to the problem of alcoholism.

We know of course that the alcoholic is a sick person. That is a very simple phrase. It is today a phrase that is widely and generally accepted, and yet you and I know that it was not so long ago that the alcoholic was regarded as a nuisance, a pest, a person who could snap out of it if he really wanted to. He was regarded as a spoiled brat and as a no-good. Today we know that he is an individual who is sick, and we know that he is sick in an area of which our understanding is perhaps the least of any area in medicine, namely, illness of the emotions.

We are in some respects today in the same position with regard to emotional illness that we were fifty years ago with regard to tuberculosis. My memory does not extend quite that far back. I have been out of medical school only thirty-nine years, but from earlier literature I know that the idea persisted in the minds of some people that tuberculosis, an infectious disease which attacks people through no fault of their own, was a disgrace. Families often hid the tubercular person just as they cover up for the alcoholic today. I can remember very well, and so can every doctor on this platform, when we had the same attitude toward cancer. Cancer was regarded as a stigma, as a blight, something to be hidden, because it was a reflection upon the family. Today we know that cancer is a misfortune, and we are beginning now to realize that we must adopt the same attitude toward mental and emotional illnesses that we have slowly and painfully adopted to-

ward tuberculosis and cancer. Illness of the emotions is no mor
something to be ashamed of than is illness of the body. We should n
more hesitate to consult a psychiatrist, except for the scarcity of thes
important specialists, than we should hesitate to consult an ortho
pedist for a sore foot.

There is so much in attitudes. A movie star of a day gone by
Clara Bow, is credited with the statement that if she said her foot hur
everyone was sympathetic, but if she said, "My feet are killing me!"
they laughed. It's all in the matter of attitude, and we must learn to
consult the psychiatrist with the same attitude that we do any othe
specialist, without a feeling of shame, without a feeling that it is a
stigma. There are certain phrases that physicians are compelled to use
that we must learn to understand and to accept and to compensate for

We have to learn in medicine, and the public as a whole is going to
have to learn, of the tremendous individual differences among people
Differences in resistance, for example. Some people tire more easily
than others. Some people fall victims to infection more easily than
others because of differences in their body chemistry. There are
marked differences, as you know, in the intelligence of people, and
we must also learn to recognize that there are differences in emotional stability. There are some who can "take it" better than others
Being able to take it is generally regarded as a virtue, and so it is; it's
a fine thing if one has it. Courage also is a fine thing, and yet eminent
soldiers and military leaders have been asked, "Were you ever afraid
in battle?" and the answer, if they were honest, has usually been, "Of
course I was always afraid in battle. I'd be a fool not to be afraid in
battle. There is danger in battle."

We too must learn that there are battle situations for us, in which we
must be afraid, some of us more than others. It is no great credit
to me, as an individual, that I am not tempted by alcohol. I have my
own temptations. I am tempted by tobacco, I am tempted by food,
and there is just as much intemperance in giving way to those temptations as there is in giving way to the temptation which, to some of
you and many others, is or has been alcohol.

So we in the medical profession appreciate that we have a partnership with you. We need a partnership with you, as you do with us, to solve this problem of alcoholism. You have arrived by your own separate paths at some of the same solutions that medicine has arrived at in the treatment of alcoholism. We have learned, for example, as you have learned, the value of group therapy in many situations. I suppose the earliest indication of group therapy in medicine, at least in modern medicine, was expectant mothers' classes, where a lot of young pregnant women went together and learned all about what was happening to them and why and what to do about it.

Then the idea spread, and a very courageous doctor, who was almost laughed out of the profession, decided that there was no good reason why a man should not learn how to mix a formula and change a diaper. So we had expectant fathers' classes. And then we found group therapy a very potent factor in the field of mental and emotional health. In some of our mental institutions the device of play-acting is used, in order to allow people to express their latent hostility, if not in a constructive way at least harmlessly.

We have even applied group therapy to one of our other great temptations, the area of food, and it has been seriously suggested that "Fatties Anonymous," or something like that, be organized. I would dislike to see A.A. paraphrased too often, and in regard to lesser issues. But the fact is that overweight people can diet more cheerfully in groups than they can by themselves. I noticed in one of your bulletin items something about a lone member, and I can imagine how much more difficult it must be for lone members than it is for your groups, because the lone members do not have the direct support and sympathy of others who know what their problem is.

In medicine, we have learned a great deal about the physical treatment of the alcoholic. We have learned about nutrition and the importance of a fully rounded diet, and vitamins and minerals. We do not regard these as cures for alcoholism, for we don't believe any more that lack of vitamins is the cause of alcoholism; that's altogether too simple. But we do know that these things are necessary in the physical treatment and rehabilitation of the alcoholic. We know also that various kinds of drying out and other forms of therapy have failed. They are not enough by themselves. We need something more.

We know also that religious exhortation has failed, as has exhortation from people who have no grasp of the problem, who oversimplify, people in whose view an alcoholic is a person who is perpetually thirsty with a fierce craving for alcohol, people who do not know that a great many alcoholics hate alcohol worse than poison when they are sober, because they know that it *is* poison.

We have learned the futility of long-term pledges, which are so very, very difficult to keep. All these things you, more than any other group that I know anything about, have taught us. I have a great many friends in A.A. I suspect I have more friends in A.A. than I know anything about, because perhaps some of my friends have not yet told me that they are A.A.'s. I can recall, after some of the broadcasts we made, being stopped on the street in the village where I live near Chicago by people whom I had known for many years, and having them express to me a brief word of thanks for the broadcast. I was astonished at these people, but as time went on I became less and less astonished as I saw the effectiveness of your work, as I saw a man of great talent, a close friend of mine, a man in a creative line which I will not identify because it might possibly identify him, a man who was almost on the verge of genius. I saw alcohol make its insidious inroads upon his career, upon his relationships with his family and children, upon his standing in the community. I saw his wife covering up for him; I saw her describing his frequent illnesses, which we gradually came to know were illnesses, but not of the kind she wanted us to believe; I saw him on the verge of losing his job, and I saw him lose his job; and then I saw him surrender. I saw him throw up his hands and quit, saying, "I can't do it by myself. I've got to have help." And with the spiritual help of his clergyman and A.A., I have seen that man come back to a commanding position in his field, a man who is as sober today, as clear-eyed and bright, as any person in this audience. I'm confident he's going to stay that way. That is only one of a number that I have seen, and that other doctors have seen too.

So more and more we are beginning to realize that you have in your principles—surrender, humility, looking above for divine guidance, day-by-day sobriety, and above all anonymity—the insurance that nobody is going to get famous as a leader of Alcoholics Anonymous. These principles are all vitally important. You who have seen what alcohol can do in your lives are working together in groups and individually, and you are making a bigger impression on the problem of alcohol than has ever been made before. We need that impression in this world today, a world in which fear dominates.

Alcoholism is an escape—from what? Well, from intolerable situations in your own life, and the whole world is in an intolerable situation today. It is no wonder that alcoholism grows. Not only that, but we are in a social situation where alcoholic temptations are on every hand. I suppose this is the only convention, with perhaps the exception of the strictly religious ones, and not all of them, that is really a dry convention. I don't know whether you are welcome in convention cities. You certainly don't do the bar business any good.

People who, when I was a child, would have looked askance at anyone who took a drink are now socially serving cocktails in their homes. Our children are being brought up in a thoroughly alcoholic environment. By billboard, by radio, by television, in advertising of all kinds, the qualities of alcoholic beverages are being extolled. Put those two things together—a world living under the domination of fear and a world filled with alcohol and with alcoholic suggestion—and you can see how important it is that people realize what alcoholism really is: a deep-seated emotional illness that must be treated according to psychosomatic principles. Psychosomatic of course simply means body and soul. We hear a lot about psychosomatic medicine these days, but let me tell you that any doctor who was worth his salt, from the earliest times to these present days, was practicing psychosomatic medicine. Sir William Osler said, "It isn't so important what disease the patient has, as what kind of patient has the disease." That's one of the things that you people have realized.

So I come to you here with a great sense of appreciation for your having invited me. I come, as I say, to stand humbly before you and admire your great accomplishments, and to say to you that we in the medical profession are confident that these accomplishments will grow bigger and more significant as time goes on, because you have set your feet upon the upward paths; you have held out, and are holding out, a helping hand to those who need it.

I am no psychiatrist, but I have confidence in saying this to you as I have said to thousands of patients, that the thing we need most of all in this world today is tranquillity of mind. Various names have been given to it. Some books about it have been very popular. Some call it the power of positive thinking, some call it peace of mind, some call it peace of soul, but I'm inclined to go along with Billy Graham and call it peace with God. Those are the things we need. And an organization like yours, in a world that seems to have gone materialistically mad, gives us courage to believe that there is still hope, that there is still idealism, and that we are going to win out over many, many of our problems, one of the most serious of which is alcoholism.

CHAIRMAN: I am a Jack-of-all-trades and master of none, namely, a general practitioner, so I am a member of the American Academy of General Practice, which has its headquarters here in St. Louis. (I had to get that plug in!)

A.A. in its early days was nurtured by three outstanding doctors. You have heard Bill mention Dr. Silkworth. We all know our friend Dr. Harry Tiebout, and I would like at this time to mention our own G. Kirby Collier of New York State, who was instrumental in getting Bill W. to address the American Psychiatric Association, at which time he gave that very fine paper, "Medicine Looks at Alcoholics Anonymous," which was a milestone in medical history. So at this time I would like to pay a special tribute to G. Kirby Collier, who left us a year or so ago. Dr. Silkworth, Dr. Tiebout, and Dr. Collier were great workers for A.A. in its formative years, and we cannot say too much for any of these three men.

The next speaker in my opinion is a great physician. First he is a doctor of medicine, and then he has pursued that special branch of medicine called psychiatry. He has written many inspiring articles, the most recent one of which I would call to your attention, "The Ego Factors in the Surrender of Alcoholism." We had some reprints of this piece that we passed around to members of our groups in Rochester. We think it is one of the finest things that has been written in recent years. Of course, all of us alcoholics are endowed with this ego which Dr. Tiebout so effectively describes.

It gives me great pleasure to introduce to you Bill's friend of long standing, a great friend of A.A., a fine physician, scientist, and research man, Dr. Harry Tiebout of Greenwich, Connecticut.

DR. HARRY M. TIEBOUT: Under ordinary circumstances, I should thank the man who introduced me for his very nice remarks, but for years I've been teaching the need for ego reduction, and I'm not sure that my ego got sufficiently reduced by the introduction.

When the invitation came to speak before this group I immediately said, "Yes, I want to go." For many years, as you all know, I have been associated with A.A., and all the experiences that I had had came flashing through my mind, so there was so much to say that I didn't know quite where to begin. With your permission, I'm going to use a manuscript, so that the points I want to make will not be forgotten.

At an A.A. meeting the speaker as a rule identifies himself as an alcoholic and then proceeds to tell his story, sprinkling wisdom or humor, or both, as he goes along. I shall also tell my story, although I am less sure of matching either the wit or the wisdom of the A.A. speakers.

I joined A.A. by proxy in 1939 when a patient of mine became a member of the New York group. Well do I remember my first meeting. It was tense with excitement. A.A. was going on the air for the first time. One of the members, trying to rehabilitate himself, had talked with Gabriel Heatter, who, on hearing his story, suggested that he, the A.A. man, appear on the program "We The People." This was the night of his appearance, and it was far too thrilling and special for settling down to a regular meeting. The actual event was a bit of a letdown. The man from A.A. spoke briefly of his experiences —and it was over. A.A., however, had taken a step toward making itself known, not a very big step, to be sure; but one of the many which finally led to its present position on the national and international scene.

Later I attended other meetings, more orthodox in character, and as I did, I developed the conviction that this group had hit upon a method which solved the problem of excessive drinking. In a sense, it was an answer to my prayers. After years of butting my head against the problem of treating the alcoholic, I could now begin to hope.

In that respect my first two or three years of contact with A.A. were the most exciting in my whole professional life. A.A. was then in its miracle phase. Everything that happened seemed strange and wonderful. Hopeless drunks were being lifted out of the gutter. Individuals who had sought every known means of help without success were responding to this new approach. To be close to any such group, even by proxy, was electrifying.

In addition, from a professional point of view, a whole new avenue of treatment for the problems of alcohol had opened up. Somewhere in the A.A. experience was the key to sobriety. Here was the first authentic clue after many years of fruitless effort. The possibilities ahead were most intriguing. Perhaps I could learn how A.A. worked and thus learn something about how people stopped drinking. Yes, I shared in the general excitement of those days. I could see some daylight ahead.

My future in this regard was now clear. I would try to discover what made A.A. tick. In this quest for understanding I would never have gotten beyond first base if it had not been for Bill and many of the early members. A study of the Twelve Steps helped a little, but of far greater importance were the many insights already possessed by Bill and the others into the process through which A.A. brought about its results.

I heard of the need to hit bottom, of the necessity for accepting a higher Power, of the indispensability of humility. These were ideas which had never crossed my professional horizon and certainly had never influenced my nonprofessional thinking or attitudes. Revolutionary as they were, they nevertheless made sense, and I found myself embarked on a tour of discovery.

I began to recognize more clearly what hitting bottom really implied, and I began to do what I could to induce the experience in others, always wondering what was happening inside the individual as he went through the crisis of hitting the bottom.

Finally, fortune smiled on me again, this time from another patient. For some time she had been under my new brand of psychotherapy, designed to promote hitting bottom. For reasons completely unknown, she experienced a mild but typical conversion which brought her into a positive state of mind. Led by the newly found spiritual elements, she started attending various churches in town. One Monday morning she entered my office, her eyes ablaze, and at once commenced talking. "I know what happened to me! I heard it in church yesterday. I *surrendered*." With that word "surrender" she handed me my first real awareness of what happens during the period of hitting bottom.

The individual alcoholic was always fighting an admission of being licked, of admitting that he was powerless. If and when he surrendered, he quit fighting, admitted he was licked, and accepted the fact that he was powerless and needed help. If he did not surrender, a thousand crises could hit him and nothing constructive would happen. The need to induce surrender became a new therapeutic goal. The miracle of A.A. was now a little clearer, though the reason was still obscure why the program and the fellowship of A.A. could induce a surrender which could in turn lead to a period of no drinking.

As might be expected, I enjoyed a thrill of my own. I was getting in on what was happening, all of it an enjoyable experience. Still questing eagerly, I shifted my therapeutic attack. The job now was to induce surrender. But I ran into a whole nest of resistances to that idea. Totally new territory had to be explored. As I continued my tour it became ever more apparent that in everyone's psyche there existed an unconquerable ego which bitterly opposed any thought of defeat. Until that ego was somehow reduced or rendered ineffective no likelihood of surrender could be anticipated. The shift in emphasis in hitting bottom to surrender, to ego reduction, occurred during the first five or six years of my initial contact with A.A.

I well remember the first A.A. meeting to which I spoke on the subject of ego reduction. A.A., still very much in its infancy, was celebrating a third or fourth anniversary of one of the groups. The speaker immediately preceding me told in detail of the efforts of his local group, which consisted of two men, to get him to dry up and become its third member. After several months of vain efforts on their part, and repeated nose dives on his, the speaker went on to say, "Finally I got cut down to size, and I've been sober ever since." When my turn came to speak I used his phrase, "cut down to size," as a text around which to weave my remarks. Before long, out of the corner of my eye, I was conscious of a disconcerting stare. It was coming from the previous speaker. Looking a little more directly I could see his eyes fixed on me in wonder. It was perfectly clear that he was utterly amazed that he had said anything that would make sense to a psychiatrist. The look of incredulity never left his face during my entire talk. The incident had one value in my eyes. It showed that two people, one approaching the matter clinically, and the other relying on his own intuitively experienced report of what had happened to him, both came up with exactly the same observation: the need for ego reduction.

During the past decade my own endeavors have centered primarily upon this problem of ego reduction. How far I have been able to explore the territory is not at all certain. I have made, however, a little progress, and in the minutes remaining I shall try, first, to acquaint you with some of my findings, and second, to relate them to the A.A. scene as I see it.

As I have already stated, the fact of hitting bottom to produce a surrender which cut the ego to size was evident fairly soon. In time two additional facts manifested themselves. The first was that a reduced ego has marvelous recuperative powers. The second was that surrender is an essential disciplinary function and experience.

The first is merely repeating a fact known to you all. It is common knowledge that a return of the full-fledged ego can happen at any time. Years of sobriety are no insurance against its resurgence. No A.A., regardless of his veteran status, can ever relax his guard against the encroachments of a reviving ego. Recently one A.A., writing to another, reported that he was suffering, he feared, from "halo-tosis," a reference to the smugness and self-complacency which so easily can creep into the individual with years of sobriety behind him.

The assumption that one has all the answers, and the contrary, that one needs to know no answers, but just to follow A.A., are two indicators of trouble. In both cases open-mindedness is notably absent. Perhaps the commonest manifestation of the return of ego is witnessed in the individual who falls from his pink cloud, a state of mind familiar to you all. The blissful pink cloud state is a logical aftermath of surrender. The ego, which is full of striving, just quits, and the individual senses peace and quiet within. The result is an enormous feeling of release, and the person flies right up to his pink cloud and thinks he has found heaven on earth. Everyone knows he is doomed for a fall. But it is perhaps not equally clear that it is the ego slowly making its comeback which forces the descent from the pink cloud into the arena of life, where, with the help of A.A., he can learn how to become a sober person and not an angel. I could go on with many more examples familiar to you all, to show you the danger of ever assuming that the ego is dead and buried. Its capacity for rebirth is utterly astounding and must never be forgotten.

My second finding, that surrender is a disciplinary experience, requires explanation. In recent articles I have shown that the ego, basically, must be forging continuously ahead, and that it operates on the unconscious assumption that it, the ego, should never be stopped. It takes for granted that it is right to go ahead. It has no expectation of every being stopped and hence no capacity to adjust to that eventuality. Stopping says in effect, "No, you cannot continue," which is the essence of disciplinary control. The individual who cannot take a stopping is fundamentally an undisciplined person. The function of surrender in A.A. is now clear. It produces that stopping by causing individuals to say, "I quit. I give up my headstrong ways. I've learned my lesson." Very often for the first time in that individual's adult career he has encountered the necessary discipline which halts him in his headlong pace. And this happens because we can surrender and truly feel, "Thy will, not mine, be done." When that is true we have become in fact obedient servants of God. The spiritual point, at that moment, is a reality. We have become members of the human race.

I have now presented the two points I wished to make, namely, first, the ego is revivable, and second, surrender is a disciplinary experience. I next wish to discuss their significance to A.A. as I see it.

Primarily, they say quite simply that A.A. can never be just a miracle. The single act of surrender can produce sobriety by its stopping effect upon the ego. Unfortunately, that ego will return unless the individual learns to accept a disciplined way of life, which means that a tendency for ego comeback is permanently checked. This is not new to A.A. members; they have learned that a single surrender is not enough. Under the wise leadership of the founding fathers, the need for continued endeavor to maintain that miracle has been steadily stressed. The Twelve Steps, repeated inventories, not just one, and the Twelfth Step itself, a routine reminder that one must work at deserving sobriety, are all essential. Moreover, it is referred to as Twelfth Step work, which is exactly what it is. But this time the miracle is for the other fellow.

The Traditions are also part of a non-miracle aspect of A.A. They represent, as Bill has said, the meanings and the lessons of experience. They serve as guides for the inexperienced. They check the ways of the innocent and the unwary. They bring the individual down to earth and present him with the facts of reality. They say, "Pay heed to the teachings of experience or you will court disaster." It is not without reason that we talk with a sober voice of experience. My stress on the non-miracle elements of A.A. has a purpose. When I first made my acquaintance with A.A., I rode the pink cloud with most of its members. I, too, went through a period of disillusionment and, fortunately for me, I came out with a faith far stronger than anything a pink cloud can supply.

Mind you, I'm not selling miracles short. They do loosen up the individual. I know however, now, the truth of the Biblical saying, "By their fruits ye shall know them." Only through hard toil and labor can lasting results be obtained. As a consequence of the need for hard work to supplement any miracle, my interest in the non-miracle features is strong.

I can accept more truly the necessity of organization and of structure to curb as well as to guide. I believe there must be meetings like this one to provide the sense of belonging to a big working organization, of which each individual is but a part. And I believe that any group or individual who fails to participate in the enterprise of the organization is rendering himself and his group a disservice by not submitting to the disciplinary values inherent in those activities. He may be keeping himself free of entanglements but he is also keeping the ego unstopped. His chances of remaining sober are not of a high order. He is really going it alone and may be needing another miracle, which may not come off the next time.

In closing, let me reaffirm my proxy membership in A.A. I have been in on its glowing start and I have shared in its growing pains. And now I have reached the state of deep conviction in the soundness of the A.A. process, including its miracle aspects. I have tried to convey to you some of my observations on the nature of that process. I hope they will help in making the A.A. experience not just a miracle but a way of life which is filled with eternal value. A.A. has, I can assure you, done just that for me. Thank you.

V

Religion Looks at
Alcoholics Anonymous

THE society of Alcoholics Anonymous is spiritually as well as
morally centered. Nearly every A.A. member comes to believe in
and depend upon a higher Power which most of us call God. In A.A.
practically no full recovery from alcoholism has been possible without this all-important faith. God, *as we understand Him,* is the
foundation upon which our fellowship rests.

We present here the St. Louis addresses of two of the oldest and
finest friends in religion that A.A. may ever know—Father Edward
Dowling of the Jesuit order, whose personal example and influence
have meant so much to thousands of our members and to A.A. as a
whole, and Dr. Samuel M. Shoemaker, the Episcopal clergyman who
in our pioneering time instructed certain of our older members in
most of the spiritual principles which are today embodied in the
Twelve Steps of Alcoholics Anonymous.

BILL: With deep joy, I present to you Father Ed Dowling who
lives at the Jesuit House right here in St. Louis. Father Ed, knowing
whence comes his strength, is definitely allergic to praise. Nonetheless
I think that certain facts about him should be put into our record—
facts that new generations of A.A.'s ought to hear, read, and know.

Father Ed helped to start the first A.A. group in this town; he was
the first clergyman of his faith to note the surprising resemblance
between the spiritual Exercises of St. Ignatius (founder of the Jesuit

253

order) and the Twelve Steps of Alcoholics Anonymous. As a result, he was quick to write in 1940 the first Catholic recommendation of A.A. of which we have any knowledge.

Since then, his labor for us has been a prodigy. Not only have his recommendations been heard world-wide, but he has himself worked at A.A. and for A.A. Travels, A.A. meetings, wise and tender counsel —these works can be measured in thousands of miles and thousands of hours.

In my entire acquaintance, our friend Father Ed is the only one from whom I have never heard a resentful word and of whom I have never heard a single criticism. In my own life he has been a friend, adviser, great example, and the source of more inspiration than I can say.

Father Ed is made of the stuff of the saints. Now here he is.

FATHER DOWLING: I forgot to bring my store teeth, so if I am not being understood just wave a handkerchief and I'll try to do something about it. I asked my friend of very recent vintage, Dr. Shoemaker, to say a prayer for me and for you during this talk, and he said, "God is with you." I think you know what he meant, and it is reassuring, and I hope in the spirit of the Eleventh Step, through prayer and meditation, to try to improve our conscious contact with God.

May I suggest a few thoughts on the three words of our assignment: "God," "we," and "understand." And, if you will listen with your hearts, as I know you have during this whole meeting, rather than with just your ears, I think God will bless us.

My trying to understand God somehow reminds me of a definition of psychiatry which I heard just a day or two ago. It is "the id being examined by the odd," and I think that there could be our breakdown of topics: The *id* is the primary reservoir of power, or *God. Examined* could mean *understood*. And the *odd* is *us*.

First of all, to look at us: We are three things, I think—alcoholics, Alcoholics Anonymous, and agnostic.

Alcoholic means to me that we have the tremendous drive of fear, which is the beginning of wisdom. We have the tremendous drive of shame, which is the nearest thing to innocence. One of the early members of the Irish groups likes to quote some author whose name I forget but who said, "Alcohol doth do more than Milton can to make straight the ways of God to man."

Alcoholics Anonymous—not merely alcoholics, but Alcoholics Anonymous. Bill spoke last night of the outside antagonist in Alcoholics Anonymous, John Barleycorn. But I have always felt that there is an inside antagonist who is crueler, and that is the corporate sneer for a phony, and who of us is not a phony? I think that in all groups you have the problem of people of lynx-eyed virtue.

A third qualification is that I think we are all agnostic. I believe there are several groups, qualitatively, in A.A. There are the devout who did not seem to be able to apply their old-line religious truths. They were agnostic as to application. They are people like the priest who passed the man in the ditch before the good Samaritan helped him. A very good priest friend of mine says, "I really think that the first thing we will say when we get to Heaven is, 'My God, it's all true!'" I think all of us are rusty in some phases of our application of beliefs. Then there are the sincere eighteen-carat agnostics who really have difficulty with the spiritual hurdle.

The next word is *understand*. As we move from an obscure and confused idea of God to a more clear and distinct idea, I think we should realize that our idea of God will always be lacking, always to a degree be unsatisfying. Because to understand and to comprehend God is to be equal to God. But our understanding will grow. I am sure that Bill, sitting in that chair, and Dr. Bob, whose angel is probably sitting on that oddly misplaced empty chair, are growing in the knowledge of God. There is an old German saying that applies here: "Very few of us know how much we have to know in order to know how little we know." I'm sure Dr. Bob and Bill would certify to that.

There is a negative approach from agnosticism. This was the approach of Peter the Apostle. "Lord, to whom shall we go?" I doubt if there is anybody in this hall who really ever sought sobriety. I think we were trying to get away from drunkenness. I don't think we should despise the negative. I have a feeling that if I ever find myself in Heaven, it will be from backing away from Hell. At this point, Heaven seems as boring as sobriety does to an alcoholic ten minutes before he quits.

However, there are positive approaches, and the Twelfth Step mentions one: experience. (I still weep that the elders of the movement have dropped the word "experience" for "awakening.") Experience is one of the ways. It is mentioned in the Twelfth Step, and in the Second Step in another way. Now experience can be of two kinds. One kind is a sudden, passive insight like Bill's experience and like the *Grapevine* story of that Christmas Eve in Chicago. Those are all in the valid pattern of Saul's sudden passive insight as he was struck from his horse on the road to Damascus. There are other types, probably dearer to God since they are commoner, and those are our routine active observations. "I am sober today." This meeting this morning, this convention this week, as experience distills and condenses, have been born of suffering. The other night Bernard Smith, Chairman of A.A.'s Trustees (I get that hierarchy all mixed up), said something which to me was so good that I took it down. He said, "The tragedy of our life is how deep must be our suffering before we learn the simple truths by which we can live."

Some time before Whittaker Chambers became a well-known character, in his sister publication—he was on *Time* then—he wrote in *Life* an article called "The Devil." Quoting Satan, Whittaker Chambers says this: "And yet it is at this very point that man, that monstrous midget, still has the edge on the Devil. He suffers. Not one man, however base, quite lacks the capacity for the specific suffering which is the seal of his divine commission."

The second approach to understanding is mentioned in the Second Step, "Came to believe. . . ." I've known some of my Catholic friends who at that Step said, "Well, I believe already, so I don't have to do anything." And in a great burst of kindness they kept on drinking to let the Protestants catch up with them!

Belief is capitalizing on the experience of others. Blessed are the lazy, for they shall find their short cuts. The world can now capitalize on the A.A. experience of two decades. Newman says that the essence of belief is to look outside ourselves. Dr. Tiebout seems to think that, psychiatrically, the great problem is the turning of our affection away from self, outward. Faith is hard, as hard and as easy as sobriety, and has been called the greatest of our undeveloped resources.

What experience should we seek? What beliefs should we accept in our quest for God? The third word then would be *God*. Bill early wrote a letter—I have it—in which he said, "How far the alcoholic shall work out his dependence on God is none of A.A.'s business. Whether it is in a church or not in a church, whether it is in that church or this church, is none of A.A.'s business." In fact, he implied, "I don't think it's any of the members' business. It's God's business." And the A.A.'s business is charted in the Eleventh Step. Seek through meditation and prayer to find God's will and seek the power to follow it out.

I would like to share with you what I have found to be God's will. I believe the problem which half the people in this room have had in attaining sobriety I have had in attaining belief and faith. Where do you start? Well, I believe there's something to be said about starting at the nearest manifestation of God. Where is God nearest to me? Francis Thompson answers in his poem, "In No Strange Land":

> Does the fish soar to find the ocean,
>   The eagle plunge to find the air—
> That we ask of the stars in motion
>   If they have rumor of thee there?
>
> Not where the wheeling systems darken,
>   And our benumbed conceiving soars!—
> The drift of pinions, would we harken,
>   Beats at our own clay-shuttered doors.

We know A.A.'s Twelve Steps of man toward God. May I suggest God's Twelve Steps toward man as Christianity has taught them to me.

The first step is decribed by St. John. The Incarnation. The word was God and the word became flesh and dwelt amongst us. He turned His life and His will over to the care of man as He understood him. The second step, nine months later, closer to us in the circumstances of it, is the birth, the Nativity. The third step, the next thirty years, the anonymous hidden life. Closer, because it is so much like our own. The fourth step, three years of public life.

The fifth step, His teaching, His example, our Lord's Prayer. The sixth step, bodily suffering, including thirst, on Calvary.

The next step, soul suffering in Gethsemane; that's coming close. How well the alcoholic knows, and how well He knew, humiliation and fear and loneliness and discouragement and futility. Finally death, another step closer to us, and I think the passage where a dying God rests in the lap of a human mother is as far down as divinity can come, and probably the greatest height that humanity can reach.

Down the ages He comes closer to us as head of a sort of Christians Anonymous, a mystical body laced together by His teachings. "Whatsoever you do to the least of these my brethren so do you unto me." "I can fill up with is wanting in the sufferings of Christ." "I was in prison and you visited me." "I was sick and I was hungry and you gave me to eat."

The next step is the Christian Church, which I believe is Christ here today. A great many sincere people say, "I like Christianity, but I don't like Churchianity." I can understand that. I understand it better than you do because I'm involved in Churchianity and it bothers me too! But, actually, I think that sounds a little bit like saying, "I do love good drinking water but I hate plumbing." Now, who does like plumbing? You have people who like sobriety, but they won't take A.A.

And then, the eleventh steps is several big pipe lines or a sacraments of God's help.

And the twelfth step, to me, is the great pipe line or sacrament of Communion. The word that was God became flesh and becomes our food, as close to us as the fruit juice and the toast and the coffee we had an hour ago.

Oh, we know the story of an alcoholic's flight from God, and his movement toward Him. "Lord, give me sobriety, but not yet!" "Lord, I believe, help Thou mine unbelief!" I don't think there's an A.A. in this room who isn't worrying about one of those steps. "Lord, let me make that step, but not yet!" The picture of the A.A.'s quest for God, but especially God's loving chase for the A.A., was never put more beautifully than in what I think is one of the greatest lyrics and odes in the English language. It was written by a narcotic addict, and alcohol is a narcotic. It's a poem by Francis Thompson called "The Hound of Heaven." Let me just give you a few of the lines and I'll sit down.

> I fled Him, down the nights and down the days;
>   I fled Him down the arches of the years;
> I fled Him down the labyrinthine ways
>   Of my own mind; and in the midst of tears
> I hid from Him and under running laughter.
>   Up vistaed hopes I sped;
>   And shot, precipitated
>   Adown titanic glooms of chasmèd fears,
> From those strong Feet that followed, followed after.

And here's his description of God:

>   But with unhurrying chase
>   And unperturbèd pace,
>   Deliberate speed, majestic instancy
>   They beat—and a Voice beat
>   More instant than the Feet—
>   "All things betray thee, who betrayest Me."

And I'll skip to:

>   "Naught shelters thee, who wilt not shelter Me."

And:

> "Lo, naught contents thee, who content'st not Me."

> In the rash lustihead of my young powers,
>   I shook the pillaring hours
> And pulled my life upon me; grimed with smears,
> I stand amid the dust o' the mounded years—
> My mangled youth lies dead beneath the heap.
> My days have crackled and gone up in smoke,
> Have puffed and burst as sun-starts on a stream.

Now the long chase comes at last to an end:

> That Voice is round me like a bursting sea:

And the voice says, in conclusion:

> "And is thy earth so marred,
>   Shattered in shard on shard?
> Lo, all things fly thee, for thou fliest Me!
>   Strange, piteous, futile thing,
> Wherefore should any set thee love apart?
> Seeing none but I makes much of naught" (He said),

> "And human love needs human meriting:
>   How hast thou merited—
> Of all man's clotted clay the dingiest clot?
>   Alack, thou knowest not
> How little worthy of any love thou art!
> Whom wilt thou find to love ignoble thee
>   Save Me, save only Me?"

And this I find consoling:

> "All which I took from thee I did but take,
>   Not for thy harms,
> But just that thou mightst seek it in My arms.
>   All which thy child's mistake
> Fancies as lost, I have stored for thee at home:
>   Rise, clasp My hand, and come!"

And the alcoholic or the nonalcoholic answers:

> Halts by me that footfall:
> Is my gloom, after all,
> Shade of His hand, outstretched caressingly?

And God's answer:

> "Ah, fondest, blindest, weakest,
> I am He Whom thou seekest!
> Thou dravest love from thee, who dravest me."

Thank you.

BILL: Sitting just beyond Father Ed is another man we'd all like to be like. I have been wondering how many hours some of us in this room, including me, have spent in criticizing the men of religion. Yet they have taught us all that we know of things spiritual. It is through Sam Shoemaker that most of A.A.'s spiritual principles have come. He has been the connecting link: it is what Ebby learned from Sam, and then told me, that makes the connection between Sam, a man of religion, and ourselves. How well I remember that first day I caught sight of him. It was at a Sunday service in his church. I was still rather gun-shy and diffident about churches. I can still see him standing there before the lectern. His utter honesty, his tremendous forthrightness, struck me deep. I shall never forget it. I want to introduce Sam to you as one of the great channels, one of the prime sources of influence, that have gathered themselves together into what is now A.A. Here he is.

DR. SAMUEL SHOEMAKER: God bless you.

Whenever Bill gives me a chance to talk to you A.A.'s he says certain things about me to you which, if I said like things about him in your hearing, he would say was very bad for him. The rest of us suffer from egotism just as much as any alcoholic does, and it's just as bad for us, I'm afraid, to be flattered.

I got well flattered the other day. When I first got here a gal that I had never met before said to me, "Are you an alcoholic?" and I said, "No," and she said, "Well, you talk like one!"

Now just to get this record straight, I have always felt that Bill gave me a great deal more credit for having anything to do with getting this amazing outfit started than I really should have been given. But Bill's perceptions are very deep, and as we have noticed in many of the meetings where he has spoken to us, his memories are very sharp. So I just cheerfully accept these allegations of his because one of the most joyous things in my whole very joyous life has been the association that I have had with the people in A.A. And I am deeply grateful for the privilege of being here with you for this tremendous occasion.

Last autumn at his twentieth anniversary dinner, I first heard Bill give the story of the various strands which, woven together, have made the strong cable of A.A. We all know by now that the first thing that got into his mind as offering any real hope was talking with some men in whom there was the beginning of a real religious experience. One of them is here now. They had begun to find this through the old Oxford Groups in its earlier and, I think, better days. Much of its work centered at that time in my old parish, Calvary, on Gramercy Park in New York.

I take it that it began to be clear quite early in the life of A.A. that Dr. Jung's simple declaration that science had no answer, and Dr. Silkworth's incalculable help from the medical angle, and William James' great wisdom in his *Varieties of Religious Experience,* still left the need for a spiritual factor that would create a kind of synthesis and offer a kind of positive dynamic. The problem was: how to translate the spiritual experience into universal terms without letting it evaporate into mere ideals and generalities. And so, immediately after Step One, which concerned the unmanageableness of life, came Step Two: We came to believe in a power greater than ourselves that could restore us to sanity. The basis of that belief was not theoretical; it was evidential. Right before us were people in whose lives were the beginnings of a spiritual transformation. You could question the interpretation of the experience, but you couldn't question the experience itself.

In the third and fourth chapters of Acts is the story of the healing of a lame man by Peter and John. A lot of the ecclesiastics wanted to know how this came about. The Apostles told them that it was through the name of Christ that this man was healed. The story says, "And beholding the man which was healed standing with them, they could say nothing against it." Now you can fight a theory about an experience, but you've got to acknowledge the experience itself.

A.A. has been supremely wise, I think, in emphasizing the reality of the experience, and acknowledging that it came from a higher Power than human, and leaving the interpretation part pretty much at that. It would have been easy and must have been something of a temptation to go into the theological side. Here was evidence of spiritual power. All right then, let's define the power. But that would have run against several possible difficulties. If A.A.'s had said more, some people would have wanted them to say a great deal more and define God in a way acceptable and congenial to themselves. It would have taken only two or three groups like this, dissenting from one another, to wreck the whole business. Moreover, there were people with an unhappy association with religion, a dead church or a dull parson, or some churchgoing people whose workaday weekday lives did not support their Sunday professions. That would have added another factor to be overcome, as if we didn't have enough already. Also, there are the agnostics and the atheists, who either say that they don't know anything at all about these ultimate realities or that they disbelieve in God altogether.

I would like to quote for those who believe themselves still to be without faith in God a wonderful word from the Roman Catholic Spanish philosopher Unamuno y Jugo, who said, "Those who deny God deny Him because of their despair at not finding Him." For an outfit like A.A. to become dogmatic would have been fatal, I think. So they stuck to the inescapable experiences and told people to turn their wills and their lives over to the care of God *as they understood Him*. That left the theory and the theology, as Father Ed has just been saying to us, to the churches to which people belong. If they belonged to no church and could hold no consistent theory, then they had to give themselves to the God that they saw in other people. That's not a bad way to set in motion the beginnings of a spiritual experience. Maybe that's what we all do at the point where religion changes over for us from a mere tradition to a living power.

I believe in the psychological soundness of all this. Don't think it applies to alcoholics alone. I think it applies to everybody who is seeking genuine spiritual faith and experience. When one has done the best he can with intellectual reasoning, there yet comes a time for decision and for action. It may be a relatively simple decision, such as to enter fully into the experiment. I think the approach is much more like science than it is like philosophy. We don't so much try to reason it out in abstract logic. We choose a hypothesis. We act as if it were true and see whether it works. If it doesn't we discard it, and if it does we are free to call the experiment a success.

You can consider an idea in a vacuum, whether it be in the privacy of your own room or in an academic classroom or indeed in a pulpit, and you can discuss the truth of a theory forever, and it may do you no good. But when you let truth go into action, when you hurl your life after your held conception of truth, then things start to happen. If it is genuine truth it will accomplish things on the plane of actual living. If God is what Christ said He is, He is more eager to help us than we are to be helped. He does not trespass on man's freedom, and we can reject Him and deny Him and ignore Him as long as we like. But when we open the door on a spiritual search with our whole lives thrown into it, we shall find Him always there ready to receive our feeblest approaches and our most selfish and childish prayers and our always entirely unworthy selves. He is always ready to get down to business with us. The experimental approach seems to me to be the essence of our finding the help of a higher Power. We first lean on another human being who seems to be finding the answer, and then we lean on the higher Power that stands behind him.

William James, in the famous passage in *Varieties of Religious Experience,* says this: "The crisis of self surrender is the throwing of our conscious selves on the mercy of powers which, whatever they may be, are more ideal than we are actually, and make for our redemption. Self surrender has been and always must be regarded as the vital turning point of the religious life." That was almost the turning point in my own thinking, that sentence. He goes on to say, "One may say that the whole development of Christianity in inwardness has consisted in little more than the greater and greater emphasis attached to this crisis of self surrender." That, of course, becomes the heart of all real religion. Most of us come to God in the first instance from a need. If you want to say so, we come selfishly. But I would like to point out that before we can possibly be of any use to anybody else we must find the beginnings of an answer for ourselves, so that kind of selfishness may represent a necessary step in progress.

There is a great hue and cry today on the part of some people about those who seek benefits from God. I would like to know where in Heaven's name a bewildered and defeated person is going to go for the help he desperately needs if he doesn't go to God for it. Of course he is concerned about himself. He can't help it. He ought to be. He must be, if he is ever going to be made useful to other people. But later on he must also grow up and stop just *using* God and begin to ask God to *use him*. Stop asking God to do what *he* wants, and begin to try to find out what it is that God wants. Many people tell you they've given up faith. They prayed for something they wanted and it didn't come, and either there is no God or else He has no interest in them. What childish nonsense! How can anybody expect God to acquiesce in the half-baked prayers that a lot of us send up to Him. He would have the world in a worse chaos than it is now in five minutes.

Real prayer is not telling God what *we* want. It is putting ourselves at His disposal so that He can tell us what He wants. Prayer is not trying to get God to change His will. It is trying to find out what His will is, to align ourselves or realign ourselves with His purpose for the world and for us. That's why it is so important for us to *listen* as well as *talk* when we pray. That's why it is good to begin these meetings with silence. Oftentimes we come feverishly and willfully, and we have just got to quiet down before God can do anything for us. While our own voices are clamorous and demanding, there is no place for the voice of God. That is the thing most of us nonalcoholics get drunk on, just willfulness, just wanting life on our own terms, and it is as neurotic as any neurosis ever was. Everybody that is away from God and tries to do his own will in defiance of God is half-crazy. Till our own clamorous, demanding voices quiet down we cannot hear the voice of God. When we let willfulness cool out of us, God can get His will across to us as far as we need to see ahead of us. Dante said, "In His will is our peace."

There are a lot of people who don't like the weakness that is implied in that word "surrender." I was deeply thankful to hear Dr. Tiebout use that word. People like to think they are strong characters who can take care of their own destinies. That is always fictitious thinking. Everybody in this world is some kind of weakling, and if he thinks he is not, then pride is his weakness, and that is the greatest weakness of all.

People may think that they *have* overcome, or else they have *never* been overcome by the overtly disreputable sins, but who of us avoids selfishness and self-centeredness and the love of adulation and the love of power and pride? I think that a man is fortunate whose problems are of such a kind that they really get him into trouble, so he has got to do something about it. Temper and pride and laziness and scornfulness and irritability and indifference to human trouble and God-awful littleness—which is the worst thing about most of us in a day when everybody is meant to be bigger—these things get us non-alcoholics into difficulties, and they are just as bad as anything that ever got you alcoholics into difficulties. Nobody is strong, and the people who think they are strong are only self-deceived.

We act as if character and reasonably good behavior were the end of all existence. The real questions in life which underlie these matters of behavior are definitely of a religious nature. And they have only a religious answer, an answer that comes from God. Where did I come from, and what am I supposed to be doing here, and where do I go when I die? Those are questions which, unanswered, leave us without direction, without moorings, and without values. Science hasn't got any answer to those things, and philosophy only has the answers of good human guesses. Religious faith is the one candle in man's darkness in the mystery of life. If Christ came down from Heaven to represent God and speak for Him, we have got an answer. The lesser revelations to prophets and seers are of the same nature, but not of the same authority—as Father Ed has been suggesting to us—but all truly wise men begin with the acknowledgment of their finiteness, their darkness, and their needs. When we get through to God, by whatever name we call Him, or rather when we let Him get through to us, then we begin finding light and the answer.

I think the great need of our time is for vast, world-wide spiritual awakening. There are many signs that it is upon us. Western man is gradually getting it through his head that he owes the greatest of all human blessings, the blessing of liberty, to God and religion.

When Benjamin Franklin was in Paris at the end of the eighteenth century, he took his son around one day to call on Voltaire. As they were leaving, he asked Voltaire to give the boy a blessing. I could think of better men than Voltaire to ask for a blessing, but that is what he did. Voltaire put his bony old hands on that boy's head and said, "God and liberty, my son. Remember those words." Those words are correlative. There is an indissoluble connection between the two. I think that the gradual perception of that fact, as well as the realization of our personal insecurity, lies behind the greatly increased interest in religion that characterizes our time.

I believe that there are four universal factors in all genuine spiritual awakenings: conversion, prayer, fellowship, and witness. By conversion I mean the place where a person turns toward God. Where he begins to want to be honest about himself in the light of his religion. I don't mean perfection; I mean the search for it and the start toward it. That start is within the reach of us all.

But that is only the beginning. You know what a lot of religious people are like? They are like a lot of people sitting around a railroad station thinking they are on a train. Everybody is talking about travel, and you hear the names of stations and you have got tickets, and there is the smell of baggage around you and a great deal of stir, and if you sit there long enough you almost think you are on a train. But you are not. You only start to get converted at that point where you get on the train and get pulled out of the station. And you *do* get pulled out; you do not walk out.

Prayer, either private or group or public, is the place where we get in touch with God and God's power. God's power is always there, as there is always potential electricity in a wire that's plugged into a socket that is in touch with a dynamo. But you don't get the power until you close the circuit by turning the switch. Prayer, in ways which to me are theoretically quite unfathomable but which are always open to us actually, turns on the switch, opens up the power by closing the circuit. We do not so much "get what we want" as find out what we should do. Awakening—in the individual or in companies or in nations—always includes discovering the power that is in prayer.

Somehow we never can do this alone. From the first, Christ drew about Him a company. To join Him, you had also to join that company. The church has always been a scratch company of sinners. It is not the best people in the community gathered together for self-congratulation; it is the people who know they have a great need gathered to find its answer in worship toward God and fellowship with one another. The church is not a museum; it is a hospital. That is why we can all belong to it and all should.

Two old pagans went into an Episcopal Church one day, and they got in just in time to hear the minister say, "We have left undone those things we ought to have done and we have done the things we ought not to have done, and there is no health in us," and they said, "We're in the right place!"

Get over the idea that because you go to church you are good. You go to church to try to get in touch with God and let God redeem you, and incidentally you try to get good by the grace of God and not by your own bootstraps.

Then comes witness, by life and by word. I think there are a lot of self-righteous people in the world who think they are being a tremendously good influence, but they are so much like everybody else in the world, there is not much edge, there is not much difference. When a spiritual experience has begun that changes us deeply inside, it makes us more humble and conscious that we are not very good at all. Then I think people begin to get interesting. They wonder what happened to them and they begin asking questions, and then is the time to open up by the witness of words. We do not preach to other people, we do not talk down to them, God knows we do not point to ourselves as answers, but we share the beginnings of a victory. Every real believer shares in Twelfth Step work. Every real believer wants to get his belief across to other people, and he will take the trouble to try to learn to do it by life and by word.

To me A.A. is one of the great signs of spiritual awakening in our time. It is experimental in nature, not dogmatic. But none can doubt that God is what has made A.A. what it is today, what inspires it, what keeps it going, what is that perfectly intangible but absolutely unmistakable spirit that we have felt again and again since we have been here in St. Louis. I am thankful that the church has so widely associated itself with A.A., because I think A.A. people need the church for personal stabilization and growth, but also because I think the church needs A.A. as a continuous spur to greater aliveness and expectation and power. They are meant to complement and supplement each other.

I believe that A.A. will go on serving men and women as long as it may be needed, if it keeps open to God for inspiration, open to one another for fellowship, and open to people outside for service. I think A.A. has been wise to confine its organized activity to alcoholics, but

I hope and I believe that we may yet see a wide effect of A.A. on medicine, on psychiatry, on correction, on education, on the ever-present problem of human nature and what we shall do about it, and not least of all on the church itself.

I believe that A.A. has derived its inspiration and impetus indirectly from the insights and beliefs of the church. Perhaps the time has come for the church to be reawakened and revitalized by the insights and practices found in A.A. I don't know any fields of human endeavor in which the Twelve Steps are not applicable and helpful. I believe A.A. may yet have a much wider effect upon the world of our day than it has already had and may contribute greatly to the spiritual awakening which is on the way but which has come none too soon, for the world of our time is not sitting pretty.

And so on this occasion, when A.A. turns a historic corner, when the leadership will fall upon a wider company than in the past, let us give thanks to God for His goodness to us, for the way He has guided and prospered and used and enriched and developed this wonderful force in our time, and for all the promise that A.A. holds out for un-counted thousands and perhaps millions in the future.

God bless A.A. forever.

BILL: It is a commonplace of A.A. to say that our leaders do not rule by mandate—they lead by example. Surely we have been led this morning by a magnificent example—an example without which this Society might never have been. I think it is altogether fitting if, as my concluding part of this session, I recite to you the prayer of Francis, one of the saints whose example is so near and so dear to us all:

"Lord, make me a channel of thy peace, that where there is hatred, I may bring love; that where there is wrong, I may bring the spirit of forgiveness; that where there is error, I may bring truth; that where there is doubt, I may bring faith; that where there is despair, I may bring hope; that where there are shadows, I may bring light; that where there is sadness, I may bring joy. Lord, grant that I may seek rather to comfort than to be comforted; to understand than to be understood; to love than to be loved. For it is by giving that one receives. It is by self-forgetting that one finds. It is by forgiving that one is forgiven. And it is by dying that one awakens to eternal life."

VI

A Friend Looks at
Alcoholics Anonymous

THE friends of A.A. are legion. Their immense good will and
often their direct help has been indispensable to our progress.

Mr. Bernard B. Smith, the New York attorney whose address follows, has been notable for years because of the skilled devotion which
he, as a Trustee and as a Chairman of A.A.'s General Service Board,
has long given our world affairs. His is an example of the kind of
friendship which has always caused A.A. to prosper and to grow.

THE INDIVIDUAL, A.A., AND SOCIETY

BY BERNARD B. SMITH
Chairman, General Service Board of Alcoholics Anonymous
1951-1956

(Based on talks by Mr. Smith at the first six General Service Conferences)

As the time approached when I would cease to serve as Chairman, I found myself thinking of many things—of those exciting, early struggling days when A.A. was taking form; of the many friendships that A.A. has made possible for me, a nonalcoholic; of the countless heartwarming experiences that have been mine within the fellowship of A.A.; of the wonder that, in so short a time, A.A. could have produced a General Service Conference with so large a part of our Society represented by its chosen delegates.

More than anything else, perhaps, I thought of the miracle of timing in A.A., how things seem to get started in A.A. only when the time is ripe; how we may be vexed at things delayed only to realize and appreciate later that they were delayed solely because the time for doing them had not yet arrived.

And I thought of the finger of God determining our course—as individuals, as a fellowship, and in our relation to the world about us. Clearly, I thought, the Twelve Steps of A.A. must have been spiritually conceived to meet a serious and growing challenge to all of us, nonalcoholic as well as alcoholic. What is that challenge? It is the challenge to a generation that would deny the spiritual basis for human existence and accept in its place a currently socially accepted basis that is mechanistic and materialistic. It is a challenge to which A.A. will never yield, for the tenet of its faith and, indeed, its exist-

274

ence is founded on the certainty of a spiritual basis for life on earth.

I confess that when I was first exposed to A.A. I did not think in terms of broad social concepts or the application of great spiritual truths to the problems all men share in their pursuit of what each may dimly regard as happiness.

The circumstances of this first exposure were rather prosaic. The early members of A.A. and certain of their nonalcoholic friends, conscious of the need to create a simple but effective service structure for the fledgling movement, needed a lawyer to help frame the document leading to incorporation of the Alcoholic Foundation, now known as the General Service Board of A.A.

A friend of mine who was—and is—a member of A.A. suggested that I meet Bill. I shall never forget that first meeting in my office, late one afternoon fifteen years ago, and the evening we then spent together. And I shall always be grateful to my friend who brought Bill and me together on that memorable afternoon and evening, for in some mysterious way I was ready for Bill's message. I learned something then from Bill for which all of my life up to then seems to have been a kind of preparation. What Bill was getting through to me was the then-startling fact that in A.A., when men cease to drink by applying the Twelve Steps to their lives, they are in effect beginning to live on a spiritual basis.

And it struck me, as a nonalcoholic, that A.A. was a way of life for me, too, and for countless others like me who had never sought escape in a bottle or in those other refuges to which men turn from the pressures of a materialistic world. The still-drinking alcoholic, as should be clear to all who observe mankind today, has no monopoly on unhappiness or on the feeling that life lacks purpose and fulfillment.

In all the years since that first meeting with Bill, wonderful years, when it has been my privilege to serve as a member and as Chairman of the General Service Board, I have never lost my initial awareness that A.A. is more than a fellowship for recovered alcoholics, that it is indeed a way of life for all who have lost their way in a troubled world.

I have frequently attempted to define the fellowship of A.A., with little success, until one day while in England I listened to a broadcast delivered by Canon C. E. Raven, a noted British religious leader. In the course of this broadcast, Canon Raven set forth the conditions of a true fellowship in these words:

Three conditions are necessary for true fellowship: The possession of a common ideal involving a complete release from selfishness and division. The discharge of a common task big enough to capture the imagination and give expression to loyalty. And the comradeship, the "togetherness," thus involved as we find out the joy and power of belonging to an organic society and engaging in a whole-time service. We can find it at its fullest extent where the ideal is highest and most exacting, where the task extends and integrates every ounce of our strength and every element of our being, where the comradeship is so solid and deep that we respond one to another without conscious effort, realize the unspoken need, and react to it spontaneously and at once.

Under such conditions, all the vitality that we usually waste upon our jealousies and our vanities—upon keeping up appearances and putting other people in their proper place—becomes available for creative use.

These words have meaning for A.A., I believe, not only as a definition of a true fellowship and of our goals and attitudes but as reminders that A.A. is not a static, passive social organism but, in its largest sense, a dynamic, creative force that releases our latent power to live and act constructively.

Not long ago I was flying high over the deserts of our great Southwest. Here and there, almost out of nowhere, were tiny patches of lush, green growth, surrounded by great expanses of brown, lifeless desert. My mind turned to the great springs of water lying under this desert expanse which, if tapped, would cause the entire desert to flower. And I thought that God provides the water but we have to dig the wells.

Those green, lush patches I likened to our groups where, with the faith derived from the Twelve Steps, we dug the wells that caused patches in the desert of life to flower. And I reflected how we have learned that we, alone, could not transform the desert in which we lived; we could not dig that well alone. For in A.A. the whole is truly greater than the sum of all its parts. The infusing power of the group, of our fellowship, draws something more out of each of us than any of us by himself can supply. Each of us in turn draws out of the spiritual reservoir of our fellowship the added courage and will which makes each one the stronger and our fellowship the greater.

What we can draw by living according to the tenets of A.A. is something more than what the materialist regards as happiness.

Recently I had occasion to examine the definition of happiness in a new, unabridged dictionary. To my surprise, the first definition listed "good luck, good fortune, prosperity." This materialistic definition is a long way from the concept of happiness to be found in A.A.

The second definition in that dictionary, however, was directly applicable to the kind of happiness men and women seek and find in A.A., the kind that can be sustained, by living in accordance with the Twelve Steps. This definition reads: "A state of well-being characterized by relative permanence, by dominantly agreeable emotion, ranging in value from mere content to positive felicity, and by a natural desire for its continuation."

Measured in terms of this definition I believe that those who live by the principles of A.A. enjoy a greater measure of happiness than any class or group of people to which I have ever been exposed.

I gave a great deal of thought to these definitions. I reflected, for example, that dictionary definitions follow current socially accepted usage, and I was disturbed by the fact that the first definition of happiness should be couched in such materialistic terms as "good luck, good fortune, prosperity."

So I examined a number of dictionaries published in the 1890's. I found that the word "prosperity" appeared in none of these reference works under the definition of "happiness." I then happened upon a standard dictionary published in 1927. By this time the definition "good luck, good fortune, prosperity" had not only appeared but reached second place. And by 1943 it had reached first place, supplanting that definition of happiness by which we in A.A. prefer to be blessed, and a totally material conception of happiness had now been accepted as a definition of the goal of men and women in modern society.

One might say, therefore, that our Twelve Steps, judged by the socially accepted standard of happiness of this age, are steps backward. But they are steps backward into the universal heart of man, back into the true spirit of man. The world will have moved forward when our dictionary definition of happiness is revised backward.

Truths emerging in a materialistic society are bound at times to be paradoxical. Consider, for example, the simple statement: "I am an alcoholic." The first time a man or woman stands before us and says, "I am an alcoholic," he speaks those words when he no longer drinks alcohol. Thus, when the time comes that members *describe* themselves as alcoholics, society ceases to *regard* them as such. Yet it is only at the moment when a member ceases to drink that he asserts the right to describe himself as an alcoholic.

When alcoholics live materialistically and drink excessively, they refuse to accept the label of "alcoholic." Yet when they cease to drink and when they say to themselves and to the world, "We are alcoholics," the world refuses to see them as such.

What an unthinking world may look upon as defeat, alcoholics in A.A. know as a triumph of the spirit, a triumph of humility over false pride and self-centeredness. How few human beings ever have the courage to stand up before their neighbors and, in humility, describing themselves truthfully, to say: "This is what I really am."

There are two moments in which utterance of the words "I am an alcoholic" have great significance. There is the first time a member speaks those words at an A.A. meeting. There is, however, another and earlier time which is perhaps of even greater significance. That is the moment when a man says to his sponsor, in the darkness and desperation of his soul, "I am an alcoholic." And this moment points to another paradox in A.A.

The paradox is that the member of A.A. approaches his suffering alcoholic brother not from the superiority and strength of his position of recovery but from the realization of his own weakness. The member talks to the newcomer not in a spirit of power but in a spirit of humility and weakness. He does not speak of how misguided the still suffering alcoholic is; he speaks of how misguided he once was. He does not sit in judgment of another but in judgment of himself as he had been.

Society, in referring to the alcoholic, employs the expression "the enslavement of alcohol." For the A.A. member, this statement is in a very special sense paradoxical too, if indeed it is true at all. In sober fact, the member was never enslaved by alcohol. Alcohol simply served as an escape from personal enslavement to the false ideals of a materialistic society. Yet if we accept society's definition of the alcoholic's earlier state as enslavement by alcohol, the A.A. member can no longer resent it, for it has served to set him free from all the materialistic traps with which the paths through the jungle of our society are set. For the alcoholic first had to face materialism as a disease of society before he could free himself of the illness of alcoholism and be free of the social ills that made him an alcoholic.

Men and women who use alcohol as an escape are not the only ones who are afraid of life, hostile to the world, fleeing from it into loneliness. Millions who are not alcoholics are living today in illusory worlds, nurturing the basic anxieties and insecurities of human existence rather than face themselves with courage and humility. To these people, A.A. can offer as a cure no magic potion, no chemical formula, no powerful drug. But it can demonstrate to them how to use the tools of humility, honesty, devotion, and love, which indeed are the heart of the Twelve Steps of our recovery.

There is still another paradoxical statement by human society which has special application to A.A. That statement is the saying that "A chain is as strong as its weakest link." The accepted connotation is that a chain is strong only if it has no weak links.

The paradox of this statement as applied to A.A. is that, in A.A., the chain *is* as strong as its weakest link. For the endless chain of A.A. grows in strength to the extent that it is able to reach the weak links, the still-suffering alcoholic men and women about us. It is upon this paradoxical truth that the assurance of the survival of the fellowship rests. The perpetuation of A.A. is grounded in the so-called weakness of those human beings who escape the materialistic bases of society through the medium of alcohol.

It is because we know of the tremendous impact that A.A. can have on generations that will follow us that we have been so painstaking in building a structure of service of A.A. in the General Service Board, the General Service Conference, and the many service agencies that perform the essential daily tasks of carrying the A.A. message throughout the world. It is with good reason that Bill has described this structure of service as a legacy, deserving of the same attention and understanding accorded the First Legacy of the Twelve Steps and the Second Legacy of Twelve Traditions.

But this Third Legacy of Service has a string to it. And the string is that we are granted the use of this legacy for our lifetime upon the condition that we will not only look after it but increase its spiritual content for the generations that will follow us. Each succeeding generation, as it receives this legacy, must similarly protect it if they wish to employ it and gain life by it and pass it on to the next generation with an enriched spiritual content.

The General Service Conference of A.A. is, of course, the practical instrument for preserving, enhancing, and administering this great Third Legacy of Service. The concept of the Conference from the beginning has been simple and compelling. It is grounded in the belief that all of us who have been associated with A.A. during its early growth and development owe an obligation to society. That obligation is to insure that this fellowship survives, that this flame of faith, this beacon light of hope for the world, must never be extinguished.

We may not need a General Service Conference to insure our own recovery. But we do need it to insure the recovery of the alcoholic who still stumbles in the darkness, seeking the light. We need it to insure the recovery of some newborn child, inexplicably destined to alcoholism. We need it to provide, in keeping with the Twelfth Step, a permanent haven for all alcoholics who in the ages ahead can find in A.A. that rebirth which brought its first members back to life.

We need it because we are conscious of the devastating effect of the human urge for power and prestige which must never be permitted to invade A.A. We need a Conference to insure A.A. against government while insulating it against anarchy; we need it to protect the fellowship against disintegration while preventing overintegration. We need it so that Alcoholics Anonymous and Alcoholics Anonymous alone may be the ultimate repository of its own Twelve Steps, its Twelve Traditions, and all of its Services.

We need a Conference to insure that changes within A.A. come only as a response to the needs and wants of all A.A., and not of any few. We need it to insure that the doors of the halls of A.A. shall never have locks on them, so that all people with an alcoholic problem for all time to come may enter these halls unmasked and feel welcome. We need it to help insure that Alcoholics Anonymous never asks of anyone who needs help what his or her race is, what his or her creed is, or what his or her social position is.

I have considered it a priceless privilege and a great inspirational experience to have been able to serve A.A. as Chairman of the General Service Board for so many years, a position which also enabled me to serve as Chairman of the first six General Service Conferences. When I retired as Chairman, following the Sixth Conference in April, 1956, I did not feel that I was stepping out of A.A. No one who is a part of A.A., as I feel I have been, steps out. He just steps aside. He continues to serve in the ranks, giving of himself as humbly and as ably as he can.

I did not tender my resignation as Chairman because I no longer wanted to be Chairman. I have enjoyed the responsibility. I have found, as a nonalcoholic, great self-fulfillment in the trust that so many have granted to me. To state one more paradox, I am resigning as Chairman out of my love for, and devotion to, A.A. For I declared many years go, and have continued to believe, that A.A. must insulate itself against the "proprietary right to serve." No man must have the right to remain in office in A.A. indefinitely.

The very fact that no one has sought my resignation, and indeed that the contrary is happily true, is all the more reason to reaffirm the tradition of rotation in all A.A. service positions. Some day this tradition that no one should serve as chairman for an indefinite period may prove more valuable than we appreciate today. Certainly it is in keeping with the expanding unwritten body of tested tradition that is being accepted throughout A.A.: that while A. A. is important to the existence of the individual, no individual must be vital to the existence of A.A. It is A.A. that is important, important to those whom society has rejected and to those who have rejected society, important indeed to all of human society as a symbol of the power of the great spiritual reservoir upon which all may draw who aspire to a true way of life.

This precious message which we have received, and by which we try to live, has resulted in our achieving a far greater measure of human happiness than is the lot of the average human being who walks the earth today and who has not been subjected to the acute suffering of alcoholism. We must, however, as individuals and as a fellowship, always be concerned with the structure of service of Alcoholics Anonymous which protects and expands our way of life. For we will continue to owe to the generations yet unborn a solemn obligation to insure that this way of life is available to them, as it has been to us.

As a nonalcoholic and as a student of those great social movements from which we derive the best of our heritage today, I regard the fellowship of Alcoholics Anonymous as the outstanding spiritual phenomenon of our century. I see in the concept of living which is embodied in Alcoholics Anonymous a glorious hope for all of mankind. For the members of this fellowship are truly witnesses of the living truth that man can live the life of the spirit and still function effectively in a materialistic world.

And so this first generation in the life of A.A. draws to a close. It is rich in its faith, large in its numbers, and dedicated to its purpose. I am grateful that I have been privileged to observe its emergence in our society.

In now stepping aside as Chairman of A.A.'s movement-wide service agency, I confess to only one regret. And that is that I did not have the skill or the gifts that would have enabled me to do more than the little I have tried to do to further the purposes of this great and enduring fellowship.

APPENDICES

APPENDIX A

How to Get in Touch with Alcoholics Anonymous and the Al-Anon Family Groups

In the United States and Canada, most towns and cities have A.A. groups. In such places, A.A. can be located through the local telephone directory, newspaper office, or police station, or by contacting local priests or ministers. In large cities, groups often maintain local offices where alcoholics or their families may arrange for interviews or hospitalization. These so-called Intergroup Associations are found under the listing "A.A." or "Alcoholics Anonymous" in telephone directories.

In New York, U.S.A., Alcoholics Anonymous maintains its international service center. This consists of the General Service Board of A.A., whose Trustees administer A.A.'s General Service Office, A.A. World Services, Inc., and our monthly magazine, The A.A. Grapevine.

If you cannot find A.A. in your locality, a letter addressed to Alcoholics Anonymous, Box 459, Grand Central Station, New York, N.Y. 10017 U.S.A., will receive a prompt reply from this world center, referring you to the nearest A.A. group. If there is none nearby, you will be invited to carry on a correspondence which will do much to insure your sobriety no matter how isolated you are.

Should you be the relative or friend of an alcoholic who shows no immediate interest in A.A., it is suggested that you write the Al-Anon Family Groups, Inc., P.O. Box 182, Madison Sq. Station, New York, N.Y. 10010 U.S.A. This is a world clearinghouse for the Al-Anon Family Groups, composed largely of the wives, husbands, and friends of A.A. members. This headquarters will give you the location of the nearest Family Group and will, if you wish, correspond with you about your special problems.

APPENDIX B

WHY ALCOHOLICS ANONYMOUS IS ANONYMOUS

BY BILL

This article will be best understood by first recalling the anonymity Traditions. Tradition Eleven reads: "Our public relations policy is based on attraction rather than promotion; we need always maintain personal anonymity at the level of press, radio, films, and TV." Tradition Twelve states: "Anonymity is the spiritual foundation of all our traditions, ever reminding us to place principles before personalities."

As never before, the struggle for power, importance, and wealth is tearing civilization apart—man against man, family against family, group against group, nation against nation.

Nearly all those engaged in this fierce competition declare that their aim is peace and justice for themselves, their neighbors, and their nations. "Give us power," they say, "and we shall have justice; give us fame and we shall set a great example; give us money and we shall be comfortable and happy." People throughout the world deeply believe such things and act accordingly. On this appalling dry bender, society seems to be staggering down a dead-end road. The stop sign is clearly marked. It says "Disaster."

What has this got to do with anonymity, and Alcoholics Anonymous?

We of A.A. ought to know. Nearly every one of us has traversed this identical dead-end path. Powered by alcohol and self-justification, many of us have pursued the phantoms of self-importance and money right up to the disaster stop sign. Then came A.A.

We faced about and found ourselves on a new highroad where the direction signs said never a word about power, fame, or wealth. The new signs read, "This way to sanity and serenity. The price is self-sacrifice."

Our textbook, *Twelve Steps and Twelve Traditions,* states that "anonymity is the greatest protection our society can ever have." It also says that "the spiritual substance of anonymity is sacrifice."

Let's turn to A.A.'s twenty years of experience and see how we arrived at those beliefs now expressed in our Traditions Eleven and Twelve.

At the beginning we sacrificed alcohol. We had to, or it would have killed us. But we couldn't get rid of alcohol unless we made other sacrifices. Big shot-ism and phony thinking had to go. We had to toss self-justification, self-pity, and anger right out the window. We had to quit the crazy contest for personal prestige and big bank balances. We had to take personal responsibility for our sorry state and quit blaming others for it.

Were these sacrifices? Yes, they were. To gain enough humility and self-respect to stay alive at all we had to give up what had really been our dearest possession—our ambition and our illegitimate pride.

But even this was not enough. Sacrifice had to go farther. Other people had to benefit too. So we took on some Twelfth Step work; we began to carry the A.A. message. We sacrificed time, energy, and our own money to do this. We could not keep what we had unless we gave it away.

Did we demand that our new prospects give us anything? Were we asking them for power over their lives, for fame for our good work, or for a cent of their money? No, we were not. We found that if we demanded any of these things our Twelfth Step work went flat. So these natural desires had to be sacrificed; otherwise our prospects got little or no sobriety. Nor, indeed, did we.

Thus we learned that sacrifice had to bring a double benefit, or else little at all. We began to know about the kind of giving of ourselves that has no price tag on it.

When the first A.A. group took form, we soon learned a lot more about this. We found that each of us had to make willing sacrifices for the group itself, sacrifices for the common welfare. The group, in turn, found that it had to give up many of its own rights for the protection and welfare of each member, and for A.A. as a whole. These sacrifices had to be made or A.A. could not continue to exist.

Out of these experiences and realizations, the Twelve Traditions of Alcoholics Anonymous began to take shape and substance. Gradually we saw that the unity, the effectiveness, and even the survival of A.A. always would depend upon our continued willingness to give up our personal ambitions and desires for the common safety and welfare. Just as sacrifice meant survival for the individual, so did sacrifice mean unity and survival for the group and for A.A.'s entire fellowship.

Viewed in this light, A.A.'s Twelve Traditions are little else than a list of sacrifices which the experience of twenty years has taught us that we must make, individually and collectively, if A.A. itself is to stay alive and healthy.

In our Twelve Traditions we have set our faces against nearly every trend in the outside world. We have denied ourselves personal government, professionalism, and the right to say who our members shall be. We have abandoned do-goodism, reform, and paternalism. We refuse outside charitable money and have decided to pay our own way. We will co-operate with practically everybody, yet we decline to marry our society to anyone. We abstain from public controversy and will not quarrel among ourselves about those things that so rip society asunder: religion, politics, and reform. We have but one purpose, to carry the A.A. message to the sick alcoholic who wants it.

We take these attitudes not at all because we claim special virtue or wisdom; we do these things because hard experience has told us that we must— if A.A. is to survive in the distraught world of today. We also give up rights and make sacrifices because we ought to, and, better yet, because we want to. A.A. is a power greater than any of us; it must go on living or else uncounted thousands of our kind will surely die. This we know.

Now where does anonymity fit into this picture? What is anonymity anyhow? Why do we think it is the greatest single protection that A.A. can ever have? Why is it our greatest symbol of personal sacrifice, the spiritual key to all our Traditions and to our whole way of life?

The following fragment of A.A. history will reveal, I deeply hope, the answer we all seek. Years ago a noted ball player sobered up through A.A. Because his comeback was so spectacular, he got a tremendous personal ovation in the press, and Alcoholics Anonymous got much of the credit. His full name and picture, as a member of A.A., was seen by millions of fans. It did us plenty of good, temporarily, because alcoholics flocked in. We loved this. I was specially excited because it gave me ideas.

Soon I was on the road, happily handing out personal interviews and pictures. To my delight, I found I could hit the front pages, just as he could. Besides, he couldn't hold his publicity pace, but I could hold mine.

I only needed to keep traveling and talking. The local A.A. groups and newspapers did the rest. I was astonished when recently I looked at those old newspaper stories. For two or three years I guess I was A.A.'s number one anonymity breaker.

So I can't really blame any A.A. who has grabbed the spotlight since. I set the main example myself, years ago.

At the time, this looked like the thing to do. Feeling justified, I ate it up. What a bang it gave me when I read those two-column spreads about "Bill the Broker," full name and picture, the guy who was saving drunks by the thousands!

Then this fair sky began to be a little overcast. Murmurs were heard from A.A. skeptics who said, "This guy Bill is hogging the big time. Dr. Bob isn't getting his share." Or, again, "Suppose all this publicity goes to Bill's head and he gets drunk on us?"

This stung. How could they persecute me when I was doing so much good? I told my critics that this was America and didn't they know I had the right of free speech? And wasn't this country and every other run by big-name leaders? Anonymity was maybe okay for the average A.A. But co-founders ought to be exceptions. The public certainly had a right to know who we were.

Real A.A. power-drivers (prestige-hungry people, folks just like me) weren't long in catching on. They were going to be exceptions too. They said that anonymity before the general public was just for timid people; all the braver and bolder souls, like themselves, should stand right up before the flash bulbs and be counted. This kind of courage would soon do away with the stigma on alcoholics. The public would right away see what fine citizens recovered drunks could make. So more and more members broke their anonymity, all for the good of A.A. What if a drunk was photographed with the Governor? Both he and the Governor deserved the honor, didn't they? Thus we zoomed along down the dead-end road.

The next anonymity-breaking development looked even rosier. A close A.A. friend of mine wanted to go in for alcohol education. A department of a great university interested in alcoholism wanted her to go out and tell the general public that alcoholics were sick people, and that plenty could be done about it. My friend was a crack public speaker and writer. Could she tell the general public that she was an A.A. member? Well, why not? By using the name Alcoholics Anonymous she would get fine publicity for a good branch of alcohol education and for A.A. too. I thought it an excellent idea and therefore gave my blessing.

A.A. was already getting to be a famous and valuable name. Backed by our name and her own great ability, she produced immediate results. In nothing flat her own full name and picture, plus excellent accounts of her educational project and of A.A., landed in nearly every large paper in North America. The public understanding of alcoholism increased, the stigma on drunks lessened, and A.A. got new members. Surely there could be nothing wrong with that?

But there was. For the sake of this short-term benefit, we were taking on a future liability of huge and menacing proportions. Presently an A.A. member began to publish a crusading magazine devoted to the cause of Prohibition. He thought Alcoholics Anonymous ought to help make the world bone dry. He disclosed himself as an A.A. member and freely used the A.A. name to attack the evils of whiskey and those who made it and drank it. He pointed out that he too was an "educator," and that his brand of education was the "right kind." As for putting A.A. into public controversy, he thought that was exactly where we should be. So he busily used A.A.'s name to do just that. He broke his anonymity, of course, to help his cherished cause along.

This was followed by a proposal from a liquor trade association that an A.A. member take on a job of "education." People were to be told that too much alcohol was bad for anyone and that certain people—the alcoholics— shouldn't drink at all. What could be the matter with this?

The catch was that our A.A. friend had to break his personal anonymity; every piece of publicity and literature was to carry his full name as a member of Alcoholics Anonymous. This of course would be bound to create the definite public impression that A.A. favored "education," liquor trade style.

Though these two developments never happened to get far, their implications were nevertheless terrific. They spelled it right out for us. By hiring out to another cause, and then declaring his A.A. membership to the whole public, it was in the power of any A.A. to marry Alcoholics Anonymous to practically any enterprise or controversy at all, good or bad. The more valuable the A.A. name became, the greater the temptation would be.

Further proof of this was not long in showing up. Another member started to put us into the advertising business. He had been commissioned by a life insurance company to deliver a series of twelve "lectures" on Alcoholics Anonymous over a national radio hookup. This would of course advertise life insurance and Alcoholics Anonymous—and naturally our friend himself—all in one good-looking package.

At A.A. Headquarters, we read the proposed lectures. They were about 50 per cent A.A. and 50 per cent our friend's personal religious convictions. This could create a false public view of us. Religious prejudice against A.A. would be aroused. So we objected.

Our friend shot back a hot letter saying that he felt "inspired" to give these lectures and that we had no business to interfere with his right of free speech. Even though he was going to get a fee for his work, he had nothing in mind except the welfare of A.A. And if we didn't know what was good for us, that was too bad. We and A.A.'s Board of Trustees could go to the devil. The lectures were going on the air.

This was a poser. Just by breaking anonymity and so using the A.A. name for his own purposes, our friend could take over our public relations, get us into religious trouble, put us into the advertising business.

This meant that any misguided member could thus endanger our society any time or any place simply by breaking anonymity and telling himself how much good he was going to do for us. We envisioned every A.A. advertising man looking up a commercial sponsor, using the A.A. name to sell everything from pretzels to prune juice.

Something had to be done. We wrote our friend that A.A. had a right of free speech too. We wouldn't oppose him publicly, but we could and would guarantee that his sponsor would receive several thousand letters of objection from A.A. members if the program went on the radio. Our friend abandoned the project.

But our anonymity dike continued to leak. A.A. members began to take us into politics. They began to tell state legislative committees—publicly, of course—just what A.A. wanted in the way of rehabilitation, money, and enlightened legislation.

Thus, by full name and often by pictures, some of us became lobbyists. Other members sat on benches with police court judges, advising which drunks in the line-up should go to A.A. and which to jail.

Then came money complications involving broken anonymity. By this time, most members felt we ought to stop soliciting funds publicly for A.A. purposes. But the educational enterprise of my university-sponsored friend had meanwhile mushroomed. She had a perfectly proper and legitimate need for money and plenty of it. Therefore, she asked the public for it, putting on a drive to this end. Since she was an A.A. member and continued to say so, many contributors were confused. Some thought A.A. was in the educational field. Others thought A.A. itself was raising money, when indeed it was not and did not want to. So A.A.'s name was used to solicit funds at the very moment we were trying to tell people that A.A. wanted no outside money. This precedent set in motion all sorts of public solicitations by A.A.'s for money—money for drying-out farms, Twelfth Step enterprises, A.A. boarding houses, clubs, and the like—powered largely by anonymity breaking.

Seeing what happened, my friend, wonderful member that she is, tried to resume her anonymity. Because she had been so thoroughly publicized, this has been a hard job. It has taken her years. But she has made the sacrifice, and I here want to give her deep thanks on behalf of us all.

Next we were startled to learn that we had been drawn into partisan politics, this time for the benefit of a single individual. Running for public office, a member splashed his political advertising with the fact that he was an A.A. and, by inference, sober as a judge! A.A. being popular in his state, he thought it would help him win on election day.

Probably the best story in this class tells how the A.A. name was used to back up a libel lawsuit. A member whose name and professional attainments are known on three continents got hold of a letter which she thought damaged her professional reputation. She felt something should be done about this and so did her lawyer, also an A.A. They assumed that both the public and A.A. would be rightfully angry if the facts were known. Soon several newspapers headlined how Alcoholics Anonymous was rooting for one of its lady members, named in full, of course, to win her suit for libel. Shortly after this a noted radio commentator told a listening audience, estimated at twelve million people, the same thing. This again proved that the A.A. name could be used for purely personal purposes, this time on a nation-wide scale.

The old files at A.A. Headquarters reveal many scores of such experiences with broken anonymity. Most of them point up the same lessons.

They tell us that we alcoholics are the biggest rationalizers in the world, and that, fortified with the excuse that we are doing great things for A.A., we can, through broken anonymity, resume our old and disastrous pursuit of personal power and prestige, public honors, and money—the same implacable urges that when frustrated once caused us to drink, the same forces that are today ripping the globe apart at its seams. These lessons make clear, moreover, that enough spectacular anonymity breakers could someday carry our whole society down into that ruinous dead end with them.

So we are certain that if such forces ever rule our Fellowship we will perish too, just as other societies have perished throughout human history. Let us not suppose for a moment that we recovered alcoholics are so much better or stronger than other folks, or that because in twenty years nothing has ever happened to A.A. nothing ever can.

Our really great hope lies in the fact that our total experience, as alcoholics and as A.A. members, has at last taught us the immense power of these forces for self-destruction. These hard-won lessons have made us entirely willing to undertake every personal sacrifice necessary for the preservation of our treasured Fellowship.

This is why we see anonymity at the general public level as our chief protection against ourselves, the guardian of all our Traditions, and the greatest symbol of self-sacrifice that we know.

Of course no A.A. need be anonymous to family, friends, or neighbors. Disclosure there is usually right and good. Nor is there any special danger when we speak at group or semipublic A.A. meetings, provided press reports reveal first names only.

But before the general public—press, radio, films, television, books, and the like—the revelation of full names and pictures is not for us. Here the lid can and must stay down.

We now fully realize that 100 per cent personal anonymity before the public is just as vital to the life of A.A. as 100 per cent sobriety is to the life of each and every member. This is not the counsel of fear; it is the prudent voice of long experience. I am sure that we are going to listen and that we shall make every needed sacrifice. Indeed we have been listening. Today only a dwindling handful of anonymity breakers remain.

I say all this with what earnestness I can. I say this because I know what the temptation of fame and money really is. I can say this because I was once a breaker of anonymity myself. I thank God that years ago the voice of experience and the urging of wise friends took me away from that perilous path into which I might have led our entire society. Thus I learned that the temporary or seeming good can often be the deadly enemy of the permanent best. When it comes to survival for A.A., nothing short of our very best will be good enough.

We want to maintain 100 per cent anonymity for still another potent reason, one often overlooked. Instead of securing us more publicity, repeated self-serving anonymity breaks could severely damage the wonderful relation we now enjoy with press and public alike. We could wind up with a poor press and very little public confidence.

For many years news channels all over the world have showered A.A. with enthusiastic publicity, a never ending stream of it. Editors tell us why this is. They give us extra space and time because their confidence in A.A. is firm. The very foundation of that high confidence is, they say, our continual insistence on personal anonymity at the press level.

Never before had news outlets and public relations people heard of a society that refused personally to advertise its leaders or members. To them this strange and refreshing novelty has alway been proof positive that A.A. is on the square; that nobody has an angle. This, they tell us, is the prime reason for their great good will. This is why, in season and out, they continue to carry the A.A. message of recovery to the whole world.

If through enough anonymity lapses we finally caused the press, the public, and our alcoholic prospects themselves to wonder about our motives, we would surely lose this priceless asset, and along with it countless prospective members. Alcoholics Anonymous would not then be getting more good publicity; it would be getting less and worse. The handwriting on the wall is clear. Most of us can already see it, and I am fully confident that the rest of us soon will.

APPENDIX C

The Conference Charter

This General Service Conference Charter, as shown below, is a body of principles and relationships through which A.A. can function as a whole.

The Conference itself is not incorporated, and its Charter is not a legal instrument. Its principles are traditional, and its power to serve A.A. is based upon experience, custom, and usage rather than upon the binding commitments of law. It is an informal agreement between Alcoholics Anonymous and its Trustees setting forth the means by which A.A. can give world-wide service.

The service arms of the Conference, such as the General Service Board, A.A. World Services, Inc., and the A.A. Grapevine, Inc., are of course separately incorporated and legally related to each other. But these arrangements have been made only for the purpose of holding funds, making necessary contracts, and insuring good routine management.

For purely Conference purposes, the several trustees, directors, and staff members who actively man the services of the General Service Office are Conference members with special duties and are entitled to one vote each. Thus the trustees are Conference members who have custodial duties; the A.A. World Services and A.A. Grapevine directors and staffs are Conference members having service or editorial duties.

Traditionally, the trustees of the General Service Board will name their own successors, subject to the advice and consent of the Conference or a committee thereof.

Traditionally, though not legally, a two-thirds vote of a quorum of the Conference will be considered binding upon the trustees or any element of the board's corporate services. But a simple majority vote of the Conference will be a suggestion only to the General Service Board.

This Charter may be amended at any time by a three-quarters vote of all Conference members.

While the Conference may mold and direct its world services, it may never mandate or govern the Fellowship of Alcoholics Anonymous.

Such is the essence of the Charter for the General Service Conference of Alcoholics Anonymous.

The Charter itself follows.

CHARTER
THE GENERAL SERVICE CONFERENCE OF
ALCOHOLICS ANONYMOUS
(UNITED STATES AND CANADA)

1. *Purpose:* The General Service Conference of Alcoholics Anonymous is the guardian of the world services and of the Twelve Traditions of Alcoholics Anonymous. The Conference shall be a service body only; never a government for Alcoholics Anonymous.

2. *Composition:* The Conference (U.S. and Canada) shall be composed of area delegates, the trustees of the General Service Board, directors of A.A. World Services and A.A. Grapevine, staff members of the Grapevine and General Service Office, and foreign delegates as the Conference may wish to invite.

Other Sections of the Conference may sometimes be created in foreign lands as the need arises out of language or geographical considerations. The U.S. and Canada Section of the General Service Conference will then become the Senior Section, related to the other Sections by ties of mutual consultation and a cross linking of delegates.

But no Conference Section shall ever be placed in authority over another. All joint action shall be taken only upon a two-thirds vote of the combined Sections. Within its boundaries each Conference ought to be autonomous. Only matters seriously affecting A.A.'s worldwide needs shall be the subject of joint consideration.

3. *Conference Relation to A.A.:* The Conference will act for A.A. in the perpetuation and guidance of its world services, and it will also be the vehicle by which the A.A. movement can express its views upon all matters of vital A.A. policy and all hazardous deviations from A.A. Tradition. Delegates should be free to vote as their conscience dictates; they should also be free to decide what questions should be taken to the group level,

whether for information, discussion, or their own direct instruction.

But no change in Article 12 of the Charter or in the Twelve Traditions of A.A. or in the Twelve Steps of A.A. may be made with less than the written consent of three-quarters of the A.A. groups as described in the resolution adopted by the 1955 Conference and Convention.

4. *Conference Relation to the General Service Board and its Corporate Services:* The Conference will replace the founders of Alcoholics Anonymous, who formerly functioned as guides and advisers to the General Service Board and its related service corporations. The Conference will be expected to afford a reliable cross section of A.A. opinion for this purpose.

To effectively further this same purpose it will be understood, as a matter of tradition, that a two-thirds vote of a Conference quorum shall be considered binding upon the General Service Board and its related corporate services. A quorum shall consist of two-thirds of all the Conference members registered.

But no such vote ought to impair the legal rights of the General Service Board and the service corporations to conduct routine business and make ordinary contracts relating thereto.

It will be further understood, regardless of the legal prerogatives of the General Service Board, as a matter of tradition, that a three-quarters vote of all Conference members may bring about a reorganization of the General Service Board and the directors and staff members of its corporate services, if or when such reorganization is deemed essential.

Under such a proceeding, the Conference may request resignations, may nominate new trustees, and may make all other necessary arrangements regardless of the legal prerogatives of the General Service Board.

5. *Area Assemblies: Composition of:* Assemblies, designated as area assemblies, are composed of the elected general service representatives of all A.A. groups desiring to participate, district committee members, and area committee officers in each of the delegate areas of the United States and Canada.

Each delegate area will always be entitled to one assembly. But areas of large A.A. populations and/or whose geography presents communication problems will be entitled to additional assemblies, as provided by "The A.A. Service Manual," or by any further amendment thereto.

6. *Area Assemblies: Purpose of:* Area Assemblies convene every two years for the election of area committee members, from which are elected delegates

to the General Service Conference of Alcoholics Anonymous. Such area assemblies are concerned only with the world service affairs of Alcoholics Anonymous.

7. *Area Assemblies: Method of Electing Area Committee Members and Delegates:* Whenever practicable, committee members are elected by written ballot without personal nomination. And delegates are selected from among such committee members by a two-thirds written ballot or by lot, as provided in "The A.A. Service Manual."

8. *Area Assemblies: Terms of Office for Group General Service Representatives, Area Committee Members and Delegates:* Unless otherwise directed by the Conference, these terms of office shall all be concurrent and of two years' duration each. In approximately half the areas, assembly elections will be held in the even years; the remaining assemblies will elect in the odd years, thus creating rotating Panels of the Conference as further described in "The A.A. Service Manual."

9. *The General Service Conference Meetings:* The Conference will meet yearly in the City of New York, unless otherwise agreed upon. Special meetings may be called should there be a grave emergency. The Conference may also render advisory opinions at any time by a mail or telephone poll in aid of the General Service Board or its related services.

10. *The General Service Board: Composition, Jurisdiction, Responsibilities:* The General Service Board of Alcoholics Anonymous shall be an incorporated trusteeship, composed of alcoholics and nonalcoholics who elect their own successors, these choices being subject, however, to the approval of the Conference or a committee thereof. Candidates for alcoholic regional trustee are, however, first selected by the areas in the region. Then, at the General Service Conference, voters consisting of delegates from the region involved, plus an equal number of voters—one-half to come from the Conference Committee on Trustees and one-half to come from the Trustees' Nominating Committee—make a selection of a nominee by a two-thirds written ballot or by lot. This nominee is then elected to the General Service Board, the trustees being obligated by tradition to do so. For trustees-at-large in the U.S. and in Canada, the Board will specify certain business or professional qualifications. The procedure is then as follows. Each Conference area may select one candidate, or two or more areas may jointly propose a single candidate via Third Legacy procedure. Résumés of all candidates will be reviewed for eligibility by the Trustees' Nominating

Committee. At the General Service Conference, delegates from each region will caucus prior to the nomination, using Third Legacy procedure, to reduce the number of candidates to one for each region in the U.S. and two for each region in Canada. A maximum of six candidates for trustee-at-large, U.S., and a maximum of four candidates for trustee-at-large, Canada, will be presented to the voting members of the Conference for nomination. Voting members of the Conference will be all delegates from the nominating country (U.S. or Canada) and all members of the Trustees' Nominating Committee. These nominees are then elected to the General Service Board, the trustees being obligated by tradition to do so.

The General Service Board is the chief service arm of the Conference, and is essentially custodial in its character.

Excepting for decisions upon matters of policy, finance, or A.A. Tradition, liable to seriously affect A.A. as a whole, the General Service Board has entire freedom of action in the routine conduct of the policy and business affairs of the A.A. service corporations and may name suitable committees and elect directors to its subsidiary corporate service entities in pursuance of this purpose.

The General Service Board is primarily responsible for the financial and policy integrity of its subsidiary services: A.A. World Services, Inc., and A.A. Grapevine, Inc., and for such other service corporations as the Conference may desire to form, but nothing herein shall compromise the Grapevine editor's right to accept or reject material for publication.

The charter and bylaws of the General Service Board, or any amendments thereto, should always be subject to the approval of the General Service Conference by a two-thirds vote of all its members.

Except in a great emergency, neither the General Service Board nor any of its related services ought ever take any action liable to greatly affect A.A. as a whole, without first consulting the Conference. It is nevertheless understood that the Board shall at all times reserve the right to decide which of its actions or decisions may require the approval of the Conference.

11. *The General Service Conference: Its General Procedures:* The Conference will hear the financial and policy reports of the General Service Board and its related corporate services. The Conference will advise with the trustees, directors, and staff members upon all matters presented as affecting A.A. as a whole, engage in debate, appoint necessary committees,

and pass suitable resolutions for the advice or direction of the General Service Board and its related services.

The Conference may also discuss and recommend appropriate action respecting serious deviations from A.A. Tradition or harmful misuse of the name "Alcoholics Anonymous."

The Conference may draft any needed bylaws and will name its own officers and committees by any method of its own choosing.

The Conference at the close of each yearly session will draft a full report of its proceedings, to be supplied to all delegates and committee members; also a condensation thereof which will be sent to A.A. groups throughout the world.

12. *General Warranties of the Conference:* In all its proceedings, the General Service Conference shall observe the spirit of the A.A. Tradition, taking great care that the Conference never becomes the seat of perilous wealth or power; that sufficient operating funds, plus an ample reserve, be its prudent financial principle; that none of the Conference members shall ever be placed in a position of unqualified authority over any of the others; that all important decisions be reached by discussion, vote, and whenever possible, by substantial unanimity; that no Conference action ever be personally punitive or an incitement to public controversy; that though the Conference may act for the service of Alcoholics Anonymous, it shall never perform any acts of government; and that, like the Society of Alcoholics Anonymous which it serves, the Conference itself will always remain democratic in thought and action.

(This Charter was unanimously adopted by the 1955 Conference and was updated by the 1968, 1969, 1970, 1971, 1974, 1975, and 1978 Conferences.)

APPENDIX D

Text of the Lasker Award

The American Public Health Association presents a Lasker Award for 1951 to Alcoholics Anonymous in recognition of its unique and highly successful approach to that age-old public health and social problem, alcoholism.

Since its founding sixteen years ago, Alcoholics Anonymous has brought recovery to more than 120,000 chronic drinkers formerly thought hopeless. Today this world fellowship of 4,000 groups, resident in 38 countries, is rehabilitating 25,000 additional persons yearly. In emphasizing alcoholism as an illness, the social stigma associated with this condition is being blotted out.

Alcoholics Anonymous works upon the novel principle that a recovered alcoholic can reach and treat a fellow sufferer as no one else can. In so doing, the recovered alcoholic maintains his own sobriety; the man he treats soon becomes a physician to the next new applicant, thus creating an ever expanding chain reaction of liberation, with patients welded together by bonds of common suffering, common understanding, and stimulating action in a great cause.

This is not a reform movement, nor is it operated by professionals who are concerned with the problem. It is financed by voluntary contributions of its members, all of whom remain anonymous. There are no dues, no paid therapists, no paid professional workers. It enjoys the good will and often the warm endorsement of many medical and scientific groups—no mean achievement in itself for any organization run entirely by laymen.

Historians may one day point to Alcoholics Anonymous as a society which did far more than achieve a considerable measure of success with alcoholism and its stigma; they may recognize Alcoholics Anonymous to have been a great venture in social pioneering which forged a new instrument for social action; a new therapy based on the kinship of common suffering; one having a vast potential for the myriad other ills of mankind.

REPORTS ON A.A.

APPENDIX E:a

A New Approach to Psychotherapy in Chronic Alcoholism

by W. D. Silkworth, M.D.
New York, New York

(First medical paper ever written about A.A. Reprinted from *Journal-Lancet*,
July, 1939, Minneapolis, Minnesota)

The beginning and subsequent development of a new approach to the problem of permanent recovery for the chronic alcoholic has already produced remarkable results and promises much for the future. This statement is based upon four years of close observation. As this development is one which has sprung up among alcoholic patients themselves and has been largely conceived and promoted by them, it is felt that this new treatment can be reported freely and objectively.

The central idea is that of a fellowship of ex-alcoholic men and women banded together for mutual help. Each member feels duty bound to assist alcoholic newcomers to get upon their feet. These in turn work with still others, in an endless chain. Hence there is a large growth possibility. In one locality, for example, the fellowship had but three members in September, 1935; eighteen months later the three had succeeded with seven more. These ten have since expanded to ninety.

It is much more than a sense of duty, however, which provides the requisite driving power and harmony so necessary for success. One powerful factor is that of self-preservation. These ex-alcoholics frequently find that unless they spend time in helping others to health they cannot stay sober themselves. Strenuous, almost sacrificial work for other sufferers is often imperative in the early days of their recovery. This effort proceeds entirely on a good will basis. It is an avocation. There are no fees or dues of any kind, nor do these people organize in the ordinary sense of the word.

These ex-alcoholic men and women number about one hundred at present. One group is scattered along the Atlantic seaboard with New York as a center. Another and somewhat larger body is located in the Middle West. Many walks of life are represented, though business and professional types predominate. The unselfishness, the extremes to which these men and women go to help each other, the spirit of democracy, tolerance, and sanity which prevails, are astonishing to those who know something of the alcoholic personality. But these observations do not adequately explain why so many gravely involved people are able to remain sober and face life again.

The principal answer is: Each ex-alcoholic has had, and is able to maintain, a vital spiritual or "religious" experience. This so-called "experience" is accomplished by marked changes in personality. There is always, in a successful case, a radical change in outlook, attitude, and habits of thought, which sometimes occurs with amazing rapidity, and in nearly all cases these changes are evident within a few months, often less.

That the chronic alcoholic has sometimes recovered by religious means is a fact centuries old. But these recoveries have been sporadic, insufficient in numbers or impressiveness to make headway with the alcoholic problem as a whole.

The conscious search of these ex-alcoholics for the right answer has enabled them to find an approach which has been effectual in something like half of all the cases upon which it has been tried. This is a truly remarkable record when it is remembered that most of them were undoubtedly beyond the reach of other remedial measures.

The essential features of this new approach, without psychological embellishment, are:

1. The ex-alcoholics capitalize upon a fact which they have so well demonstrated, namely: that one alcoholic can secure the confidence of another in a way and to a degree almost impossible of attainment by a nonalcoholic outsider.

2. After having fully identified themselves with their "prospect" by a recital of symptoms, behavior, anecdotes, etc., these men allow the patient to draw the inference that if he is seriously alcoholic, there may be no hope for him save a spiritual experience. They cite their own cases and quote

medical opinion to prove their point. If the patient insists he is not alcoholic to that degree, they recommend he try to stay sober in his own way. Usually, however, the patient agrees at once. If he does not, a few more painful relapses often convince him.

3. Once the patient agrees that he is powerless, he finds himself in a serious dilemma. He sees clearly that he must have a spiritual experience or be destroyed by alcohol.

4. This dilemma brings about a crisis in the patient's life. He finds himself in a situation which, he believes, cannot be untangled by human means. He has been placed in this position by another alcoholic who has recovered through a spiritual experience. This peculiar ability, which an alcoholic who has recovered exercises upon one who has not recovered, is the main secret of the unprecedented success which these men and women are having. They can penetrate and carry conviction where the physician or the clergyman cannot. Under these conditions, the patient turns to religion with an entire willingness and readily accepts, without reservation, a simple religious proposal. He is then able to acquire much more than a set of religious beliefs; he undergoes the profound mental and emotional change common to religious "experience." (See William James' *Varieties of Religious Experience*.) Then, too, the patient's hope is renewed and his imagination is fired by the idea of membership in a group of ex-alcoholics where he will be enabled to save the lives and homes of those who have suffered as he has suffered.

5. The fellowship is entirely indifferent concerning the individual manner of spiritual approach so long as the patient is willing to turn his life and his problems over to the care and direction of his Creator. The patient may picture the Deity in any way he likes. No effort whatever is made to convert him to some particular faith or creed. Many creeds are represented among the group and the greatest harmony prevails. It is emphasized that the fellowship is nonsectarian and that the patient is entirely free to follow his own inclination. Not a trace of aggressive evangelism is exhibited.

6. If the patient indicates a willingness to go on, a suggestion is made that he do certain things which are obviously good psychology, good morals and good religion, regardless of creed:

a. That he make a moral appraisal of himself, and confidentially discuss his findings with a competent person whom he trusts.

b. That he try to adjust bad personal relationships, setting right, so far as possible, such wrongs as he may have done in the past.
c. That he recommit himself daily, or hourly if need be, to God's care and direction, asking for strength.
d. That, if possible, he attend weekly meetings of the fellowship and actively lend a hand with alcoholic newcomers.

This is the procedure in brief. The manner of presentation may vary considerably, depending upon the individual approach, but the essential ingredients of the process are always much the same. When presented by an ex-alcoholic, the power of this approach is remarkable. For a full appreciation one must have seen the work and must have known these patients before and after their change.

Considering the presence of the religious factor, one might expect to find unhealthy emotionalism and prejudice. This is not the case, however; on the contrary, there is an instant readiness to discard old methods for new ones which produce better results. For instance, it was early found that usually the weakest approach to an alcoholic is directly through his family or friends, especially if the patient is drinking heavily at the time. The ex-alcoholics frequently insist, therefore, that a physician first take the patient in hand, placing him in a hospital whenever possible. If proper hospitalization and medical care is not carried out, this patient faces the danger of delirium tremens, "wet brain," or other complications. After a few days' stay, during which time the patient has been thoroughly detoxicated, the physician brings up the question of permanent sobriety and, if the patient is interested, tactfully introduces a member of the ex-alcoholic group. By this time the prospect has self-control, can think straight, and the approach to him can be made casually, with no intervention by family or friends. More than half of this fellowship have been so treated. The group is unanimous in its belief that hospitalization is desirable, even imperative, in most cases.

What has happened to these men and women? For years, physicians have pursued methods which bear some similarity to these outlined above. An effort is made to procure a frank discussion with the patient, leading to self-understanding. It is indicated that he must make the necessary readjustment to his environment. His co-operation and confidence must be secured. The objectives are to bring about extraversion and to provide someone to whom the alcoholic can transfer his dilemma.

In a large number of cases, this alcoholic group is now attaining these very objectives because their simple but powerful devices appear to cut deeper than do other methods of treatment for the following reasons:

1. Because of their alcoholic experiences and successful recoveries they secure a high degree of confidence from their prospects.

2. Because of this initial confidence, identical experience, and the fact that the discussion is pitched on moral and religious grounds, the patient tells his story and makes his self-appraisal with extreme thoroughness and honesty. He stops living alone and finds himself within reach of a fellowship with whom he can discuss his problems as they arise.

3. Because of the ex-alcoholic brotherhood, the patient, too, is able to save other alcoholics from destruction. At one and the same time, the patient acquires an ideal, a hobby, a strenuous avocation, and a social life which he enjoys among other ex-alcoholics and their families. These factors make powerfully for his extraversion.

4. Because of objects aplenty in whom to vest his confidence, the patient can turn to the individuals to whom he first gave his confidence, the ex-alcoholic group as a whole, or the Deity. It is paramount to note that the religious factor is all important even from the beginning. Newcomers have been unable to stay sober when they have tried the program minus the Deity—or at least a "greater Power" than themselves, the group itself.

The mental attitude of these people toward alcohol is interesting. Most of them report that they are seldom tempted to drink. If tempted, their defense against the first drink is emphatic and adequate. To quote from one of their number, once a serious case at this hospital, but who has had no relapse since his "experience" four and one-half years ago:

Soon after I had my experience, I realized I had the answer to my problem. For about three years prior to December 1934 I had been taking two and sometimes three bottles of gin a day. Even in my brief periods of sobriety, my mind was much on liquor, especially if my thoughts turned toward home, where I had bottles hidden on every floor of the house. Soon after leaving the hospital, I commenced to work with other alcoholics. With reference to them, I thought much about alcohol, even to the point of carrying a bottle in my pocket to help them through severe hangovers. But from the first moment of my experience, the thought of taking a drink myself hardly ever occurred. I had the feeling of being in a position of neutrality. I was not fighting to stay on the water wagon. The problem was removed; it simply ceased to exist for me. This new state of mind came about in my case at once and automatically. About six weeks after leaving the hospital my wife asked me to fetch a small utensil which stood on a shelf in our kitchen. As I fumbled for it, my hand grasped a bottle, still partly full. With a start of surprise and gratitude, it flashed upon me that not once during the past weeks had the thought of liquor being in my home occurred to me. Considering the extent to which alcohol had dominated my thinking, I call this no less than a miracle. During the past four years of sobriety I have seriously considered drinking only a few times. On each occasion, my reaction was one of fear, followed by the reassurance which came with my new found ability to think the matter through, to work with another alcoholic, or to enter upon a brief period of prayer and meditation. I now have a defense against alcoholism which is positive so long as I keep myself spiritually fit and active, which I am only too glad to do.

Another interesting example of reaction to temptation comes from a former patient, now sober three and one-half years. Like most of these people, he was beyond the reach of psychiatric methods. He relates the following incident:

Though sober now for several years, I am still bothered by periods of deep depression and resentment. I live on a farm, and weeks sometimes pass in which I have no contact with the ex-alcoholic group. During one of my spells, I became violently angry over a trifling domestic matter. I deliberately decided to get drunk, going so far as to stock my guest house with food, thinking to lock myself in when I had returned from town with a case of liquor. I got in my car and started down the drive, still furious. As I reached the gate I stopped the car, suddenly feeling unable to carry out my plan. I said to myself, "At least I have to be honest with my wife." I returned to the house and announced I was on my way to town to get drunk. She looked at me calmly, never saying a word. The absurdity of the whole thing burst upon me and I laughed. And so the matter passed. Yes, I now have a defense that works. Prior to my spiritual experience I would never have reacted that way.

The testimony of the membership as a whole sums up to this: For the most part, these men and women are now indifferent to alcohol, but when the thought of taking a drink does come, they react sanely and vigorously.

This alcoholic fellowship hopes to extend its work to all parts of the country and to make its methods and answers known to every alcoholic who wishes to recover. As a first step, they have prepared a book called *Alcoholics Anonymous.* A large volume of 400 pages, it sets forth their methods and experience exhaustively, and with much clarity and force. The first half of the book is a text aimed to show an alcoholic the attitude he ought to take and precisely the steps he may follow to effect his own recovery. He then finds full directions for approaching and working with other alcoholics. Two chapters are devoted to family relations and one to employers for the guidance of those who surround the sick man. There is a powerful chapter addressed to the agnostic, as the majority of the present members were of that description. Of particular interest to the physician is the chapter on alcoholism dealing mostly with its mental phenomena, as these men see it.

By contacting personally those who are getting results from the book, these ex-alcoholics expect to establish new centers. Experience has shown that as soon as any community contains three or four active members, growth is inevitable, for the good reason that each member feels he must work with other alcoholics or perhaps perish himself.

Will the movement spread? Will all of these recoveries be permanent? No one can say. Yet, we at this hospital, from our observation of many cases, are willing to record our present opinion as a strong "Yes" to both questions.

APPENDIX E:b

THERAPEUTIC MECHANISM OF ALCOHOLICS ANONYMOUS [1]

BY HARRY M. TIEBOUT, M.D.
Greenwich, Connecticut

(Reprinted by permission from *The American Journal of Psychiatry*, January, 1944. Dr. Harry's first paper on the subject of Alcoholics Anonymous. Three recent papers are indexed at the close of this one.)

Alcoholics Anonymous is the name applied to a group of ex-alcoholics who, through a therapeutic program which includes a definite religious element, have successfully combated alcoholism. The group stems from the efforts of one man, Mr. "X," who in 1934 found an answer to his drinking problem in a personal religious experience. This experience he was able to translate into terms which were meaningful for others. Since then, many alcoholics have become sober by using his approach.

The work of Alcoholics Anonymous has a threefold aspect. First, the group has weekly gatherings where experiences are related and problems discussed. Second, all are urged to read their book, *Alcoholics Anonymous,* which contains their basic tenets and must be read if one is to arrive at any understanding of their program. Third, the members work with prospects who are making their initial contact with the group. Helping others is a two-way situation since it not only assists the beginner in his first efforts but also aids the helper, who derives from his efforts something which is essential for his continued sobriety.

Statistics at the New York office of the organization read as follows:

[1] Read at the ninety-ninth annual meeting of the American Psychiatric Association, Detroit, Michigan, May 10-13, 1943.

> 5 recovered at the end of the first year.
> 15 recovered at the end of the second year.
> 40 recovered at the end of the third year.
> 100 recovered at the end of the fourth year.
> 400 recovered at the end of the fifth year.
> 2000 recovered at the end of the sixth year.
> 8000 recovered at the end of the seventh year.

Alcoholics Anonymous claims a recovery rate of 75 per cent of those who really try their methods. This figure, coupled with their mushroom growth, commands respect and demands explanation.

While fully cognizant of the fellowship values of the group, of the help accruing to each member from his efforts to help new ones, and of the general atmosphere of hope and encouragement which emanates from any successfully treated person, I regard them as accessory to the central therapeutic force, religion—a truth which, hopefully, will become clear by the end of the paper, and a realization of which developed from many long talks with Mr. "X."

My first contact with the group came through the medium of a thirty-four-year-old woman patient who had been under my care at Blythewood for several months. She had been a chronic alcoholic for many years and, despite intelligence, family position, and early successes, had literally hit the gutter, after a steady decline in her fortunes had left her all but penniless. Although no patient ever wanted to get well more desperately or co-operated more wholeheartedly in a treatment program than she, the results were very unsatisfactory. Finally, it became clear that she possessed a character structure which, despite her best efforts and mine, persisted unshaken and was clearly responsible for the continuance of her drinking. One day a copy of *Alcoholics Anonymous,* while yet in multilith form, came into my hands. I read it, and found it contained a most accurate description of the character problem I had been facing in my patient. In an effort to jar her a bit, I gave her the book to read. To my surprise she was so greatly impressed that she arranged to go to an Alcoholics Anonymous meeting and very shortly became an active and successful member of the group. Even more surprising was the discovery that, with the process of assimilation of that program, her character structure, which had been blocking any help, dissolved and was replaced by one which enabled its possessor to remain dry.

Something had taken place under my very nose which could not be doubted and which could not be explained away as mere coincidence. I found myself facing the question: What had happened? My answer is that the patient had had a religious or spiritual experience. The answer, however, did not prove particularly enlightening and it was not until much later that I began to appreciate the real meaning of the answer.

Before attempting to explain how further understanding of the significance of the religious factor developed, it is necessary to discuss the character structure which had dissolved. Despite most reports to the contrary, there is a growing recognition of certain common qualities which are regularly present in alcoholics excepting those who have a frank underlying mental condition. Characteristic of the so-called typical alcoholic is a narcissistic egocentric core, dominated by feelings of omnipotence, intent on maintaining at all costs its inner integrity. While these characteristics are found in other maladjustments, they appear in relatively pure culture in alcoholic after alcoholic. In a careful study of a series of cases, Sillman recently reported that he felt he could discern the outlines of a common character structure among problem drinkers and that the best terms he could find for the group of qualities noted was "defiant individuality" and "grandiosity." In my opinion, those words were accurately chosen. Inwardly the alcoholic brooks no control from man or God. He, the alcoholic, is and must be master of his destiny. He will fight to the end to preserve that position.

Granting then the more or less constant presence of these character traits, it is easy to see how the person possessing them has difficulty in accepting God and religion. Religion by its demand that the individual acknowledge the presence of a God challenges the very nature of the alcoholic. But, on the other hand, and this point is basic to my paper, *if* the alcoholic can *truly accept* the presence of a Power greater than himself, he, by that very step, modifies at least temporarily and possibly permanently his deepest inner structure and when he does so without resentment or struggle, then he is no longer typically alcoholic. And the strange thing is that if the alcoholic can sustain that inner feeling of acceptance, he can and will remain sober for the rest of his life. To his friends and family, he has gotten religion! To psychiatrists, he has gotten a form of self-hypnosis or what you will. Regardless of what has occurred inside the alcoholic, he can now stay dry. Such is the Alcoholics Anonymous contention, and I believe it is based upon facts.

Let us go back to my patient and describe her after her experience in Alcoholics Anonymous. In her original state she corresponded perfectly with the description already given of the alcoholic character structure. After Alcoholics Anonymous began to take hold, changes in her personality became apparent. The aggression subsided materially, the feeling of being at odds with the world disappeared, and with it vanished the tendency to suspect the motives and attitudes of others. A sense of peace and calm ensued with real lessening of inner tension; and the lines of her face softened and became gentler and more kindly. That hard inner core was being altered, altered sufficiently to bring about the patient's sobriety for a period of five years.

What was the nature of the experience which stirred this patient when she joined Alcoholics Anonymous? The answer is that some sort of religious or spiritual force was awakened. Mr. "X" states that the success of the group with any alcoholic depends upon the degree to which the individual goes through a conversion or spiritual activation. His own experience was of the sweeping, cataclysmic type which lifted him out of a slough of despond and transported him to heights of ecstatic joy and happiness where he stayed for some hours. This state was then succeeded by a feeling of peace, serenity, and the profound conviction that he was freed from the bondage of liquor. He states that roughly 10 per cent enter Alcoholics Anonymous on the strength of such an experience. The remaining 90 per cent who stay dry achieve the same result by developing slowly and much more gradually the spiritual side of their nature through following the various steps in the program already outlined. According to Alcoholics Anonymous experience, the speed with which the spiritual awakening takes place is no criterion of either depth or permanence of cure. The religious leavening, however little at first, starts the process; the program helps to bring it to a successful conclusion.

What then is a spiritual awakening? Here the personal experience of Mr. "X" is again informative. A man of energy, drive, and great ability, in his thirties, he found himself completely bogged down by drink. For at least five years he fought the downhill process that was going on in him without success. Two weeks before his last hospital stay, he was visited by a former alcoholic crony who had achieved sobriety through Buchmanism.

Mr. "X" tried unsuccessfully to avail himself of his friend's teachings and finally decided he would get sobered up by entering a well-known drying-out place where he could clear his brain of liquor and have a chance to try out his friend's ideas with his, Mr. "X's," system free from the drag of alcohol. He was desperate, depressed, with all the fight knocked out of him. He was willing to try anything because he knew that the alternative facing him was a state hospital and a life of permanent insanity. The evening of his first day of admission, he was again visited by his friend, who once more expounded the principles which he felt had brought him health. After he left, Mr. "X" sank into an even deeper depression, which he describes as a "profound sense of melancholy and utter hopelessness." Suddenly in this agony of spirit, he cried aloud, "If there is a God, let Him show himself now." And with this plea his religious experience started. He points out, and I think rightfully, that it was not until he became utterly humble that he could and did turn to God for the help that was there.

In other words, in light of Mr. "X's" own experience, a religious or spiritual awakening is the act of giving up one's reliance on one's omnipotence. The defiant individuality no longer defies but accepts help, guidance, and control from the outside. And as the individual relinquishes his negative, aggressive feelings toward himself and toward life, he finds himself overwhelmed by strongly positive ones such as love, friendliness, peacefulness, and pervading contentment, which state is the exact antithesis of the former restlessness and irritability. And the significant fact is that with this new mental state the individual is no longer literally "driven to drink."

Further insight into the phenomenon of spiritual change came from another patient, whose case I now wish to cite. He is a man in his early forties. From a family of wealth, and the youngest of several children, he was the pampered darling of a neurotic, hypochondriacal mother. Drinking began in late adolescence. Almost at once he learned to rely upon liquor to help him meet social situations, and as the years rolled on, this reliance became more pronounced. Finally after one prolonged spree, he was admitted to Blythewood.

He proved to be an exceedingly responsive patient, readily acknowledging his alcoholic tendency, and quickly becoming interested in Alcoholics Anonymous. After residence of about a month, he left quite convinced that he had the problem in hand. Within a short time, however, nipping set in and four months later he returned after some weeks of steady drinking. Again he showed himself responsive to interviews, but it now became apparent that there was a real battle ahead and that it was exactly the same battle previously faced in the patient first discussed. The traits already described reared themselves as insuperable barriers to therapy.

During the weeks that we were discussing these obstacles the patient began again to nip on the sly and finally went off on a full-fledged spree. He was brought back to Blythewood to terminate it. As is usual with all alcoholics, as he sobered up he was filled with remorse, guilt, and a tremendous sense of humility. The defiant personality was licked by the very excesses of its own behavior and, in that mood, he was utterly sure he would never take another drop. On the third day of his recuperation, however, he informed me during an interview that I had better do something about it, and when I asked him what "it" referred to, he replied, "My old feeling is coming back over me; I can feel myself closing in from you and all that has just happened." The indifference to his problem, the aggressive sureness, the utter lack of any real sense of humility and guilt, all the character traits which he had come to identify with the frame of mind that led to drinking were returning and crowding out the feelings, the thoughts, almost the sensations which filled him as he came out of his drinking bout. He knew that if these returning feelings again took hold of him sooner or later he would go on another alcoholic spree. He realized that somehow he must cling to the attitudes he had as he came out of the bout.

The next day he began his interview with the statement, "Doc, I've got it." He then went on to report his experience of the previous night. This experience I label, for want of a better term, "a psychological awakening." What happened was a sudden flash of understanding about himself as a person. This occurred around eleven o'clock, and he lay in bed, wide awake until four o'clock in the morning fitting his new insights and understanding to his knowledge of himself.

It is not easy to reconstruct the events of that five-hour period, yet those events constituted a major experience in the life of that patient which gave him a basic appreciation of himself as an alcoholic. Moreover, for the first time, he could see himself as he had always been, and in addition he could sense the sort of person he must become if he were to remain sober. Without being aware of it at the time, he had switched from a completely egocentric subjective point of view to an objective, mature understanding of himself and his relationship to life.

In retrospect, it is apparent that the patient became aware of his basic egocentricity. For the first time he was able to penetrate behind the façade of his rationalizations and defense reactions and to see that always hitherto he had put himself first. He was literally unaware that other souls existed except insofar as they affected him. That they, too, might have separate existences, similar yet different from his, just never had taken on the aspect of reality. Now he no longer felt himself the omnipotent being who viewed the world only in relation to himself. Instead, he could see himself in relation to the world and could realize that he was but a small fraction of a universe peopled by many other individuals. He could share life with others. He had no further need to dominate and to fight to maintain that domination. He could relax and take things easy.

His new orientation can best be described in the patient's own words. As he put it, "Why, Doc, do you know I've been a fraud all my life, and I never knew it. I used to think I was interested in people, but that wasn't really so. I wasn't interested in my mother as a person who was sick. I didn't realize that she as a person might be suffering; I only thought what will happen to me when she is gone. People used to point me out as a dutiful son and an example, and I believed it. But there wasn't anything to it. I was just anxious to keep her near, because she made me feel better. She never criticized me and always made me feel that whatever I did, I was O.K."

New insights illuminated his previous relationships with people. With respect to this point, he remarked, "Do you know, I'm beginning to feel closer to people. I can think of *them* sometimes. And I feel easier with them, too. Maybe that's because I don't think they're fighting me, since I don't feel I'm fighting them. I now think maybe they can really like me."

Other enlightenments about himself and his relationship to the world could be cited, but they would only add further proof that the thinking of this patient for the first time in his life had become truly objective. This switch to objectivity is, however, but half the story. Associated with the switch, there was an equally striking alteration in the prevailing feeling tone. In words that were reminiscent of Mr. "X's" in his spiritual experience, the patient described his new attitudes, "I feel wonderful but not like I do when I've been drinking. It's very different from that; I feel quiet, not excited and wanting to rush around. I'm more content to stay put, and I don't think I'm going to worry so much. I'm relaxed, yet I feel better able to cope with life now than I ever did." He then went on, "I have a different feeling about God. I don't mind the idea of Some One up there running things now that I don't want to run them myself. In fact, I'm kind of glad that I can feel there is a Supreme Being who can keep things going right. I guess maybe this is something like that spiritual feeling which they talk about. Whatever it is, I hope it stays because I never felt so peaceful in all my life."

In this statement, the patient manifests a different attitude toward God, and he also shows that he has become aware of the fact that, as he ceases the effort to maintain his individuality, he can relax and enjoy life in a quiet, yet thoroughly satisfying way. Such feelings are, as he intimates, distinctly spiritual in quality, and he was correct in their appraisal, because he has been able to remain dry for a period of nearly a year. The change to objectivity and the altered feeling tone have proved to be what he needed to stay sober. Despite this relatively brief period of sobriety, the patient feels that he is on much firmer footing. Hitherto, during periods of dryness, he was constantly fighting liquor. Now he has real peace of mind, because he knows what it takes to keep thinking soberly.

This case is cited because it represents an individual who underwent a rapid psychological reorientation, the result of which was an entirely new and different life pattern and life outlook. While one can question the permanence of this new pattern, there can be no question as to the fact that the experience itself occurred.

Of even greater significance for the purpose of this paper is the fact that the patient, as a result of his experience, used the same words to describe his new feelings as did Mr. "X" following his religious experience, and as did my other patient after the activities of Alcoholics Anonymous began to take hold and work upon her. Mr. "X" informs me that of the 10 per cent who have a rapid awakening, some achieve it on the basis of a true religious experience and others as a result of a sweeping psychological event such as happened to my patient. The other 90 per cent attain the same result more gradually, as did the woman patient cited. Irrespective of the path by which that outcome is achieved, there seems no doubt that all end up with this feeling of peace and security, which they link with the spiritual side of life. The narcissistic component in the character is submerged, at least for the time being, and in its place there is a much more mature and objective person, who can meet life situations positively and affirmatively without escape into alcohol. According to Mr. "X," all members of Alcoholics Anonymous who succeed in remaining dry, sooner or later undergo the same change in personality. They must lose the narcissistic element permanently; otherwise the program of Alcoholics Anonymous works only temporarily.

Here let me make two additional observations. First, there is all the difference in the world between a true, emotional, religious feeling and the vague, groping, skeptical, intellectual belief which passes as a religious feeling in the minds of many people. Regardless of his final conception of that Power, unless the individual attains in the course of time a sense of the reality and the nearness of a Greater Power, his egocentric nature will reassert itself with undiminished intensity, and drinking will again enter into the picture. Second, most of the individuals who finally reach the necessary spiritual state do so merely by following the Alcoholics Anonymous program and without ever consciously experiencing any sudden access of spiritual feeling. Instead they grow slowly but surely into a state of mind which, after it has been present for a time, they may suddenly recognize is greatly different from the one they formerly had. To their surprise, they discover that their point of view and outlook has taken on a very real spiritual coloring.

The central effect, therefore, of Alcoholics Anonymous is to develop in the person a spiritual state which will serve as a direct neutralizing force upon the egocentric elements in the character of the alcoholic. If and when that state becomes completely integrated into new habit patterns, the patient will remain dry. Mr. "X" says that this process of integration takes place over a period of years, and that if there is no noticeable change in personality structure after six months, the spiritual side will probably succumb to a return of the submerged alcoholic self. In other words, unless the religious impetus of Alcoholics Anonymous effects a change in the deeper personality components, the influence of the program is not lasting. Significantly, this change, which is typical, takes place without psychiatric help; yet, as Mr. "X" describes it, it has characteristics which we, as psychiatrists, hope for in our improved patients. Briefly, he sums up his observations with the words, "The alcoholic must gain in objectivity and maturity, otherwise he doesn't stay sober."

In conclusion, it is my belief that the therapeutic value of the Alcoholics Anonymous approach arises from its use of a religious or spiritual force to attack the fundamental narcissism of the alcoholic. With the uprooting of that component, the individual experiences a whole new series of thoughts and feelings which are of a positive nature, and which impel him in the direction of growth and maturity. In other words, this group relies upon an emotional force, religion, to achieve an emotional result, namely, the over-throwing of the negative, hostile set of emotions and supplanting them with a positive set in which the individual no longer need maintain his defiant individuality, but instead can live in peace and harmony with and in his world, sharing and participating freely.

One final comment. Present-day psychiatry is properly chary of purely emotional cures. Until any change is firmly linked up with the mind and the intellect, the cure is considered suspect. The emphasis today is on anal-ysis which relies upon the mind to ferret out the causes for the failure to achieve a state of synthesis, which is actually an emotional condition of feeling free of conflict and strain. It is presumed that, as the blocking emo-tions are uncovered and freed through analysis, positive, synthetic ones will appear instead. It is just as logical, though, to change emotions by using emotions and then, after the change has been brought about, to bring the mind and intellect into play to anchor the new set of emotions into the structure of the personality. In a sense, this is what occurs in Alcoholics Anonymous; religion plays upon the narcissism and neutralizes it to pro-duce a feeling of synthesis. In referring to his own spiritual experience, Mr. "X" often calls it a "great synthesizing experience in which everything for the first time became clear to me. It was as though a great cloud had lifted and everything took on an indescribable illumination." My second patient, in reference to this point, said this: "I feel all of one piece now. I feel all together, not rushing around in all directions at once." And it was in the light of his new set of emotions that the patient could and did re-spond more satisfactorily to a discussion of what his previous difficulties had been and what he could do now to avoid any further trouble. After his synthesizing experience, he was for the first time really able to do an honest, decent job of self-understanding.

The lesson for psychiatrists is clear, it seems to me. Although we ad-mittedly deal with emotional problems, we, as a group which tends to be intellectual, distrust emotions too much. We are self-conscious and a little ashamed, when we are forced to use them, and always apologetic with our confreres if we suspect they have reason to think our methods are too emotional. In the meantime, others, less bound by tradition, go ahead to get results denied to us. It is highly imperative for us as presumably open-minded scientists to view wisely and long the effects of others in our field of work. We may be wearing bigger blinders than we know.

Recent papers by Dr. Tiebout:

"The Role of Psychiatry in the Field of Alcoholism," 1951.
"Surrender Versus Compliance in Therapy," 1953.
"The Ego Factors in Surrender in Alcoholism," 1954.

APPENDIX E:c

DISCUSSION BEFORE THE MEDICAL SOCIETY OF THE STATE OF NEW YORK

BY FOSTER KENNEDY, M.D.

We have heard a truly moving and eloquent address, moving in its form and in its facts.[1]

I have no doubt that a man who has cured himself of the lust for alcohol has a far greater power for curing alcoholism than has a doctor who has never been afflicted by the same curse.

No matter how sympathetic and patient the doctor may be in the approach to his patient, the patient is sure to either feel, or imagine, condescension to himself or get the notion that he is being hectored by one of the minor prophets.

This organization of Alcoholics Anonymous calls on two of the greatest reservoirs of power known to man, religion, and that instinct for association with one's fellows which Trotter has called the "herd instinct."

Religious faith has been described by Matthew Arnold as a convinced belief in a power greater than ourselves that makes for righteousness, and a sense of helpfulness from this can be acquired through a kind of spiritual conversion which might well be called a variety of religious experience.

The sick man's association with those who, having been sick, have become or are becoming well is a therapeutic suggestion of cure and an obliteration of his feeling of being, in society, a pariah; and this tapping of deep internal forces is shown by the great growth of this sturdy and beneficent movement. Furthermore, this movement furnishes an objective of high emotional driving power in making every cured drunkard a missionary to the sick.

[1] Refers to Bill's paper of 1944, which had just been read.

We physicians, I think, have always had difficulty in finding an occupation for our convalescent patients of sufficient emotional driving power by which to replace the psychical results of the alcohol that has been withdrawn.

These men grow filled with a holy zeal and their very zealousness keeps the missionary steady while the next man is being cured.

I think our profession must take appreciative cognizance of this great therapeutic weapon. If we do not do so we shall stand convicted of emotional sterility and of having lost the faith that moves mountains, without which medicine can do little.

APPENDIX E:d

1939 BOOK REVIEW OF ALCOHOLICS ANONYMOUS

BY DR. HARRY EMERSON FOSDICK; also a quotation
from his autobiography.

This extraordinary book deserves the careful attention of anyone interested in the problem of alcoholism. Whether as victims, friends of victims,
physicians, clergymen, psychiatrists, or social workers, and there are many
such, this book will give them, as no other treatise known to this reviewer
will, an inside view of the problem which the alcoholic faces. Gothic cathedral windows are not the sole things which can be truly seen only from
within. Alcoholism is another. All outside views are clouded and unsure.
Only one who has been an alcoholic and has escaped the thralldom can
interpret the experience.

This book represents the pooled experience of one hundred men and
women who have been victims of alcoholism—many of them declared
hopeless by the experts—and who have won their freedom and recovered
their sanity and self-control. Their stories are detailed and circumstantial,
packed with human interest. In America today the disease of alcoholism is
increasing. Liquor has been an easy escape from depression. As an English
officer in India, reproved for his excessive drinking, lifted his glass and said,
"This is the swiftest road out of India," so many Americans have been
using hard liquor as a means of flight from their troubles until to their
dismay they discover that, free to begin, they are not free to stop. One
hundred men and women, in this volume, report their experience of enslavement and then of liberation.

The book is not in the least sensational. It is notable for its sanity, restraint, and freedom from overemphasis and fanaticism. It is a sober, careful, tolerant, sympathetic treatment of the alcoholic's problem and of the

successful techniques by which its co-authors have won their freedom. The group sponsoring this book began with two or three ex-alcoholics, who discovered one another through a kindred experience. From this personal kinship a movement started, ex-alcoholic working for alcoholics without fanfare or advertisement, and the movement has spread from one city to another. This book presents the practical experience of this group and describes the methods they employ.

The core of their whole procedure is religious. They are convinced that for the hopeless alcoholic there is only one way out—the expulsion of his obsession by a Power greater than himself. Let it be said at once that there is nothing partisan or sectarian about this religious experience. Agnostics and atheists, along with Catholics, Jews, and Protestants, tell their story of discovering the Power greater than themselves. "WHO ARE YOU TO SAY THAT THERE IS NO GOD," one atheist in this group heard a voice say when, hospitalized for alcoholism, he faced the utter hopelessness of his condition. Nowhere is the tolerance and open-mindedness of the book more evident than in its treatment of this central matter on which the cure of all these men and women has depended. They are not partisans of any particular form of organized religion, although they strongly recommend that some religious fellowship be found by their participants. By religion they mean an experience which they personally know and which has saved them from their slavery, when psychiatry and medicine had failed. They agree that each man must have his own way of conceiving God, but of God Himself they are utterly sure, and their stories of victory in consequence are a notable addition to William James' *Varieties of Religious Experience*.

Altogether the book has the accent of reality and is written with unusual intelligence and skill, humor and modesty mitigating what could easily have been a strident and harrowing tale.

Dr. Fosdick Again Recommends Us

In his autobiography, *The Living of These Days* (Harper, 1956), Dr. Fosdick has generously said:

"Alcoholics Anonymous, grown to its present astonishing strength, is a godsend to us ministers. How can we understand an alcoholic—his compulsive desire for liquor, the hopeless captivity against which he futilely contends, one determined decision after another to stop drinking ending in collapse? When we talk to an alcoholic, he knows that never having been in his place we cannot understand his plight. But when an ex-alcoholic, who has been in the depths himself and has taken the Twelve Steps to freedom, talks to an alcoholic, amazing results can follow and have followed in countless thousands of lives.

"Month after month I read the *Grapevine*, A.A.'s official journal—about the most moving collection of testimonies to the possibility of personal transformation of which I know. Moreover, these testimonies bear witness to religion's reality, for Alcoholics Anonymous is deeply religious. That Eleventh Step is an essential factor in its program: 'Sought through prayer and meditation to improve our conscious contact with God, as we understand Him, praying only for knowledge of His will for us and the power to carry that out.' The meetings of Alcoholics Anonymous are the only place, so far as I know, where Roman Catholics, Jews, all kinds of Protestants, and even agnostics get together harmoniously on a religious basis. They do not talk theology. Many of them would say that they know nothing about it. What they do know is that in their utter helplessness they were introduced to a Power, greater than themselves, in contact with whom they found a strong resource which made possible a victory that had seemed incredible. I have listened to many learned arguments about God, but for honest-to-goodness experiential evidence of God, His power personally appropriated and His reality indubitably assured, give me a good meeting of A.A.!"

APPENDIX F

LIST OF PUBLICATIONS
ALCOHOLICS ANONYMOUS WORLD SERVICES, INC.

BOOKS

Alcoholics Anonymous (605 pages)
Alcoholics Anonymous Comes of Age (333 pages)
Twelve Steps and Twelve Traditions (190 pages)
Twelve Steps and Twelve Traditions (Pocket-size edition, 190 pages)
As Bill Sees It (The A.A. Way of Life) (332 pages)

BOOKLETS

Came to Believe . . . (128 pages)
Living Sober (96 pages)

PAMPHLETS

A.A.—44 Questions
A.A. Tradition—How It Developed
A Clergyman Asks About A.A.
Three Talks to Medical Societies by Bill W.
Alcoholics Anonymous and the Medical Profession
A.A. in Your Community
Is A.A. for You?
This Is A.A.
Questions and Answers on Sponsorship

Do You Think You're Different?
A.A. for the Woman
A.A. and the Alcoholic Employee
The Jack Alexander Article
Letter to a Woman Alcoholic
Young People and A.A.
A.A. and the Armed Services
The A.A. Member and Drug Abuse
Is There an Alcoholic in Your Life?
Inside A.A.
The A.A. Group
G.S.R.
Memo to an Inmate
The Twelve Traditions Illustrated
How A.A. Members Cooperate
A.A. in Prisons
A.A. in Hospitals
What Happened to Joe (Comic-book style)
It Happened to Alice (Comic-book style)
A Member's-Eye View of Alcoholics Anonymous
Problems Other Than Alcohol
Let's Be Friendly With Our Friends
A Brief Guide to A.A.
Speaking at Non-A.A. Meetings
Understanding Anonymity
The Co-Founders of Alcoholics Anonymous
If You Are a Professional . . .
The A.A. Member
Too Young? (Cartoon pamphlet for teenagers)

PERIODICAL
THE A.A. GRAPEVINE, INC.

The A.A. Grapevine (monthly)

Index

Akron, Ohio, First A.A. Group, 6, 7, 11, 16, 19, 21 f., 67, 69, 145 f., 149, 155 f., 190; and *Alcoholics Anonymous* (book), 164; expansion of, 76, 141; formation of, 65-75; studied by Frank Amos, 149 f.

Al-Anon Family Groups: Long Beach, 23; Richmond, 23; Toronto, 23, 33; and *Alcoholics Anonymous* (book), 164; functioning of, 31, 34, 98; how to get in touch with, 285; membership of, 229; origin of, 24; purpose of, 228 f.; and St. Louis Convention, 32, 42

Alaska, 26, 82

Alcoholic Foundation: finances of, 17, 113, 151, 153, 155, 157; as forerunner of General Service Board, 14, 198, 210, 214 f., 218; formation of, 16, 151; functions of, permitted by charter, 107; incorporation of, 275; meetings of, 154; naming of, 152; organized, 15

Alcoholics Anonymous (book): contents of, 2, 7, 17, 19, 195; finances for publication of, 18, 145, 153 f., 193, 202; importance of, for members, 22, 30, 41, 87 f., 93 f., 144, 198; use in South Africa, 85; office for, 11; ownership of, 15, 154 ff., 189 f.; preparation of, 13, 16, 43, 153; publication of, 11, 21, 76, 91, 132, 154 ff., 220; publicity of, 174 ff., 183; royalties from, 193 ff.; sales of, 156, 175 f., 178, 186 f., 220, 307 f., 309 f.; suggested titles for, 165 f., 170; translations of, 27, 29; *see also* Works Publishing, Inc.

A.A. Tradition, The (pamphlet), 204

Alcoholism: and A.A. principles, 243; and alcoholic environment, 243; and anger, 233 f.; chronic, 302 ff.; diagnosis of, 13; and discipline, 249-51; and ego-reduction, 4, 248-51, 311 ff.; and emotions, 317-19, 239, 243; as escape, 243; and group therapy, 241; medical aspect of, 206; mild, 199 f.; and objectivity, 314 f.; as "obsession plus allergy," 69 f., 72, 161; and other diseases, 239 f.; and peace of mind, 316; physical treatment of, 241 f.; and psychosomatic medicine, 243; relapse to, 97; and religious exhortation, 242; social stigma of, 239 f.; and surrender, 247, 249-51, 265, 379; and temptation, 240, 306 f.

Alexander, Jack: and *A.A.'s Twelve Steps and Twelve Traditions*, 219; and article on Alcoholics Anonymous, 16, 18, 35, 87, 89, 134, 190 f.; a trustee, 6, 208

Allis-Chalmers, 5

American Academy of General Practice, 244

American Journal of Psychiatry, 205

American Medical Association, 4, 237 f.

American Psychiatric Association, 205, 244

American Public Health Association, 4; *see also* Lasker Award

Amos, Frank, 6, 15, 149 ff., 168, 208

Anderson, Dwight, 2

Anne: wife of Dr. Bob, 6; as counselor, 73; as example, 23, 67; and early group meetings, 19, 141; trials and tribulations of, 69

Anonymity: address on by Bill W., 286-94; breaking of, 117, 208 f.; and egotism, 43, 292 f.; as escape from stigma, 75; and money, 291; origins of, 286; personal, 25; and politics, 291 f.; and pride, 287; as principle, 135; and publicity, 129, 133 ff., 288 ff.; and sacrifice, 286-88; and survival of A.A., 132;